A Handbook for Classroom Instruction that *Works*

2nd Edition

HOWARD PITLER

Bj STONE

ASCD
Alexandria, Virginia USA

McREL
Mid-continent Research for Education and Learning
Denver, Colorado USA

1703 N. Beauregard St. • Alexandria, VA 22311-1714 USA
Phone: 800-933-2723 or 703-578-9600 • Fax: 703-575-5400
Website: www.ascd.org • E-mail: member@ascd.org
Author guidelines: www.ascd.org/write

Gene R. Carter, *Executive Director*; Ron Miletta, *Interim Chief Program Development Officer*; Richard Papale, *Publisher*; Laura Lawson, *Acquisitions Editor*; Julie Houtz, *Director, Book Editing & Production*; Jamie Greene, *Editor*; Georgia Park, *Senior Graphic Designer*; Mike Kalyan, *Production Manager*; Valerie Younkin, *Desktop Publishing Specialist*; Kyle Steichen, *Production Specialist*

MCREL

Mid-continent Research for Education and Learning
4601 DTC Boulevard, Suite 500
Denver, CO 80237 USA
Phone: 303-337-0990 • Fax: 303-337-3005
Website: www.mcrel.org • E-mail: info@mcrel.org

All web links in this book are correct as of the publication date below but may have become inactive or otherwise modified since that time. If you notice a deactivated or changed link, please e-mail books@ascd.org with the words "Link Update" in the subject line. In your message, please specify the web link, the book title, and the page number on which the link appears.

PAPERBACK ISBN: 978-1-4166-1468-5   ASCD product #112013   n10/12

Also available as an e-book (see Books in Print for the ISBNs).

Quantity discounts: 10–49 copies, 10%; 50+ copies, 15%; for 1,000 or more copies, call 800-933-2723, ext. 5634, or 703-575-5634. For desk copies: www.ascd.org/deskcopy

Library of Congress Cataloging-in-Publication Data
Pitler, Howard, 1952–
   A handbook for classroom instruction that works / Howard Pitler & BJ Stone.—2nd ed.
      p. cm.
   Prev. ed. classed under title
   Includes bibliographical references and index.
   ISBN 978-1-4166-1468-5 (pbk. : alk. paper)
   1. Effective teaching—United States—Handbooks, manuals, etc. 2. Learning—Handbooks, manuals, etc. I. Stone, BJ. II. Handbook for classroom instruction that works III. Title.
   LB1025.3.H364 2012
   371.3—dc23
                                                                      2012025761

20 19 18 17 16 15 14 13 12   1 2 3 4 5 6 7 8 9 10 11 12

A Handbook for Classroom Instruction *that Works*

2nd Edition

Introduction vii

Part I: Creating the Environment for Learning. 1
    List of Figures. 2
    Chapter 1: Setting Objectives and Providing Feedback. 3
    Chapter 2: Reinforcing Effort and Providing Recognition 37
    Chapter 3: Cooperative Learning 75

Part II: Helping Students Develop Understanding. 93
    List of Figures. 94
    Chapter 4: Cues, Questions, and Advance Organizers 97
    Chapter 5: Nonlinguistic Representations. 129
    Chapter 6: Summarizing and Note Taking 152
    Chapter 7: Assigning Homework and Providing Practice. 205

Part III: Helping Students Extend and Apply Knowledge 237
    List of Figures. 238
    Chapter 8: Identifying Similarities and Differences 239
    Chapter 9: Generating and Testing Hypotheses 274

Part IV: Putting the Instructional Strategies to Use 301
    List of Figures. 302
    Chapter 10: Instructional Planning Using the
        Nine Categories of Strategies 303

Conclusion. 321

References. 322

Index. 327

About the Authors 332

A Handbook for Classroom Instruction *that Works*

2nd Edition

Introduction

The first edition of this handbook opened with the following statement: "We stand at a unique point in the history of U.S. education—a point at which the potential for truly meaningful school reform is greater than it ever has been" (Marzano, Norford, Paynter, Pickering, & Gaddy, 2001, p. 1). A decade later, we can look back and see the powerful impact that *Classroom Instruction That Works* has had on schools and districts throughout the United States and the world. The original book, which was based on a survey of thousands of comparisons between experimental and control groups and across a variety of subject areas, was able to identify nine categories of instructional strategies proven to improve student achievement. The following list shows the nine categories of instructional strategies in rank order, as listed in the first edition:

1. Identifying Similarities and Differences
2. Summarizing and Note Taking
3. Reinforcing Effort and Providing Recognition
4. Homework and Practice
5. Nonlinguistic Representations
6. Cooperative Learning
7. Setting Objectives and Providing Feedback
8. Generating and Testing Hypotheses
9. Cues, Questions, and Advance Organizers

In the first edition of *Classroom Instruction That Works*, the strategies were presented according to the magnitude of their average effect size (from largest to smallest). Focusing on the strategies in that order encouraged some schools and districts to focus primarily on the first three or four strategies—

with the highest effect sizes—without regard to *when* to use those strategies. For example, teachers were asked to focus on identifying similarities and differences as often as possible, yet they found this difficult to do in the early part of a unit when students didn't have a basic understanding of the concepts and vocabulary relevant to the topic. This focus on the strategies with the highest effect sizes often meant that those strategies at the "bottom" of the list were disregarded or considered less important. As a result, teachers might have minimized their use of key practices that help students activate background knowledge (Cues, Questions, and Advance Organizers) and use higher-order thinking skills (Generating and Testing Hypotheses).

What's New in the Second Edition?

Today, an increasing number of schools systematically and intentionally use all of these research-based strategies to best meet the needs of their students. We see districts in the process of building a common language for instruction and developing shared understandings of what good instruction looks like. In 2001, the focus was on helping individual teachers grow as professionals. A decade later, we are focusing on helping all teachers—and therefore all students—reach their fullest potential.

In the second edition of *Classroom Instruction That Works*, the nine categories of strategies are organized and presented within a framework for instructional planning. This helps teachers learn about the strategies in the context of how each might be used throughout a unit; it also highlights the point that all of the strategies are effective and should be intentionally included in planning. The framework has three components: Creating the Environment for Learning, Helping Students Develop Understanding, and Helping Students Extend and Apply Knowledge. These components were selected because they focus on the key aspects of teaching and learning.

The strategies in the first component of the framework—Creating the Environment for Learning—should be the backdrop for every lesson. When teachers create an environment for learning, they motivate and focus student learning by helping students know what is expected of them, by providing students with opportunities for regular feedback on their progress, and by assuring students that they are capable of learning challenging content and skills. Teachers encourage students to actively engage in and "own" their learning, providing opportunities for students to share and discuss their ideas, develop collaboration skills, and learn how to monitor and reflect on their learning.

The second component—Helping Students Develop Understanding—acknowledges that students come to the classroom with prior knowledge and must integrate new learning with what they already know. The strategies included in this component help teachers use students' prior knowledge as scaffolding for new learning. Acquiring and integrating information-type knowledge requires students to construct meaning, organize what they are learning, and store information. Constructing meaning is an active process. Students recall prior knowledge, make and verify predictions, correct misconceptions, fill in unstated information, and identify confusing aspects of the knowledge (Marzano & Pickering, 1997). They also organize information by recognizing patterns in the information (e.g., a sequence of events, a description) and store information most effectively by creating a mental image of it. Acquiring and integrating procedure-type knowledge involves constructing a model of the individual steps of the process or skill, developing conceptual understanding of the process and understanding and practicing its variations, and using the skill or process fluently or without much conscious thought (Ibid.).

Strategies in the third component of the framework—Helping Students Extend and Apply Knowledge—emphasize the importance of helping students move beyond so-called right-answer learning to an expanded understanding and use of concepts and skills in real-world contexts. These strategies help students become more efficient and flexible in using what they have learned. They involve the use of complex reasoning processes, which are necessary for students to use knowledge meaningfully (Ibid.). Figure A illustrates where the nine categories of strategies fit within the framework.

How to Use This Handbook

This handbook is intended to be used as a supplement to the second edition of *Classroom Instruction That Works* (Dean, Hubbell, Pitler, & Stone, 2012). Our objective is to provide educators with more in-depth examples that will bring the strategies, skills, and information from that book to life in their classrooms, schools, and districts. Although you can use this handbook without reading *Classroom Instruction That Works*, we recommend that you use both books in conjunction with each other. Our intent here is to provide practical applications and examples, but it is equally important for you to understand the classroom recommendations presented in the primary text for each category of instruction.

FIGURE A

The Framework for Instructional Planning

Creating the Environment for Learning

Setting Objectives
and Providing
Feedback

Reinforcing Effort
and Providing
Recognition

Cooperative Learning

**Helping Students
Develop Understanding**

Cues, Questions, and
Advance Organizers

Nonlinguistic Representations

Summarizing and Note Taking

Assigning Homework
and Providing Practice

**Helping Students
Extend and
Apply Knowledge**

Identifying Similarities
and Differences

Generating and Testing
Hypotheses

This handbook can be used as a self-study guide that targets the effective use of specific strategies in each component of the framework, or it can be used as part of a group book study. It is aligned with the three framework components presented earlier. Discussion of each of the strategies includes the following:

1. **Why This Strategy?** Each strategy is introduced with an explanation about why it has a positive impact on student achievement, how it fits within a high-quality instructional plan, and what research indicates is best practice for its use.

2. **Reflecting on My Current Practice.** We ask questions designed to help you reflect on how and why you currently use each strategy in your classroom in order to stimulate your thinking about the intentionality of your practice.

3. **Bringing the Strategy to Life in the Classroom.** Our intent is to help you see what each strategy looks like in the classroom when used with intentionality and in line with research recommendations. Our

goal is to help you connect recommendations for and examples of each strategy's use with your classroom practice. This will help you see how each strategy is supported by and supportive of other strategies in a well-designed lesson.

4. **Rubrics and Checklists.** Each strategy is accompanied by a rubric that allows you to gauge your own practice, seeing where you currently are and how you can grow as a professional. The rubric is designed so that a 3 represents best practice as indicated by research. A 4 indicates both teacher best practice as described in a 3 and how that practice transfers into student behaviors. Each strategy is also accompanied by a checklist that can be used to gauge how students view instruction and the impact it has on their learning.

5. **Tools, Templates, and Protocols.** As a way to help you broaden your instructional practice, we provide a variety of tools, templates, and protocols. For example, tools are available to help you assess your current practice and to build a professional growth plan. Some strategies include blackline masters and examples that can be customized for your particular content area and grade level.

As mentioned before, this handbook can be used for self-study. You can work through the various components at your own pace and identify your own plan of action. Although implementing some of the ideas in this book will benefit your students—and each strategy has individual merit based on sound research—the real power comes in bringing all of the strategies together with intentionality to provide the best opportunity for your students to excel. Using this handbook in conjunction with *Classroom Instruction That Works* has the potential to transform your teaching to a brand new level.

An alternative approach is to form study groups, possibly as part of a professional learning community. The study group format is one of the best ways to build skills and increase confidence in the strategies because it requires collegial support structures that encourage analysis, discussion, problem solving, and solution sharing in ways that are consistent with best practices in staff development. Study groups fulfill two salient functions relative to the use of this handbook:

- They provide a context for teachers to discuss and reflect upon the extent and effectiveness with which strategies are implemented.
- They provide an opportunity for teachers to use the strategies with structured peer support.

We talk about the importance of oral discourse with students in a number of the strategies. Working in study groups provides the same oral discourse for teachers.

Some educators might question how study groups are possible within the structure of K–12 schooling; they wonder how study groups can function in the context of how the school day is arranged. To help you envision how you might use study groups in your building, consider the following scenario.

A majority of the faculty at Haystead Middle School agreed to use the *Handbook for Classroom Instruction That Works* (2nd ed.) as the focus of study during the upcoming school year. Those faculty members who volunteered to work on the project organized themselves into study groups of four to six individuals. Each group agreed to meet for two hours every other week during both semesters of the school year. Some groups met during the school day on released time; others met after contract hours. Because of her interest in the project and to demonstrate her support for it, the principal joined one of the groups. She arranged the school schedule to allow teachers to meet during common planning periods, and she arranged for group members to receive recertification credit upon completion and acceptance of a paper describing their learning at the end of each semester.

Meeting dates, times, and locations were agreed upon at the first meeting, during which a group leader was also selected. The group leader was responsible for making sure meetings began and ended on time; arranging for meeting rooms, materials, and refreshments; and completing a summary sheet at the end of each session outlining what had been discussed, who had attended, and the goals for the next meeting. These summary sheets were forwarded to the principal, who then met with team leaders monthly so group members could exchange ideas, coordinate efforts, and share resources. Although the group leaders were volunteers, they were given a stipend of $300 per semester in partial recognition of the responsibilities they had assumed.

The groups realized it made logical sense to begin studying the book sequentially, starting with the strategies of Setting Objectives and Providing Feedback, the first category of strategies presented in the part of the framework dedicated to creating the environment for learning. Prior to the first scheduled meeting, each group member was required to read the section on Setting Objectives. The first order of business at the first meeting was to share individual responses to the Reflecting on Current Practice questions (see Figure 1.1 on pages 6–7). For some teachers, this discussion was enough to provide them with ideas about various ways to use the information presented. Other teachers felt they would be best served by doing some action research related to specific strategies. Following the meeting, one or more members of the group identified a strategy, hypothesized the effect of using that strategy with their students, and then actually tried it out in the classroom. After the strategy was implemented, data were collected using the Student Checklist (see Figure 1.3 on page 17) and by examining student work. The data were then brought back to the next group meeting, which was spent analyzing and interpreting the data and implications for classroom practice.

Periodically, and at the end of each semester, each study group evaluated its progress in terms of individual members' learning and the overall effect on student learning. In addition, the groups came together in the larger professional learning community to share their action research and learn from one another.

Designing an Approach That Works for You

Ultimately, professional development is personal. No two teachers are alike, just as no two students are alike. Therefore, no two teachers need exactly the same information to enhance their performance. The same is true at the school level. Though some teachers might be best served working independently, many need and crave the interaction and collegiality of the group approach. Working in a study group, as part of a professional learning community (PLC), also helps a school create a common language for instruction and mutual understanding of the strategies.

The previous scenario was presented to stimulate your thinking regarding the use of this handbook and to provide one possible approach. Individual schools and teachers can design study programs that meet their individual needs and learning styles, keeping in mind that the end target is building collective efficacy as a school and a district. The important thing is to look at instruction as an intentional act.

When we wrote the second edition of *Classroom Instruction That Works*, we didn't create the instructional strategies. Rather, we looked at those strategies that research identifies as highly effective, categorized them, and then highlighted what best practices would look like for each one. This book will help to intentionally embed the strategies into your classroom pedagogy. As we stated previously, each section includes a rubric showing a continuum of practice from "Not Evident" to "Exemplary." It is highly likely that you are already using every one of these strategies in your daily practice. With that in mind, we hope this handbook will help you move along the continuum toward best practice in each strategy, with the ultimate goal of improving student achievement for every child in every classroom in the country.

Part I

Creating the Environment for Learning

The categories of strategies in this section reflect the first priority of a teacher: to create an environment in which students know what is expected of them, have opportunities for regular feedback on their progress, and receive constant messages that they are a vital part of the classroom and are capable of learning even the most challenging content and processes.

These three categories are useful for motivating and focusing student learning and for helping students learn how to work collaboratively with others. They also promote student reflection and ownership of learning.

The strategies in this section include

- Setting Objectives and Providing Feedback
- Reinforcing Effort and Providing Recognition
- Cooperative Learning

Every day, when students enter the school building, they ask themselves two important questions: "Will I be accepted?" and "Can I do the work?" If students cannot answer in the affirmative to both of these questions, then it makes it difficult for them to be successful. Teachers can use the strategies in this section to create a learning environment in which students know what they are supposed to be learning, have clear direction on how well they are progressing toward that learning objective, understand their role as learners, and have an engaging and interactive place to learn. The intentional application of these strategies makes it much more likely for students to be able to answer those two questions with a resounding *yes*.

List of Figures

Chapter 1

1.1   Reflecting on Current Practice: Setting Objectives 6

1.2   Teacher Rubric: Setting Objectives. 14

1.3   Student Checklist: Setting Objectives 17

1.4   Assessing Myself: Setting Objectives 18

1.5   Professional Growth Plan: Setting Objectives. 20

1.6   Learning Objectives Worksheet 22

1.7   Reflecting on Current Practice: Providing Feedback. 25

1.8   Sample Graded Mathematics Quiz 27

1.9   Excerpt from Student Rubric 28

1.10   Teacher Rubric: Providing Feedback 30

1.11   Student Checklist: Providing Feedback. 33

1.12   Assessing Myself: Providing Feedback. 34

1.13   Professional Growth Plan: Providing Feedback 36

Chapter 2

2.1   Reflecting on Current Practice: Reinforcing Effort 42

2.2   Charting Effort and Achievement 48

2.3   Graphing Effort and Achievement. 48

2.4   Teacher Rubric: Reinforcing Effort. 51

2.5   Student Checklist: Reinforcing Effort 54

2.6   Assessing Myself: Reinforcing Effort 55

2.7   Professional Growth Plan: Reinforcing Effort. 56

2.8   Reflecting on Current Practice: Providing Recognition 59

2.9   Guidelines for Praise 64

2.10   Teacher Rubric: Providing Recognition. 67

2.11   Student Checklist: Providing Recognition 70

2.12   Assessing Myself: Providing Recognition 71

2.13   Professional Growth Plan: Providing Recognition 73

Chapter 3

3.1   Reflecting on Current Practice: Cooperative Learning 78

3.2   Teacher Rubric: Cooperative Learning. 83

3.3   Student Checklist: Cooperative Learning 87

3.4   Assessing Myself: Cooperative Learning 89

3.5   Professional Growth Plan: Cooperative Learning 91

1

Setting Objectives
and Providing Feedback

Setting Objectives

Students learn most efficiently when they know the objectives of a specific lesson or learning activity. This makes intuitive sense. If students are aware of the intended outcome, then they know where their focus should lie. When setting objectives, teachers simply give students a target for their learning. Students can gauge their individual starting points in relation to the learning objective and determine what needs their attention and where they might need help from the teacher or others. This clarity helps decrease anxiety about their ability to succeed. In addition, students build intrinsic motivation when they set personal learning objectives.

Why This Strategy?

The process of setting learning objectives begins with knowing the specific standards, benchmarks, and supporting knowledge students in your school or district are required to learn. Common Core State Standards and curriculum documents are generally the source for this information. If your school or district does not have a curriculum that is clearly aligned with an established set of standards, then this is an essential step to ensure students receive the same important content from teacher to teacher. The content that is taught should not be dependent on the teachers to whom students are assigned. Teaching the wrong content well does not, obviously, lead to robust student achievement gains. Likewise, teaching the right content poorly does not result in positive development. Schools and districts need to look at both the "what" and the "how" of instruction to maximize student achievement.

3

Standards are typically written at a fairly general level. Indeed, many are stated identically at the elementary, middle, and high school levels. For example, the Common Core College and Career Readiness Anchor Standard 5 for Writing in the cluster of Production and Distribution of Writing is as follows: "Develop and strengthen writing as needed by planning, revising, editing, rewriting, or trying a new approach." A similar standard from the McREL Compendium of Standards in Language Arts is "Uses the general skills and strategies of the writing process." This standard is taught in every grade, pre-K through 12. It is far too broad to be a good and focused objective. A benchmark under that standard for grades 3–5 is as follows: "Prewriting: Uses prewriting strategies to plan written work (e.g., uses graphic organizers, story maps, and webs; groups related ideas; takes notes; brainstorms ideas; organizes information according to type and purpose of writing)." Though this is more specific, it is still too broad to be a clear target for students.

Under that benchmark, however, are a number of knowledge and skills statements, one of which is "Uses graphic organizers to plan written work." The following objective might be stated to students: "We are learning about the prewriting process and how to use graphic organizers to help us plan our work. Yesterday we learned how concept maps can help us organize our work. In our activity today we are going to learn about and use a storyboard to help us plan our writing." Don't assume that your students recognize the connection between using a storyboard and planning for their writing. Using a storyboard is an activity; using graphic organizers as a tool in the prewriting process is the objective. Many students won't make this connection unless it is stated explicitly. The learning activity is very important, but we encourage you to think of activities as being in service to your objectives. Help your students understand that schooling is more than just a series of activities. Therefore, the posted objective for this example should be "We will use graphic organizers to plan our writing." The agenda that accompanies the learning objective might be

1. Review purpose of prewriting.
2. Use the storyboard graphic organizer provided to map out your story.
3. Share your storyboard with your writing buddy.

The following four recommendations provide guidance for teachers as they create a learning evironment for student success. Teacher are encouraged to

1. **Set learning objectives that are specific but not restrictive.** It is important for the teacher to set learning goals/objectives for students,

but it is also important for the goals/objectives to be general enough that they provide some flexibility.

2. **Communicate the learning objectives to students and parents.** Once the teacher has established and shared the learning objectives, it is important to have those objectives presented in student-friendly language and visible during the lesson.

3. **Connect the learning objectives to previous and future learning.** The teacher should explain how learning objectives connect with previous lessons or units and with the larger picture of a particular unit or course.

4. **Engage students in setting personal learning objectives.** Once the teacher has established and shared the learning objectives, it is important for students to have the opportunity to adapt the objectives to their personal needs and desires.

Reflecting on My Current Practice

The questions listed in Figure 1.1 are provided as a means to assist you as you implement the instructional practices for setting objectives.

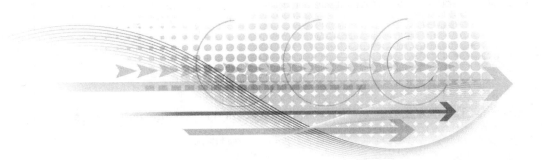

FIGURE 1.1
Reflecting on Current Practice: Setting Objectives

1. Do I write the objective in student-friendly language that clearly reflects the content that students will learn and/or the skills they will acquire?

2. Do I ensure the objective reflects the content and skills to be learned rather than a list of activities?

3. Do I ensure the objective tightly aligns with information in the Common Core, state, or district standards?

4. Do I create objectives that set the stage for rigorous, age-appropriate learning?

5. Do I include opportunities to determine students' existing knowledge and skills as well as misconceptions related to the objective?

6. Do I provide learning activities in the lesson that tightly align with the objective?

FIGURE 1.1
Reflecting on Current Practice: Setting Objectives *(continued)*

7. Do I reference the objective throughout the lesson?

8. Do I post the objective in clear sight of all students for reference throughout the lesson?

9. Do I state the objective and allow students to make sense of what they will be learning and doing?

10. Do I help students connect the activity they are doing with the learning objective?

11. Do I help students make connections between the objective and those of previous lessons/units so it is clear how they all fit in the overall course?

Bringing the Strategy to Life in the Classroom

Recommendation One:
Set learning objectives that are specific but not restrictive.

In the following vignette, see how Mr. Wallace and Mr. Miles revise their thinking about teaching an activities-based unit to one that truly focuses on a specific learning objective. They are able to accomplish this by providing the guidance their students need through a learning objective that is stated in terms of what students are expected to learn, not in terms of activities they are expected to complete. When objectives are too restrictive, they become a series of disconnected activities.

During their common planning time, Mr. Wallace and Mr. Miles discuss the content and skills to be taught in PE during the physical fitness unit. Over the summer, the district focused professional development on writing specific learning objectives that were not restrictive. After attending this training, they realized that in previous years, they had really been teaching specific skills—not objectives.

The teachers discuss what they want their students to know, understand, and be able to do by the end of the unit on physical fitness. When they taught the same unit the previous year, they simply put their students through a series of activities. As a result of their professional development, they knew they needed to focus their efforts on ensuring students see the activities (such as monitoring heart rate during and after exercise, charting times for one-mile runs, and strength testing) as part of a larger, overarching unit. Mr. Wallace and Mr. Miles realize they have been teaching discrete activities, whereas what they really need to do is create an umbrella that encompasses all of these activities under one clear objective: "We will learn how to develop an individual fitness goal by interpreting the results of our physical fitness assessments." They also realize that their past practice restricted student learning to only a series of activities without a clear purpose.

Recommendation Two:
Communicate the learning objectives to students and parents.

Too often in classrooms, we see teachers who clearly explain an activity without making the intentional connection between the activity and the learning objective. Unless this connection is made, students see learning as a series of discrete activities without a connection to an overarching objective. In the following vignette, the teacher seems to have an engaged classroom, but the learning objective is not clearly communicated to his students. This scenario drives home the importance of clearly communicated and visible learning objectives as a tool for students to keep a keen focus on what they are supposed to be learning—not just on what they are supposed to be doing.

Principal Breckenridge walks into a 7th grade science class and sees students working in pairs with laptop computers. They are completing an online simulation about the phases of the moon and working on a related activity sheet. Mr. Breckenridge immediately notices that every student in the room seems to be highly engaged in the activity. Although there is no learning objective posted on the whiteboard, he is fairly certain he knows not only what the students are doing but also what they are supposed to be learning during this lesson.

As part of his normal walkthrough protocol, however, he heads over to a pair of students working together and asks, "What are you learning?" One student replies, "We are doing an activity about the moon." The principal says, "Yes, I see that, but what do you think your teacher wants you to learn while you are doing this activity?" Replies the student, "We are learning about the phases of the moon and how the moon's gravity affects the tides on Earth." Before Mr. Breckenridge can say thank you, the second student in the pair interrupts and says, "No we aren't. We are learning about how the Mayans used the moon as a basis for their calendar and how it was part of their religious practices."

This exchange helps Mr. Breckenridge recognize the importance of clearly stated learning objectives from the students' perspective. Both of these students are learning about the moon, but one of them will be in for a surprise on Friday when the assessment is given. Would the test cover the phases of the moon or Mayan beliefs about the moon?

We recommend that every objective is visible—either on the whiteboard, in a journal, or on an activity sheet. Why does the objective need to be visible, considering you go over it orally with your class at the start of the lesson? Think about it. Are all of your students in the room when you go over the lesson objective? Are all students focused at that time? Are some of your students visual learners, rather than auditory learners? Do some of your students have a limited attention span? The answers to these questions ultimately lead to the realization that making objectives visible may not be necessary for every student, but it truly makes a difference for many of them. In addition, if the objective is visible, it is easier to reference throughout the lesson. Asking students how an activity is helping them move toward the learning objective and how they are doing in relation to that objective is another way to personalize learning.

Communication is a two-way street. Rather than simply telling your students what you want them to learn, consider giving them some time after your explanation of the objective to talk with their "elbow partners" and verbalize what they think they will be learning and what they already know about the topic. This opportunity for oral discourse allows students to verbalize their learning, use vocabulary that is specific to the content, and listen to peers do likewise. Periodically during a lesson, it is a good idea to pause and remind students of the learning objective. This helps to keep them focused. It is also critical to avoid abruptly ending a lesson without closure (e.g., "We're done writing. Now get out your science journals."). Think about the power of summative statements such as "We said our objective was to use a storyboard to plan our writing. Turn to your partners and talk about what we just learned."

Recommendation Three:
Connect the learning objectives to previous and future learning.

As you read the vignette below, see how the teacher follows the process of communicating the learning objective, providing time for oral discourse, returning to the objective during instruction for clarification, and finally reviewing at the lesson transition point. In addition to clearly communicating the objective with her students, she intentionally makes the connection to what they have previously covered, ensuring that her students see learning not as a disconnected series of activities but as a congruent unit of instruction tied to an objective.

Ms. Matas began her 6th grade language arts lesson by writing the following objective on the whiteboard: "We will be able to write a persuasive paper and support our point of view with facts and details." Under that, she writes, "School board considers banning french fries in the school cafeteria." She tells her students, "This week, we have been learning about the elements of a persuasive paper. You know you have to establish the main point of your argument, build support through facts, and pay attention to the audience for whom you are writing. I want you to discuss at your tables what you think we will be doing today."

Karina turns to her table partners and exclaims, "No french fries at lunch! That's unconstitutional!" Jessie snipes, "Do you even know what *unconstitutional* means? I don't think there's anything in the Constitution about french fries." Tameka says, "Well, we have been studying what goes into a persuasive paper. I'm thinking Ms. Matas is going to have us write a persuasive paper to the school board trying to convince them not to take french fries away at lunch. If we are going to do that, then we'll need some facts. This isn't just some lesson from a book. This is real life, people. We need to try to convince them that french fries aren't bad."

After a minute or two of student discussion, Ms. Matas begins the lesson. She has her students count off by twos. The "ones," she explains, will write a persuasive paper defending the school board's position of removing french fries from the school lunch program. The "twos" will write a paper advocating for the position of keeping fries on the menu. She reminds her class of what they already learned about writing a persuasive paper and gives them an advance organizer to help them organize their thinking. Even though some students find it challenging to defend a position they don't like, they all begin researching facts that support their position. Some students use various websites (such as www.wolframalpha.com) to look at the nutritional values of french fries and any relation to obesity. Other students compare the nutritional value of fries with that of other menu-item foods that aren't on the list to be banned, such as mashed potatoes and corn dogs.

After 15 minutes, Ms. Matas brings the class together and reminds them that their learning objective is to write a persuasive paper with facts and details that support their position. Are they finding solid facts? How about details? She also reminds students to use their advance organizers to keep their thoughts focused. She instructs both groups to get together on opposite sides of the room and share their findings. Ms. Matas says, "Our objective is to write good persuasive papers. It isn't a competition. Remember, our objective begins with *we*, not *I*. The better your facts and details, the easier it will be for everyone in the class to craft a great persuasive paper."

Just before the bell rings, Ms. Matas asks each group to discuss what they learned during the activity. She says, "What I would like to focus on is what goes into writing a good persuasive paper. We will pick up here tomorrow."

In this scenario, Ms. Matas begins her lesson by writing the class learning objective on the whiteboard in student-friendly language. She makes a connection between the new activity and what students have already learned. She explains the objective and then asks the class to briefly discuss what they think they will be learning. After the class moves on to the assignment, she intentionally pauses to review the learning objective and to remind her class what the learning objective really is, keeping them focused on the objective and not just the activity. Finally, at the end of the class, she gives her students a few minutes to talk in small groups to review what they learned.

Recommendation Four:
Engage students in setting personal learning objectives.

In the following vignette, notice how the teacher allows her students to personalize their learning. This doesn't mean they are allowed to decide which objectives they will be learning; that is a decision made at the district or state level. Rather, within the adopted scope and sequence, she allows her students to make decisions that personalize their learning.

Ms. Parnacott's 7th grade science class is working on a unit about global climate change. The specific objective in the scope and sequence reads, "Understands the ways in which technology influences the human capacity to modify the physical environment." She translates that into student-friendly language and writes on the whiteboard, "We will be able to indentify how manmade technologies have changed our environment." After making sure her students understand what *technologies* and *environment* mean, she projects a KWL advance organizer onto the whiteboard and asks her students, one by one, to say something they already know about the topic.

After each student has an opportunity to respond, Ms. Parnacott says, "As we went around the room, I am sure you heard some things that you knew but had forgotten about. This is a way to help all of us activate our background knowledge and get on the same page as a class. Next, we are going to go around the room again. This time, I want each of you to say one thing you want to learn about how manmade technologies have changed the environment."

This time, as her students say something they want to know, she writes their responses in different colors in order to categorize them. Ms. Parnacott says, "If I wrote the one thing you wanted to know in red, go to the corner of the room by my desk. Your group is looking into how factories have changed the environment. If I wrote your response in green, move to the corner by the closet. Your group is looking into global warming. The blue group should move to the corner near the fish tank. You all focused your reponse on how cars and other transportation have changed the environment. Finally, the purple group should move to the corner by the computers. You are all interested in how agriculture has impacted the environment."

In this manner, Ms. Parnacott gives her students some flexibility in choosing an area of personal interest while staying true to the learning objective in her scope and sequence. This process takes some time at the onset of the lesson, but it is one way to make sure each student is able to personalize his or her learning within the rigors of the objective and to engage all students by acknowledging personal interests.

Rubrics and Checklists

The teacher rubric provided in Figure 1.2 is intended to be a tool used for reflection on the way in which you currently set objectives in your classroom. It is designed so that 3 represents best practice as indicated by research. A 4 indicates both teacher best practice as described in a 3 and how that practice transfers into student behaviors. You can also use this rubric as a growth tool, seeing where you are now and what the next level might look like. This will provide you with valuable information as you build your professional growth plan later.

Using the teacher rubric will give you the chance to reflect on your practice. You can also ask your students how they perceive the way you teach them to set objectives. Figure 1.3 provides a student checklist you may wish to use. Periodically give this checklist to your students, and ask them to react honestly to the statements. This checklist can help your students better understand how objectives help them learn, and it can provide valuable feedback to you about how your students view the process of setting objectives.

Tools, Templates, and Protocols

If you are using this handbook as part of a school PLC or book study, Figure 1.4 provides statements that can serve as discussion prompts. Likewise, if you are using this book for individual growth, think about these prompts as they relate to your classroom practice. For example, if your answer to the first statement is a 0 or 1, then what steps should you take to move toward the other end of the spectrum, "to a great extent"? Use your individual or team results from Figure 1.4 to form the basis of a professional growth plan (see Figure 1.5).

Use the learning objectives worksheet in Figure 1.6 as a practice tool, either within your PLC or individually. Rewrite each learning objective so it more closely follows the research-based recommendations.

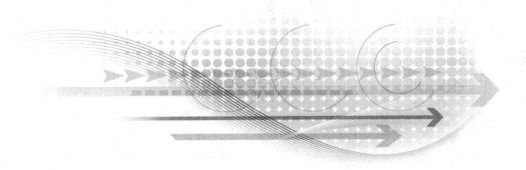

FIGURE 1.2

Teacher Rubric: Setting Objectives

Set learning objectives that are specific but not restrictive: *Common Core, state, and local standards or curriculum documents are generally the source for this information. Teachers must unpack their standards document to drill down to more specific statements of knowledge and skills. Activities should directly align with the learning objective.*

4	3	2	1
I consistently set specific learning objectives for each of my lessons based on Common Core standards, state standards, or district curriculum documents. My students understand that objectives come from standards and curriculum documents and not from the textbook.	I consistently set specific learning objectives for each of my lessons based on Common Core standards, state standards, or district curriculum documents.	I occasionally set specific learning objectives for each of my lessons based on Common Core standards, state standards, or district curriculum documents.	I seldom set specific learning objectives for each of my lessons based on Common Core standards, state standards, or district curriculum documents.
I consistently identify the knowledge and skills my students are expected to know within the objective. My students can explain the knowledge and skills they are expected to learn.	I consistently identify the knowledge and skills my students are expected to know within the objective.	I occasionally identify the knowledge and skills my students are expected to know within the objective.	I seldom identify the knowledge and skills my students are expected to know within the objective.
I consistently design and use learning activities that are directly aligned with the objective. My students can articulate the connection between an activity and the learning objective.	I consistently design and use learning activities that are directly aligned with the objective.	I occasionally design and use learning activities that are directly aligned with the objective.	I seldom design and use learning activities that are directly aligned with the objective.

FIGURE 1.2
Teacher Rubric: Setting Objectives *(continued)*

Communicate the learning objectives to students and parents: *Communicate learning objectives in student-friendly language by explicitly posting them, stating them verbally, and calling attention to them throughout a unit or lesson.*

4	3	2	1
I consistently post and discuss the learning objective in student-friendly language. My students are able to ask clarifying questions about the learning objective.	I consistently post and discuss the learning objective in student-friendly language.	I occasionally post and discuss the learning objective in student-friendly language.	I seldom post and discuss the learning objective in student-friendly language.
I consistently discuss the learning objective with my students. My students can verbalize what they are expected to learn and/or demonstrate.	I consistently discuss the learning objective with my students.	I occasionally discuss the learning objective with my students.	I seldom discuss the learning objective with my students.
I consistently reference and make connections between the learning objective and the activity during the lesson. My students can articulate the connection between what they are doing and what they should be learning.	I consistently reference and make connections between the learning objective and the activity during the lesson.	I occasionally reference and make connections between the learning objective and the activity during the lesson.	I seldom reference and make connections between the learning objective and the activity during the lesson.
I consistently communicate the learning objective with parents through newsletters, parent conferences, the school website, and/or blog postings. My students' parents understand what their children are supposed to be learning.	I consistently communicate the learning objective with parents through newsletters, parent conferences, the school website, and/or blog postings.	I occasionally communicate the learning objective with parents through newsletters, parent conferences, the school website, and/or blog postings.	I seldom or never communicate the learning objective with parents through newsletters, parent conferences, the school website, and/or blog postings.

FIGURE 1.2

Teacher Rubric: Setting Objectives *(continued)*

Connect the learning objectives to previous and future learning: *Teachers should explain how learning objectives connect with previous lessons or units and with the larger picture of a particular unit or course.*

4	3	2	1
I consistently explain to my students how learning objectives for the current lesson connect with previous lessons or units and with the larger picture of a particular unit or course. My students can communicate and discuss with one another the connections they see to previous learning.	I consistently explain to my students how learning objectives for the current lesson connect with previous lessons or units and with the larger picture of a particular unit or course	I occasionally explain to my students how learning objectives for the current lesson connect with previous lessons or units and with the larger picture of a particular unit or course.	I seldom explain to my students how learning objectives for the current lesson connect with previous lessons or units and with the larger picture of a particular unit or course.

Engage students in setting personal learning objectives: *Once the teacher has established and shared the learning objective, it is important for students to have the opportunity to adapt the objective to their personal interests.*

4	3	2	1
I consistently ask my students to personalize the objective by connecting what they will be learning to something they want to learn and/or already know. My students can personalize their learning goals and develop a plan for accomplishing their personalized goals.	I consistently ask my students to personalize the objective by connecting what they will be learning to something they want to learn and/or already know.	I occasionally ask students to personalize the objective by connecting what they will be learning to something they want to learn and/or already know.	I seldom ask students to personalize the objective by connecting what they will be learning to something they want to learn and/or already know.
I consistently have my students review their personalized goals to check their progress toward new learning. My students can discuss their progress over time.	I consistently have my students review their personalized goals to check their progress toward new learning.	I occasionally have my students review their personalized goals to check their progress toward new learning.	I seldom have my students review their personalized goals to check their progress toward new learning.

FIGURE 1.3					
Student Checklist: Setting Objectives					
		Always	Sometimes	Rarely	Never
LEARNING OBJECTIVES	I understand that the goals/learning objectives my teacher posts for the class align with standards and curriculum documents.				
	I can explain the knowledge and skills I am supposed to learn.				
	I understand how the activities I do in class connect with the learning objectives.				
COMMUNICATE	The objectives in my class are written in language I understand.				
	I know where to find my class goals/learning objectives because they are posted in the same place every day.				
	It helps me when my teacher gives us time to discuss what we are learning.				
	I can explain the connections between what I am doing and the learning objective.				
	I can explain the connections between the learning objectives in class and the information my teacher shares with my parents/guardians.				
CONNECT	I connect what I'm supposed to learn to things I already know or want to learn.				
	When my teacher gives us opportunities to discuss the learning goals, it helps me make clearer connections to prior learning.				
PERSONAL	I have a clear plan to accomplish my personal learning goals.				
	I take time to reflect on the progress I'm making toward achieving my goals and learning new things.				

FIGURE 1.4
Assessing Myself: Setting Objectives

I write the objective in student-friendly language that clearly reflects the content that students will learn and/or the skills they will acquire.

Not at all   To a great extent

0   1   2   3   4

I ensure that the objective reflects the content and skills to be learned rather than a list of activities.

Not at all   To a great extent

0   1   2   3   4

I ensure that the objective tightly aligns with information in the Common Core, state, or district standards.

Not at all   To a great extent

0   1   2   3   4

I create objectives that set the stage for rigorous, age-appropriate learning.

Not at all   To a great extent

0   1   2   3   4

I include opportunities to determine students' existing knowledge and skills as well as misconceptions related to the objective.

Not at all   To a great extent

0   1   2   3   4

FIGURE 1.4
Assessing Myself: Setting Objectives *(continued)*

I provide learning activities in the lesson that tightly align with the objective.

Not at all   To a great extent

| 0 | 1 | 2 | 3 | 4 |

I reference the objective throughout the lesson.

Not at all   To a great extent

| 0 | 1 | 2 | 3 | 4 |

I post the objective in clear sight of all students for reference throughout the lesson.

Not at all   To a great extent

| 0 | 1 | 2 | 3 | 4 |

I state the objective and allow students to make sense of what they will be learning and doing.

Not at all   To a great extent

| 0 | 1 | 2 | 3 | 4 |

I help students connect what they are learning and doing with the objective.

Not at all   To a great extent

| 0 | 1 | 2 | 3 | 4 |

I help students make connections between the objective and those of previous lessons/units so it is clear how they all fit in the overall course.

Not at all   To a great extent

| 0 | 1 | 2 | 3 | 4 |

FIGURE 1.5
Professional Growth Plan: Setting Objectives

1. What steps will I take to improve my practice of writing learning objectives in student-friendly language that clearly reflect the content that students will learn and/or the skills they will acquire?

2. How will I ensure objectives reflect the content and skills to be learned rather than a list of activities?

3. How will I ensure objectives tightly align with information in the Common Core, state, or district standards?

4. How will I more effectively create objectives that set the stage for rigorous, age-appropriate learning?

5. How will I include opportunities to determine students' existing knowledge and skills as well as misconceptions related to the objectives?

6. How will I make sure I provide learning activities that tightly align with the objectives?

FIGURE 1.5
Professional Growth Plan: Setting Objectives (continued)

7. In what ways will I reference objectives throughout lessons?

8. How and where will I post learning objectives so they are in clear sight of all students for reference throughout lessons?

9. How will I provide students with opportunities to make sense of what they will be learning and doing?

10. In what ways can I more effectively help students connect what they are learning and doing with the objectives?

11. How can I help students make connections between current objectives and those of previous lessons/units so it is clear how they all fit in the overall course?

FIGURE 1.6
Learning Objectives Worksheet

1. Students will demonstrate that they understand plot and character and are able to construct a narrative by writing a ghost story.

2. Students will demonstrate that they know three common causes of World War I, World War II, and the Vietnam conflict.

3. Students will demonstrate that they know the categories in the USDA MyPlate by creating a menu for a restaurant.

4. Working in small groups, students will create an "All About Me" slideshow presentation.

5. Make a list of sample learning objectives for this chapter. Be precise, but try to write them in a way that would allow participants to personalize the objectives.

Providing Feedback

Some education researchers believe that providing feedback is the most powerful thing a classroom teacher can do to enhance student achievement. After considering the findings from almost 8,000 studies, researcher John Hattie commented, "The most powerful single modification that enhances achievement is feedback. The simplest prescription for improving education must be 'dollops of feedback'" (1992, p. 9). We need to provide our students with feedback in a way that is corrective and helpful as they move toward the objective, without overwhelming them with truckloads of feedback at once. Keep the dollops—spoon-size portions—frequent and always targeted on the learning objective.

Why This Strategy?

Setting objectives and providing feedback work in tandem. As discussed in the previous section, teachers need to clearly identify learning objectives so students understand what they are expected to know and demonstrate. Teachers should also provide criteria or a rubric so students can identify when they have achieved those objectives (Hattie & Timperley, 2007). Feedback should be provided for tasks that are related to the learning objectives; this way, students understand the purpose of the work they are asked to do, they build a coherent understanding of a content domain, and they develop high levels of skill in a specific domain.

Imagine looking down a long, straight road to the horizon. This road represents learning, pre-K through 12. Setting objectives tells students exactly where they are going during a given lesson or unit. Once they begin down the road toward an objective, feedback keeps them on the path. If students veer onto the shoulder or take a wrong turn, corrective feedback sets them back on the road.

The following four recommendations provide guidance for teachers as they create a learning evironment for student success. Teacher are encouraged to

1. **Provide feedback that addresses what is correct and elaborates on what students need to do next.** Feedback should help students understand what is correct as well as specifics about what is incorrect. Effective feedback should also provide information about how close students come to meeting the objective and details about what they need to do to attain the next level of performance.

2. **Provide feedback appropriately in time to meet students' needs.** Providing immediate feedback can encourage students to practice, and it helps them make connections between what they do and the results they achieve.

3. **Provide feedback that is criterion referenced.** Feedback should address the knowledge that students are supposed to learn and provide information that helps them know what needs to be done to improve their performance. Rubrics are a valuable tool for providing the criterion and judging performance.

4. **Engage students in the feedback process.** Although teachers are the primary providers of feedback, students can also effectively monitor their own progress. Student-led feedback positively impacts student achievement.

Reflecting on My Current Practice

The questions listed in Figure 1.7 are provided as a means to help you implement instructional practices for providing feedback.

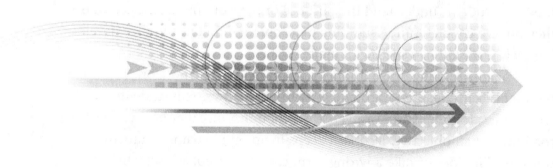

FIGURE 1.7
Reflecting on Current Practice: Providing Feedback

1. Do I provide feedback in a timely manner?

2. Do I establish and share well-defined criteria against which work or performance will be judged?

3. Do I provide feedback that is specific enough to help students improve? (In other words, does my feedback elaborate on what they already know or strengthen a skill?)

4. Do I provide feedback that aligns with the learning objective?

5. Do I provide corrective feedback as opposed to praise?

6. Do I help students develop the skills necessary to provide their own feedback?

7. After providing feedback, do I give my students the opportunity to rework until correct?

Bringing the Strategy to Life in the Classroom

Recommendation One:
Provide feedback that addresses what is correct and elaborates on what students need to do next.

As a learner, it is important to know not only if your response is right or wrong but also why. Research indicates that when a teacher only provides right/wrong feedback, there is actually a negative correlation to student achievement (Bangert-Drowns, Kulik, Kulik, & Morgan, 1991; Beesley & Apthorp, 2010). In the following vignette, see how Mr. Ward fails to provide specific feedback to Paul about the mistakes he makes and how Paul could benefit from such feedback.

Mr. Ward returns Monday's homework assignment on Thursday of the same week (see Figure 1.8). With the lack of specific feedback on the assignment, Paul knows he missed a lot of problems but doesn't understand why. He is also left with the feeling that he doesn't understand math—some people just "get" math, and he isn't one of them. In this case, specific feedback would have helped Paul immensely. He looks at problem D and understands immediately that he didn't get it right—he didn't even try. Looking at problem E, he knows he got the problem wrong, but he doesn't know why. Mr. Ward should have let Paul know that his single-digit multiplication was completely accurate; his mistake was in aligning the columns. If Paul had remembered to add a zero (as was done in the example), he likely would have come up with the correct answer. Had Paul received this kind of specific feedback, he would have understood his mistakes and been able to correct his work. He also would have understood the process more clearly and would be more likely to be successful on future work. After providing the specific feedback to Paul, Mr. Ward should have provided Paul with an opportunity to rework the missed problems to get the correct answers, thus achieving a feeling of success.

Recommendation Two:
Provide feedback appropriately in time to meet students' needs.

It is important to provide specific feedback, but it is essential to provide that feedback in a timely manner. As with much in life, timing is everything—especially when feedback can help a student complete a task correctly. As in the previous example, immediacy helps. Providing immediate feedback can encourage students to practice, and it helps them make connections between what they do and the results they achieve. An adage we often hear is "practice makes perfect." We think it is more accurate to say "practice makes permanent." Only perfect practice makes perfect performance. If students don't receive specific feedback in a timely manner, then they will keep doing their work incorrectly and reinforce bad habits. In the previous example, if Paul had received both specific and timely feedback, he would have been able to practice correctly, which would lead to more perfect performance.

FIGURE 1.8
Sample Graded Mathematics Quiz

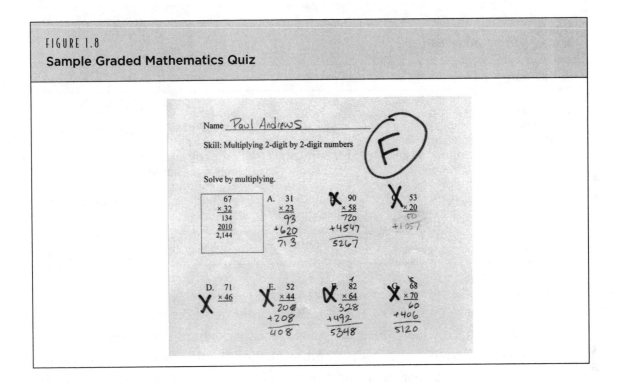

Recommendation Three:
Provide feedback that is criterion referenced.

Rubrics are not just for teachers; they also let students know up front what they need to know or be able to do. They help take the surprise or mystery out of scores and grades received. Rubrics help articulate levels of performance in terms students can understand, so they know exactly what they should know and be able to do before they begin their work. In the following vignette, see how Mr. Keller uses a rubric to provide clear criteria for his students.

Mr. Keller thinks it is important for students in his theater arts class to assess their basic acting elements. He passes out a well-defined rubric that he created on Rubistar™ (http://rubistar.4teachers.org) for these acting elements and reviews each, including the accuracy of their diction, the degree to which they use effective breathing control, the precision of their body alignment, and the depth of their concentration. Beneath each element in the rubric is a space for student self-reflection. An excerpt showing one row of the rubric is shown in Figure 1.9. He also asks students to discuss what they think it might look like if they each scored a 3 for each element of the rubric.

FIGURE 1.9
Excerpt from Student Rubric

Category	4	3	2	1
Effective breathing control	Student is consistently breathing properly and always supports his/her voice through the end of each phrase.	Student is usually breathing properly but occasionally does not support his/her voice through the end of each phrase.	Student sometimes breathes properly and only occasionally supports his/her voice through the end of each phrase.	Student is rarely breathing properly and seldom supports his/her voice through end of each phrase.

Once every two weeks, Mr. Keller collects students' rubrics and meets with students individually to provide feedback about their progress. During each conference, the student and Mr. Keller identify areas in which the student is doing well, areas that could be improved, and specific strategies for improvement.

**Recommendation Four:
Engage students in the feedback process.**

Self- and peer feedback is underused, yet it is a highly effective and flexible method of helping students think about their progress. In order for students to effectively provide feedback to themselves, they must be given clear criteria for performance and be intentionally taught how to apply those criteria to their work. The teacher should model the process through think-alouds and class discussions. He or she should not assume students can take a rubric and accurately apply it to their work.

Much like self-feedback, peer feedback requires the teacher to take time to intentionally teach and model the process. Peer feedback does not mean that students actually grade one another or score one another's papers. Instead, the goal is for students to clarify what was correct or incorrect in their classmates' work, providing their partners with clear steps to improve. In the previous example, we saw how Mr. Keller used a rubric to provide his students with clear criteria against which to self-assess. In addition to using the rubric to give students clear criteria for self-feedback, the example below shows how he used the same criteria to scaffold the process of peer feedback.

Every Friday, Mr. Keller has his students rate themselves and their acting partners on several performance elements. At the end of class every Friday, students meet with their acting partners and share their rubrics. At this meeting, they explain why they rated themselves and their partners as they did. Together, they discuss how they each might move closer to a 3 on each of the selected elements of the rubric.

Rubrics and Checklists

The teacher rubric provided in Figure 1.10 is intended to be a tool used for reflection on the way in which you currently provide feedback in your classroom. It is designed so that a 3 represents best practice as indicated by the research. A 4 indicates both teacher best practice as described in a 3 and how that practice transfers into student behaviors. You can also use this rubric as a growth tool, seeing where you are now and what the next level might look like. This will provide you with valuable information as you build your professional growth plan later.

Using the teacher rubric will give you the chance to reflect on your practice. You can also ask your students how they perceive the way you provide feedback. Figure 1.11 provides a student checklist you might want to use. Periodically give this checklist to your students, and ask them to react honestly to the statements. This checklist can help your students better understand how feedback helps them learn. It can also provide valuable information to you about how your students view the process of providing feedback.

Tools, Templates, and Protocols

If you are using this handbook as part of a school PLC or book study, Figure 1.12 provides statements that can serve as discussion prompts. Likewise, if you are using this book for individual growth, think about these prompts as they relate to your classroom practice. For example, if your answer to the first statement is a 0 or 1, then what steps should you take to move toward the other end of the spectrum, "to a great extent"? Use your individual or team results from Figure 1.12 to form the basis of a professional growth plan (see Figure 1.13).

FIGURE 1.10
Teacher Rubric: Providing Feedback

Provide feedback that addresses what is correct and elaborates on what students need to do next: *Feedback should help students understand what was correct and what was incorrect. Effective feedback should also provide information about how close students come to meeting the criterion and details about what they need to do to attain the next level of performance.*

4	3	2	1
I consistently provide corrective feedback on what is correct and incorrect and explain why. My students understand how feedback helps them get closer to the learning objective.	I consistently provide corrective feedback on what is correct and incorrect and explain why.	I occasionally provide corrective feedback on what is correct and incorrect and explain why.	I seldom provide corrective feedback on what is correct and incorrect and explain why.
I consistently give my students an opportunity to correct mistakes or redo work based on feedback. My students use the feedback I provide to revise their work.	I consistently give my students an opportunity to correct mistakes or redo work based on feedback.	I occasionally give my students an opportunity to correct mistakes or redo work based on feedback.	I seldom give my students an opportunity to correct mistakes or redo work based on feedback.

Provide feedback appropriately in time to meet students' needs: *Providing immediate feedback can encourage students to practice, and it helps them make connections between what they do and the results they achieve.*

4	3	2	1
I consistently provide corrective feedback promptly after a test or performance. My students use feedback to improve their practice.	I consistently provide corrective feedback promptly after a test or performance.	I occasionally provide corrective feedback promptly after a test or performance.	I seldom provide corrective feedback promptly after a test or performance.

FIGURE 1.10
Teacher Rubric: Providing Feedback (continued)

4	3	2	1
I consistently provide my students with feedback to help them make connections between what they are doing and the results they hope to achieve. My students use my feedback to make these connections.	I consistently provide my students with feedback to help them make connections between what they are doing and the results they hope to achieve.	I occasionally provide my students with feedback to help them make connections between what they are doing and the results they hope to achieve.	I seldom provide my students with feedback to help them make connections between what they are doing and the results they hope to achieve.

Provide feedback that is criterion referenced: *Feedback should address the knowledge that students are supposed to learn and provide information that helps them know what needs to be done to improve their performance. Rubrics are a valuable tool for providing the criterion and judging performance.*

4	3	2	1
I consistently explain what is required to reach a proficient level of performance. My students can describe what is required to reach a proficient level of performance.	I consistently explain what is required to reach a proficient level of performance.	I occasionally explain what is required to reach a proficient level of performance.	I seldom explain what is required to reach a proficient level of performance.
Prior to a unit of study, I consistently provide criteria/rubrics that describe each level of performance. My students are able to use the criteria/rubrics as a target for their performance.	Prior to a unit of study, I consistently provide criteria/rubrics that describe each level of performance.	Prior to a unit of study, I occasionally provide criteria/rubrics that describe each level of performance.	Prior to a unit of study, I seldom provide criteria/rubrics that describe each level of performance.

FIGURE 1.10
Teacher Rubric: Providing Feedback (continued)

4	3	2	1
I consistently use criteria/rubrics to judge student performance. My students can judge their own work based on the criteria/rubrics provided.	I consistently use criteria/rubrics to judge student performance.	I occasionally use criteria/rubrics to judge student performance.	I seldom use criteria/rubrics to judge student performance.

Engage students in the feedback process: *Although teachers are the primary providers of feedback, students can effectively monitor their own progress. Student-led feedback positively impacts student achievement.*

4	3	2	1
I consistently provide opportunities for my students to monitor their own progress. My students can track their progress as they are learning.	I consistently provide opportunities for my students to monitor their own progress.	I occasionally provide opportunities for my students to monitor their own progress.	I seldom provide opportunities for my students to monitor their own progress.
I consistently model techniques for my students to use as they compare their and their peers' work to the criteria/rubrics provided. My students can use the criteria/rubrics to judge their and their peers' work.	I consistently model techniques for my students to use as they compare their and their peers' work to the criteria/rubrics provided.	I occasionally model techniques for my students to use as they compare their and their peers' work to the criteria/rubrics provided.	I seldom model techniques for my students to use as they compare their and their peers' work to the criteria/rubrics provided.

FIGURE 1.11 Student Checklist: Providing Feedback					
		Always	Sometimes	Rarely	Never
CORRECTIVE	I understand how feedback helps me get closer to the learning objective.				
	When my teacher corrects my papers, I receive feedback on what is correct, what is incorrect, and why.				
	I redo my work based on the feedback my teacher gives me.				
TIMELY	My teacher grades and returns my tests and major assignments quickly after I take them or turn them in.				
	I use feedback from my teacher to make connections between what I am doing and the results I want.				
CRITERION REEFERENCED	I can describe what is required to reach a proficient level of performance.				
	I can use the criteria/rubrics my teacher provides as a target for my learning.				
	I can use the criteria/rubrics my teacher provides to judge my work.				
PERSONAL	I can use rubrics as a guide to improve my work.				
	My teacher spends class time teaching me how to judge and reflect on my work and progress.				
	I can use rubrics to judge my work and the work of my peers.				

FIGURE 1.12
Assessing Myself: Providing Feedback

I provide feedback in a timely manner.

Not at all   To a great extent

0   1   2   3   4

I establish and share well-defined criteria against which work or performance will
be judged.

Not at all   To a great extent

0   1   2   3   4

I provide feedback that is specific enough to help students improve by elaborating on
what they already know or by strengthening a skill.

Not at all   To a great extent

0   1   2   3   4

I provide feedback that aligns with the learning objective.

Not at all   To a great extent

0   1   2   3   4

I provide corrective feedback rather than praise for effort.

Not at all   To a great extent

0   1   2   3   4

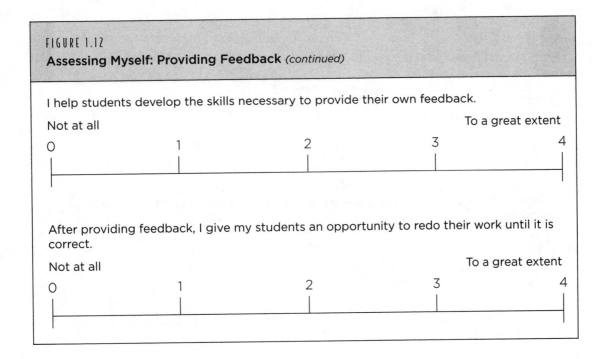

FIGURE 1.12
Assessing Myself: Providing Feedback *(continued)*

I help students develop the skills necessary to provide their own feedback.

Not at all   To a great extent

0   1   2   3   4

After providing feedback, I give my students an opportunity to redo their work until it is correct.

Not at all   To a great extent

0   1   2   3   4

FIGURE 1.13
Professional Growth Plan: Providing Feedback

1. How will I provide feedback in a timely manner?

2. How will I establish and share well-defined criteria (rubrics) against which work or performance will be judged?

3. How will I ensure the feedback I provide is specific enough to help students improve (i.e., elaborate on what they already know or strengthen a skill)?

4. How will I align my feedback with the learning objective?

5. How will I know that I am providing corrective feedback rather than praise for effort?

6. How will I help students develop the skills necessary to provide their own feedback?

7. After providing feedback, how will I give my students an opportunity to redo their work until it is correct?

2

Reinforcing Effort
and Providing Recognition

Reinforcing Effort

The strategies highlighted in this chapter continue to reflect the first priority of a teacher: to create an environment in which students are continually reminded that they are a vital part of the classroom and are capable of learning even the most challenging content and processes.

How many times have you heard or uttered statements or felt frustrated because students didn't seem to be motivated? Most teachers know intuitively that student motivation plays a critical role in the learning process. To that end, recent research has demonstrated the roles that reinforcing effort and providing recognition play in the process of motivating students (Dweck, 2006, 2010). Many students may not realize the influence effort has on their success in school. In light of this, teachers are integral in helping students recognize that effort helps them succeed. In fact, simply teaching students that added effort pays off in terms of enhanced achievement will increase student motivation. Research supports this belief; studies indicate a link between motivation and achievement (Eccles, Wigfield, & Schiefele, 1998; Greene, Miller, Crowson, Duke, & Akey, 2004; Phan, 2009). What is this link? Motivation influences how much effort students expend and how long they persist in working on tasks, and the amount of effort and persistence students put forth influences their level of academic success (Bouffard, Boisvert, Vezeau, & Larouche, 1995; Elliot, McGregor, & Gable, 1999).

Motivation influences achievement, but what influences motivation? Student motivation is complex; many variables influence whether students engage and persist in tasks, including their teachers', parents', and cultural beliefs (Wigfield & Eccles, 2000). Students' beliefs about their own competence and whether they have control over the outcome of a task—as well as their interest in the task and the reason *why* they are interested—also influence their engagement and persistence (Atkinson, 1964; Bandura, 1986; Covington, 1992; Pintrich & Schrauben, 1992; Pintrich & Schunk, 2002).

In this chapter, we focus on two strategies that are related to motivation: reinforcing effort and providing recognition. These two strategies affect one or more of the following student variables:

- Self-efficacy: beliefs about one's competency.
- Control beliefs: beliefs about one's ability to influence what is happening or will happen.
- Intrinsic motivation: motivation that comes from an individual's desire for self-satisfaction or pleasure in completing the task rather than from an external source, such as a reward.
- Task value: beliefs about one's reasons for doing a task.

Why This Strategy?

One of the greatest gifts a classroom teacher can give to his or her students is knowledge about and ongoing support related to the importance of effort. A common thread in conversations among teachers is the notion that students don't come to school ready and motivated to learn. Student readiness is related to how well students are prepared to understand and apply the underpinnings of effort (e.g., "The harder I work, the smarter I get" or "The harder I work, the more successful I will be"). Although it would be marvelous if all students grasped and put into practice the principles of hard work and satisfaction with internal rewards, the fact remains that effort is associated with a learned set of skills.

When teachers probe student thinking about effort, they are often amazed by the preconceptions held by their students. Students often explain that individual classmates are successful because the teachers like them, because they are simply lucky and always seem to do well on assignments and exams, or because they are just naturally smart. Rarely do students say that a peer does well in school because he or she works hard. This attitude is exacerbated by sports figures who, instead of commenting on how hard they have worked to achieve a high level of performance within their respective sports, will comment about how lucky they are as professional athletes. The message this conveys to students of all ages is that it is not so much about working hard to achieve a high level of proficiency as it is about simply being in the right place at the right time. Of course, nothing could be further from the truth. Though they may have some natural ability or experience some luck, individuals who achieve greatness in any area of endeavor do so because they are willing to dedicate hours to practice, and they understand that the harder they work, the better they will become. There are many gifted athletes who do not make it at the proverbial next level because they do not understand that hard work translates into greatness. This is similarly true of people in many professions.

Carol Dweck's research on student success describes teacher and student belief systems related to effort. Dweck states that people hold one of two beliefs about student intelligence. There are those, holding a fixed mind-set, who behave in a manner that reflects a belief that intelligence cannot change—some students are smart, whereas others are not. For students with a fixed mind-set, their thinking inhibits their ability to believe that effort can play a role in positively impacting their achievement. The second set of beliefs is found in individuals who possess a growth mind-set, which is a belief that intelligence can be developed through knowledge and the application of effort. Students placed in a classroom with a teacher who demonstrates a growth mind-set—believing that all students can learn and be successful—adopt that belief system and convey that thinking through tenacity and the quality of their work (Dweck, 2010).

Teachers establish a positive environment for learning by intentionally scaffolding classroom experiences that allow students to be faced with challenges. Students nurtured in this type of learning environment will, when faced with challenges both in and outside of school, respond positively knowing that they have been successful in the past. In addition, students who are not given instruction about effort or who are praised for their intellect—instead of their "stick-to-itiveness"—are less confident and will, at times, shy away from challenges for fear of failing.

The following article is taken from the sports section of Colorado's *Greeley Tribune* and provides an excellent example of the types of stories and articles that teachers can employ to teach students about the relationship between effort and achievement, the importance of working hard, and how people outside of school have faced and overcome challenges. As you read the article, note the many statements that are grounded in the philosophy of "the harder I work, the more successful I become."

> Caught in mid-swing of one of her team-high 314 kills from last season, Dulcie Stone is literally the poster child for the 2007 University of Northern Colorado volleyball team.

Not bad for the girl nobody believed in four years ago.

As one of the nine graduates from Karval High School in 2003, Stone was a standout on the Trojans volleyball team. She was a two-time All-State selection and played in the Colorado High School Activities Association All-State volleyball match as a senior. But when she mailed out tapes of herself playing volleyball to Division I schools in hopes of obtaining a scholarship, all Stone received was criticism.

Some schools said she wasn't big enough. Others told her she didn't have enough talent. Most of them just didn't believe a girl from a school with an enrollment of about 30 kids could make it on the Division I level, especially since she had never played club volleyball.

The Bears should be grateful for their oversight.

The walk-on, small-school standout UNC gave an opportunity to in 2003 is not only coming off an honorable mention All–Big Sky Conference season last year, Stone will start her redshirt senior home season at 11:30 a.m. today at Butler-Hancock Sports Pavilion as a co-captain.

"I'm so, so excited," the 5-foot-10 outside hitter said. "To be able to step out there with the Bears jersey on is amazing. Every time we have a game day I get butterflies just thinking about it."

The journey wasn't all roses, though.

Even when Stone arrived at UNC she had to overcome several obstacles, including negative comments from pessimistic teammates. For the first two years with the Bears, not only did Stone stay in Greeley when the team traveled, most of the time she didn't even participate in six-on-six drills in practice as the coaches didn't feel she was one of the best 12 players on the team at the time.

"Some of my teammates were like, 'You know, this probably isn't for you. You should just quit,'" Stone said. ". . . But I'm not a quitter. I'm not going to give up on something just because it's hard."

Stone's persistence paid off.

Before too long Stone was competing in all of the drills in practice. As a redshirt sophomore she started to travel with the team. And last year, as a redshirt junior, Stone played in all 106 games, averaging 2.96 kills and 3.35 digs per match.

Stone said anything can be accomplished if you just believe in yourself.

"Never give up on what you want to do," Stone said. "If you are just focusing on your one big goal, it's going to be really hard. But if you are focusing on little things each year, it's going to pan out."

Stone has taken that same approach into her final season. She plans to focus all of her energy on showing the rest of the teams in the Big Sky the Bears are better than the eighth-place finish they were given in the Big Sky preseason poll.

"I think it's better to be ranked as an underdog," said Stone with a smile. "It puts a little fire in you to prove people wrong."

Stone's been doing that her entire college career. I wouldn't doubt her now.

Source: From "Star Thrives Despite Doubts," by T. Wright, August 31, 2007, *The Greeley Tribune.* Copyright 2007 by Swift Newspapers, Inc. Reprinted with permission.

The following three recommendations provide guidance for teachers as they help students understand the importance of effort. Teachers are encouraged to

1. **Teach students about the relationship between effort and achievement.** Teaching about effort can positively influence students' thinking, behavior, and beliefs about their ability to succeed. This is particularly true if it helps students understand that success comes because of effort and that they alone control the amount of effort they put forth.

2. **Provide students with explicit guidance about exactly what it means to expend effort.** Teachers can help students develop an operational definition for what it means to work hard by being explicit about the actions and behaviors associated with effort in a variety of academic situations.

3. **Ask students to keep track of their effort and achievement.** A powerful way to help students make the connection between effort and success is to have them keep track of their effort and its relationship to achievement.

Reflecting on My Current Practice

The questions listed in Figure 2.1 are provided as a means to assist you as you implement the instructional practices for reinforcing effort.

FIGURE 2.1
Reflecting on Current Practice: Reinforcing Effort

1. Do I help students develop an understanding of the relationship that exists between how hard they work and their success?

2. Do I continually provide students with examples of effort and stories about people who have overcome odds and/or worked hard in order to succeed?

3. Do I ask students to provide stories about effort and success?

4. Do I break tasks into smaller component parts so students can hear about and visualize what it means to work hard? (What does working together in small groups look and sound like? What does studying hard for a quiz look and sound like?)

5. Do I use rubrics and/or lists to define what effort means in my class?

6. Do I provide students with ongoing opportunities to track their effort and relate their success to their effort?

Bringing the Strategy to Life in the Classroom

Recommendation One:
Teach students about the relationship between effort and achievement.

Helping your students understand the importance of effort through direct instruction cannot be conducted in the same manner as teaching content-related concepts and skills. Information related to effort should be a part of your planning and delivery for every lesson. This means you must be diligent in the ongoing selection and placement of relevant stories, articles, and discussions throughout the year. Providing examples and guiding targeted discussions help students create a mental image of what effort looks like and how it helps them succeed.

In the following four vignettes, notice how teachers at various grade levels provide direct instruction about the relationship that exists between effort and achievement. In the first example, which comes from a 2nd grade class, see how Mr. Payne demonstrates the importance of clearly defining what effort is both in and out of the classroom.

Mr. Payne's 2nd grade students experience difficulty while working in groups. Although Mr. Payne consistently reminds his students to stay on task and work well with one another, they often fail to work up to expectations. During a conversation with Ms. Bartholomew, his induction mentor, Mr. Payne explains how frustrated he is becoming with the lack of effort displayed by his class as they work in groups. Ms. Bartholomew smiles and asks if he has thoroughly explained what he expects.

She asks, "Did you tell them what it means to work hard? Did you discuss what it looks and sounds like when students put forth good effort in order to work well together?" Mr. Payne realizes that he has been using many catch phrases such as "work hard," "take pride in your work," and "be more committed to your work," but he has never taken the time to dissect the statements and clearly define, model, and practice what each really means.

The next day, Mr. Payne returns to class and provides a rubric that defines the phrases he has been using. He notices that even though he and his class use common language as they discuss the connections between their work and their success, a solid definition of the smaller components of effort helps his students see what he means when he says, "You need to work harder." When Mr. Payne provides his students with clear descriptions of what it means to work hard, they are able to apply the components of effort to their own work.

In order for your students to reap the benefits associated with effort, you must employ instructional practices that embed effort strands into every lesson. This means telling stories about how you persevered, how others have conquered seemingly insurmountable obstacles, and what hard work looks and feels like when it is put into practice.

In schools around the country, we see signs that say "Work Hard, Get Smart." Simply relaying this fact to students, however, has not changed beliefs or actions. Teachers, therefore, can and must provide direct instruction and ongoing support related to this powerful strategy. In the following vignette, Mr. Christopher provides explicit instruction to help students develop an understanding of the connections that exist between working hard and achievement.

Mr. Christopher was surprised by how many of his 5th grade students did not believe they could be successful in school. While planning his lessons for the upcoming week, he decides to share a story about Joba Chamberlain, a relief pitcher for the New York Yankees. Mr. Christopher reads the article to his students, stopping periodically to ask questions about what led to the pitcher's success. One student answers, "I think Joba worked hard for years and years before his hard worked paid off."

"You are right, he did work hard *and* it did pay off," replies Mr. Christopher. As the discussion continues, students share times when they worked hard both in and out of school, and they discuss the positive results of working hard. Mr. Christopher realizes that he needs to have many more conversations with his students to help them develop a belief about effort. He realizes he needs to plan weekly to include stories that emphasize the effect effort has on performance, using both national and local celebrities. He also decides to ask his students to write personal stories about times when effort made a difference in their achievement and to share those stories with classmates. He knows that when students can see the connection between effort and achievement, they will be more likely to put in that effort.

Eighth grade teacher Ms. Larson uses media and an advance organizer to highlight the four attributes of achievement—luck, other people, ability, and effort. She attends a workshop that emphasizes the importance of helping students believe in themselves and their capabilities. The information really resonates with her because she feels that many of her students do not understand the importance of effort. The next day in class, Ms. Larson shows her students small video clips from the movie *The Blind Side*. She asks students to think about how and why the main character, Michael Oher, changes over the course of the movie. Ms. Larson provides her students with an advance organizer that lists the four attributes of achievement.

Students work in teams of four and use the advance organizer to capture how Michael Oher is depicted throughout the film relative to his luck, the people in his life, his ability, and his effort. Prior to beginning the assignment, students hypothesize about which attribute contributed most to Michael's eventual success. Early in the class discussion, many students are surprised at how all of the factors play a role in Michael's success. Nevertheless, it becomes clear that without effort, he would never have made it out of poverty and into the National Football League. Ms. Larson is thus able to show her students that, although the four attributes of success are important, the one they can directly control is effort.

The final vignette offers a view of how a department or building-wide approach to helping students make the connections between effort and achievement can pay huge dividends. Members of the Valley High School English department are frustrated at how unmotivated their students are in class. "It seems that they either don't care or don't get it," states one of the teachers. A colleague counters this statement: "Honestly, I don't agree with your statement. In my class, we talk daily about working hard and doing your best. In fact, I have even given my students a rubric. They can tell you what effort looks like in my class."

Another teacher chimes in, "I think our team is missing the mark. We need to take a team approach and build on the success some teachers are seeing. What if we consistently used effort rubrics in every class here at Valley High? Students would have a very different outlook, and we would see changes in what they do and what they believe about themselves and their work. Maybe if we're successful, we can share this approach with other departments."

Although individual teachers can have a huge impact on helping their students recognize the importance of effort, the preceding vignette shows how that effect is greatly magnified when staff work together.

Recommendation Two:
Provide students with explicit guidance about exactly what it means to expend effort.

One common complaint from teachers is that their students do not study hard at home prior to a test. When asked what it means to study hard for a test, however, some teachers are unable to identify which skills are necessary to help their students. If teachers cannot clearly articulate the steps or parts of a desired practice, then how can students be expected to demonstrate the skills or perform the tasks effectively? It is paramount that teachers consider and plan for intentional instruction that helps students understand critical aspects of how to perform a given task. When teachers do this, students are able to recognize that the amount of effort applied is directly proportional to success achieved. Consider the differences in approaches applied by Ms. Hurst and Ms. Ross in the following examples. Which approach has a higher probability of giving students a clear understanding of what effort means relative to the assignment?

Ms. Hurst: "Students, you have a large test tomorrow. I want you to know that everything on the study guide will be found somewhere on the test. You must work hard today in your learning teams and study very hard tonight at home. I know you each want to succeed, so let's get to work."

Even though Ms. Hurst provides a study guide for her students and what she thinks is incentive to work hard, students are actually on their own to figure out how to study. Some of her students, especially those who have not already developed a strong set of study skills, don't know where to begin. They want to succeed, but they don't really understand the components of effort when applied to studying for a test.

Ms. Ross: "Students, you have a large test tomorrow. You have demonstrated a willingness to stay with the various tasks I have given you as you prepared for the test. Today I need you to work hard in your learning teams. Let's do a quick review. I will use Inspiration® software to capture your ideas about what it means to work hard with your team members."

Students raise their hands and begin to share what has been taught and reinforced about working hard in their learning teams. One student states, "It means we each have to be sure to do the jobs assigned." Another student says, "Everyone is responsible for contributing answers to the questions and asking for help when they are confused." A third student explains, "We have to summarize what we are learning as we answer the questions so we have a clear understanding of the materials."

Ms. Ross captures her students' ideas and recognizes them for their answers. She then asks students to begin working. At the end of the class period, she stops the students and says, "Before you leave class, I want to make sure that each of you understands what is expected of you as you study tonight. I am asking you to study hard for tomorrow's test. What does that mean?"

Students are eager to demonstrate that they understand what studying hard at home looks and sounds like. Brad says, "I know that you want us to use our notes and review them by reading a section aloud and then repeating the information to ourselves." Samantha says, "Yes, and sometimes it works better if we read a section and then make bulleted notes about what we are learning." Frederica states, "We also need to take the work that we created today in our learning teams and use the summary statements to help us review the information." Once again, Ms. Ross captures their responses with Inspiration®, and she posts the final document on the class website later that day. She ends the class by saying, "Tonight before you begin studying, go to the class website and review the list we just created to remind yourselves about what we agreed effort means in preparing for this test."

Ms. Ross provides her students with tools for success. Not only does she give them tools to use in the classroom, she also gives them specific support outside of the classroom.

Recommendation Three:
Ask students to keep track of their effort and achievement.

In order for your students to apply practices related to effort, you must first help them develop a rich understanding of the strategy. Throughout the day, the more often that students are immersed in routines and opportunities that emphasize and model the important underpinnings of effort, the better equipped they will be to view their own effort and track their progress over time.

Charting effort and achievement will reveal patterns and help students recognize the connections between the two. Students can use a simple chart to do this (Figure 2.2). The sections across the top of the chart could read *Date, Assignment, Effort,* and *Achievement.* As students view their assignments they can readily see the relationship between the effort they apply and the achievement or grade earned.

In addition to charting the relationship between effort and achievement, it is always good to ask students to describe what they learned from the experience. For example, periodically ask students to describe what they notice about the relationship between the effort they put into a project or task and the achievement that results. Figure 2.3 illustrates how a student can keep track of effort and achievement over time. Reflecting on students' experiences in this way heightens their awareness of the power of effort.

See how tracking effort and achievement over time is represented in the following vignette.

Sara wants to play basketball just like all her friends. She works hard in practice and knows that she is improving, even though it is to a lesser degree

FIGURE 2.2
Charting Effort and Achievement

Date	Assignment	Effort	Achievement
Friday, October 20	Homework: Solving linear functions	2	1
Wednesday, October 25	Quiz: Graphs of linear functions	4	2
Thursday, October 26	In-class Practice: Solving linear equations	4	3
Tuesday, October 31	Quiz: Solving linear equations	4	4

FIGURE 2.3
Graphing Effort and Achievement

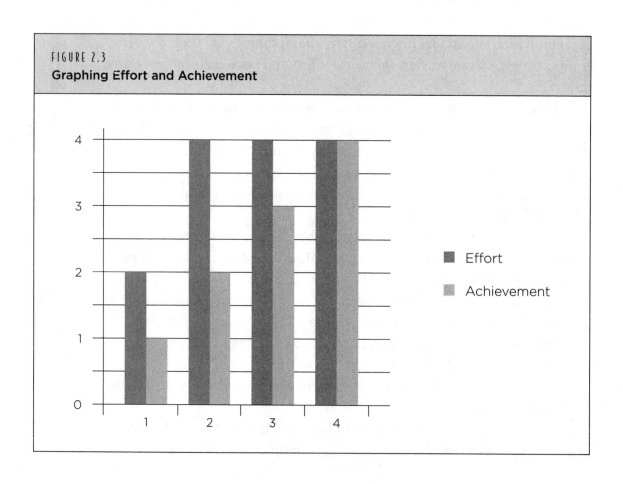

than some of her friends. Coach Cecil meets with his players individually every Monday to discuss the weekend games. Each time he meets with Sara, he refers to a chart that shows the number of shots she took, points she scored, free throws she attempted, and free throws she made. Coach Cecil explains how impressed he is with Sara's work ethic and shows her how she is slowly improving.

At the end of the season Coach Cecil meets individually with each of the players to thank them for their contributions and to encourage them to come out for basketball over the summer. When he meets with Sara, he worries about pointing only to moderate improvement over the season.

He says, "Sara, come in and sit down. I have your chart here and I realize you worked very hard to improve, and you did. I know you were hoping for greater results. Please still consider coming out for summer basketball."

Sara beams, "Coach, you can count on me for the summer team. And don't worry about my improvement, I did get better. There is another chart I have been keeping that has encouraged me throughout the season. While you were charting my progress in basketball, I was charting my speed in running sprints and saw how much I had improved. It has been a great season for me!"

Rubrics and Checklists

The teacher rubric provided in Figure 2.4 is intended to be a tool used for reflection on the way in which you currently reinforce effort in your classroom. It is designed so that a 3 represents best practice as indicated by the research. A 4 indicates both teacher best practice as described in a 3 and how that practice transfers into student behaviors. You can also use this rubric as a growth tool, seeing where you are now and what the next level might look like. This will provide you with valuable information as you build your professional growth plan later.

Using the teacher rubric will give you the chance to reflect on your practice. You can also ask your students how they perceive the way you reinforce effort. Figure 2.5 provides a student checklist you might want to use. Periodically give this checklist to your students, and ask them to react honestly to the statements. This checklist can help your students better understand how effort helps them learn, and it can provide valuable feedback to you about how your students view the process of reinforcing effort.

Tools, Templates, and Protocols

If you are using this handbook as part of a school PLC or book study, Figure 2.6 provides statements that can serve as discussion prompts. Likewise, if you are using this book for individual growth, think about these prompts as they relate to your classroom practice. For example, if your answer to the first statement is a 0 or 1, then what steps should you take to move toward the other end of the spectrum, "to a great extent"? Use your individual or team results from Figure 2.6 to form the basis of a professional growth plan (see Figure 2.7).

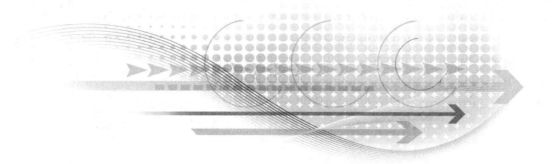

FIGURE 2.4
Teacher Rubric: Reinforcing Effort

Teach students about the relationship between effort and achievement. *Teaching about effort can positively influence students' thinking, behavior, and beliefs about their ability to succeed if it helps them understand that success comes because of effort and that they control the amount of effort they put forth.*

4	3	2	1
I understand the importance of effort and continually explain to my students how effort can positively affect school and life success. My students can identify how effort or the lack of effort has impacted their personal success.	I understand the importance of effort and continually explain to my students how effort can positively affect school and life success.	I have a limited understanding of the importance of effort and occasionally explain to my students how effort can positively affect school and life success.	I don't understand the importance of effort and use global statements that reference hard work and study habits.
I continually provide personal, local, and national stories that demonstrate the impact of effort on success. My students can identify and share stories that demonstrate the impact of effort.	I continually provide personal, local, and national stories that demonstrate the impact of effort on success.	I occasionally provide personal, local, and national stories that demonstrate the impact of effort on success.	I seldom provide personal, local, and national stories that demonstrate the impact of effort on success.
I continually monitor my students' attitudes toward the impact of effort on their success. My students monitor their attitudes toward the impact of effort on their success.	I continually monitor my students' attitudes toward the impact of effort on their success.	I occasionally monitor my students' attitudes toward the impact of effort on their success.	I seldom or never monitor student attitudes toward the impact of effort on their success.

FIGURE 2.4
Teacher Rubric: Reinforcing Effort (continued)

Provide students with explicit guidance about exactly what it means to expend effort. Teachers can help students develop an operational definition for what it means to work hard by being explicit about the actions and behaviors associated with effort in a variety of academic situations.

4	3	2	1
I continually use rubrics and checklists to help students understand what effort means in my class. My students can define what effort means to them in my class.	I continually use rubrics and checklists to help students understand what effort means in my class.	I occasionally use rubrics and checklists to help students understand what effort means in my class.	I seldom use rubrics and checklists to help students understand what effort means in my class.
I continually provide direct instruction about the role of effort so my students understand that the more purposefully and strategically they work, the more successful they will be at a task. My students can apply the principles of effort to their work.	I continually provide direct instruction about the role of effort so my students understand that the more purposefully they work, the more successful they will be at a task.	I occasionally provide direct instruction about the role of effort relative to the fact that the harder students work, the more successful they will be at a task.	I seldom provide information relative to the fact that the harder my students work, the more successful they will be at a task
I continually set high expectations related to effort that challenge my students to stay with a task until it is completed. My students set rigorous goals and identify the effort needed to achieve them.	I continually set high expectations related to effort that challenge my students to stay with a task until it is completed.	I occasionally set high expectations related to effort that challenge my students to stay with a task until it is completed.	I seldom set high expectations related to effort.

FIGURE 2.4
Teacher Rubric: Reinforcing Effort (*continued*)

Ask students to keep track of their effort and achievement. *A powerful way to help students make the connection between effort and success is to ask them to keep track of their effort and its relationship to achievement.*

4	3	2	1
I continually provide opportunities for my students to keep track of their grades/achievement relative to the amount of effort expended on tasks and tests. My students can clearly articulate how effort impacts their achievement.	I continually provide opportunities for my students to keep track of their grades/achievement relative to the amount of effort expended on tasks and tests.	I occasionally provide opportunities for my students to keep track of their grades/achievement relative to the amount of effort expended on tasks and tests.	I seldom or never provide opportunities for my student to keep track of their grades/achievement relative to the amount of effort expended on tasks and tests.
I continually provide criteria or ask my students to assist in providing criteria against which students can judge their effort and achievement. My students apply those criteria to their work.	I continually provide criteria against which my students can judge their effort and achievement.	I occasionally provide criteria against which my students can judge their effort and achievement.	I seldom or never provide criteria against which my students can judge their effort and achievement.
I continually model for my students how to reflect on the impact of their effort on overall achievement/performance, and I assist them in making changes for the future. My students model for one another the impact of how their effort impacts overall achievement.	I continually model for my students how to reflect on the impact of their effort on overall achievement/ performance, and I assist them in making changes for the future.	I occasionally model for my students how to reflect on the impact of their effort on overall achievement/performance.	I seldom if ever model for my students how to reflect on the impact of their effort on overall achievement/performance.

FIGURE 2.5
Student Checklist: Reinforcing Effort

		Always	Sometimes	Rarely	Never
IMPORTANCE OF EFFORT	I understand how my effort can impact my school and life success based on my teacher's stories and examples.				
	I understand that the more purposefully I work at a task, the more successful I will be.				
	I work strategically at a given task in order to meet the expectations set by my teacher.				
	I share stories from my life or current events that demonstrate the success of someone who has put forth a strong effort.				
	I keep track of how the effort I put forth impacts my success in this class.				
EXPLICIT GUIDANCE	I use rubrics and checklists to help me understand what expending effort means.				
	I set rigorous goals and identify the effort needed to achieve them.				
TRACKING	I keep track of my grades, progress, and effort in this class.				
	I judge the impact that my efforts have on my achievement/performance in this class.				
	I reflect on the impact of my effort on my achievement/performance and make changes for the future.				

FIGURE 2.6
Assessing Myself: Reinforcing Effort

I help students develop an understanding of the relationship that exists between how hard they work and their success.

Not at all   To a great extent

| 0 | 1 | 2 | 3 | 4 |

I continually provide students with examples of effort and stories about people who have overcome odds and/or worked hard in order to succeed.

Not at all   To a great extent

| 0 | 1 | 2 | 3 | 4 |

I ask students to provide stories about effort and success.

Not at all   To a great extent

| 0 | 1 | 2 | 3 | 4 |

I break tasks into smaller component parts so students can hear about and visualize what it means to work hard.

Not at all   To a great extent

| 0 | 1 | 2 | 3 | 4 |

I use rubrics and/or lists to define what effort means in my class.

Not at all   To a great extent

| 0 | 1 | 2 | 3 | 4 |

I provide students with ongoing opportunities to track their effort and relate their success to their effort.

Not at all   To a great extent

| 0 | 1 | 2 | 3 | 4 |

FIGURE 2.7
Professional Growth Plan: Reinforcing Effort

1. How can I help students develop an understanding of the relationship that exists between how hard they work and their success?

2. How can I continually provide students with examples of effort and stories about people who have overcome odds and/or worked hard in order to succeed?

3. How can I ask students to provide stories about effort and success?

4. How can I break tasks into smaller component parts so students can hear about and visualize what it means to work hard?

5. How can I use rubrics and/or lists to define what effort means in my class?

6. How can I provide students with ongoing opportunities to track their effort and relate their success to their effort?

Providing Recognition

Providing recognition is the process of acknowledging students' attainment of specific goals. Some teachers question if providing recognition, particularly in the form of praise, is the right thing to do. They are right to wonder; some research on praise and recognition has shown negative effects on intrinsic motivation (Henderlong & Lepper, 2002; Kamins & Dweck, 1999). Other research indicates that when teachers use an approach that bases student success on mastery of the task (i.e., a mastery-oriented approach), rather than on comparison to others' performance, praise can be used to promote student engagement and decrease behavioral problems (Moore-Partin, Robertson, Maggin, Oliver, & Wehby, 2010; Simonson, Fairbanks, Briesch, Myers, & Sugai, 2008). Furthermore, praise can positively influence intrinsic motivation if students perceive the praise to be sincere and if the praise promotes self-determination, encourages students to attribute their performance to causes they can control, and establishes attainable goals and standards (Henderlong & Lepper, 2002). Praise that is more person- or ability-oriented (rather than task- or process-oriented) can have unintended negative effects on intrinsic motivation. When students have setbacks in the domain that was praised, they may think they have lost their ability and react with helplessness. Therefore, teachers must use praise with caution.

Recognition and praise may have a more direct impact on socioemotional indicators—such as self-efficacy (beliefs about one's competency), effort, persistence, and motivation—than on learning. As a result, teachers may not see immediate academic improvements from the effective use of recognition and praise; however, the link between positive socioemotional indicators and learning suggests that fostering the former will have positive effects on the latter over time (Bouffard et al., 1995; Elliot et al., 1999; Greene et al., 2004; Phan, 2009).

Why This Strategy?

When thinking about the design and delivery of instruction, there are many times when we don't consider the importance of recognition. Although recognizing students for various reasons is something that is often done "on the fly," it is also an important strategy that should be incorporated into lesson design intentionally. In order to do so, we must first have working knowledge of what recognition is. When looking at so-called best practices in the classroom, recognition is used as a way to praise students for working toward achieving a meaningful learning objective. It can also be used to praise the hard work students apply to learn content and skills, complete a task, improve in a specific area, or reach a predetermined level of performance. Teachers who understand the power of using this strategy on an ongoing basis find that their students rise to meet the task at hand and build confidence in their ability to persevere and succeed.

A misuse of recognition often happens in classes that are controlled by well-meaning teachers who praise students for their intellect instead of the effort they are applying. When students are recognized for intelligence instead of an accomplishment, they tend to shy away from any learning activity or performance in which they may face failure. We need to help students understand they are capable of accomplishing great feats through hard work, and we need to recognize them for their tenacity and effort. This underscores the point Dweck (2010) makes about the importance of looking at students through a growth mind-set rather than through a fixed mind-set. This connection between effort and recognition is evident and is why these strategies are coupled in this category.

The following three recommendations provide guidance for teachers as they provide recognition and create a learning environment for student success. Teachers are encouraged to

1. **Promote a mastery-goal orientation.** When teachers adopt a mastery-goal orientation, they emphasize learning and meeting goals instead of comparing students' performances (i.e., performance orientation).
2. **Provide praise that is specific and aligned with expected performance and behaviors.** Praise should be specific and focus on students' attainment of established goals for performance or behavior.
3. **Use concrete symbols of recognition.** Like praise, tangible rewards can have a positive effect on intrinsic motivation if they are tied to accomplishment of objectives.

Reflecting on My Current Practice

The questions listed in Figure 2.8 are provided as a means to assist you as you implement the instructional practices for providing recognition.

FIGURE 2.8

Reflecting on Current Practice: Providing Recognition

1. Do I recognize students for their academic achievements based upon an established set of criteria or expected/desired levels of achievement?

2. Do I recognize students for how hard they work?

3. Do I ask students how they would like to be recognized for their learning?

4. Is the recognition I provide genuine and specific to the individual?

5. Do I understand the connections that exist among feedback, effort, and recognition?

6. Do I help students understand the connections among feedback, effort, and recognition?

FIGURE 2.8

Reflecting on Current Practice: Providing Recognition *(continued)*

7. Do I provide students with instruction that helps them recognize one another?

8. Do I use concrete symbols of recognition appropriately?

9. Do I provide recognition to entire groups of students even though some students in the group have not met the criteria of the learning objective?

Bringing the Strategy to Life in the Classroom

Recommendation One:
Promote a mastery-goal orientation.

A mastery-goal orientation makes the learning environment more predictable—students know what they need to do to succeed. Teachers define what it means to expend effort to achieve a goal, and students are able to expend that effort. If students are not successful in a task, then they can examine their effort and achievement to determine what they should do to improve performance. Students know they will be recognized for their achievement relative to the goal rather than for their performance relative to other students. The former provides a sense of control; the latter does not.

A mastery-goal orientation allows teachers to design tasks that are appropriate for students at different levels of learning and to personalize recognition when students accomplish their tasks. This is particularly important for struggling students who may perceive that they have few chances for success or recognition due to a history of academic failure. Such students do not believe they can be successful, and they may be reluctant to engage and persist in tasks they perceive as difficult (Diperna, 2006; Schunk, 1999; Walker, 2003; Zimmerman, 2000). Teachers can provide these students with some initial tasks that are challenging but not beyond their capabilities. After students are successful with these tasks, teachers then provide them with recognition, gradually present more challenging tasks, and link new work to these past successes (Margolis & McCabe, 2004).

The following vignette demonstrates how students placed in a learning environment that emphasizes a mastery-goal orientation can be taught to focus on the learning and to challenge themselves.

Over lunch, Kurt and Steve, two middle school teachers, are sharing stories about their 6th grade classes. Kurt states that his students seem to be more focused on competing with one another to see who is smartest or who can finish first instead of paying close attention to the learning that should be taking place. Steve agrees and says that his students seem to be all about the grade and not the learning. Additionally, some students labeled as "gifted" don't want to attempt the stretch goals. They seem to be afraid they will receive less than an *A* for a grade. The students who are struggling in class do not feel they can be successful, and some have given up. Kurt and Steve finish their lunch wondering how to move students from competing against one another and only caring about grades to being concerned about actually learning something.

Later that week, the two meet again for lunch. Kurt is excited to share a new strategy he is using. He read that students are more likely to focus on learning when they are provided with tasks that motivate and engage them. He began treating mistakes as expected parts of the learning process, and he shared more stories about people who became successful only after a string of hard-fought failures. He provides more opportunities for students to work at their own levels, and he personalizes the recognition he provides when students accomplish their tasks. He shies away from recognizing students for how they perform relative to their peers. The focus in his classroom is now on helping students achieve rigorous, attainable goals and always challenging themselves to stretch.

Kurt tells Steve that as he maintained a strong focus on treating mistakes as an expected part of learning and as a way for students to grow, he gradually saw a changed attitude from them. Some of his stronger students realized it was not about getting the *A* but more about risking and learning. When students saw that their mistakes were not called out and treated as failures, they became more likely to risk. Some of his struggling students realized that, even though earning an *A* might not be an easy goal at this time in their progression, they were really "competing" against themselves and not the bell curve to define success.

Recommendation Two:
Provide praise that is specific and aligned with expected performance and behaviors.

Many of the other strategies in this book are strongly related to content. Recognition, however, is based in the affective arena. Ultimately, what we want to do is empower students in their ability to learn something by teaching them and then recognizing their hard work toward accomplishing the learning objectives.

Think about a time when you received what you felt was effective praise. What was the situation? What was said? How did you feel? What were the results of the praise relative to your attitude toward the learning?

Conversely, think of a time when you received what you believed was ineffective praise. How was the outcome different from the time you received effective praise?

When teachers are asked about providing recognition, they typically reply that they provide recognition all the time. Delving more deeply into their responses, though, we see that much of the recognition teachers provide concerns behavior rather than improved academic performance. Teachers can certainly use recognition as a means to help students understand and portray good behavior, but we focus here on recognition that applies to academics and the effort to help students achieve their goals.

Recognition is often referred to as praise. Praise can provide students with the motivation to continue working and striving to achieve at a high level, or it can create confusion and competition. Take a moment to read the information contained in Figure 2.9, or discuss with peers how praise can and should be used in the classroom.

Read the following hypothetical examples of providing recognition in the classroom. Evaluate each example in terms of the guidelines for praise from Figure 2.9. For each example, consider whether the recognition the teacher provides is likely to be effective or ineffective. Assign specific criteria to each sample and explain your thinking.

Example #1. Dana is unable to use a table of characteristics to make connections among chemical elements. Mr. Mulder suggests that she focus on one characteristic and look for connections. When he returns later, Dana explains how she figured out a way to group the elements according to boiling point. Mr. Mulder congratulates her on finding a valid connection.

Example #2. Mr. Mulder circulates as students are working in small groups. He pauses at Station 1 and comments, "Nice work on your calculations." At Station 2, he says, "Nice work on your graphs." At Station 3, he says, "Nice work on your calculations."

Example #3. Mr. Mulder calls a student in his chemistry class to his desk and says the following: "You really did a good job working through all of the steps and checking your answers for this problem. I know you've had difficulties with multistep calculations before and sometimes settled for getting any answer down on paper, even if it wasn't correct. Your determination with this task really showed."

Example #4. Mr. Mulder looks up from his desk and calls out, "Good job, Jackson. Keep it up."

In example #1, Mr. Mulder provides his student with effective praise. The student is rewarded for attainment of specific performance criteria. The student also gains a better appreciation of her task-related behaviors and thoughts of problem solving. In example #2, the praise is ineffective. Mr. Mulder's praise shows bland uniformity, which suggests conditioned response made with minimal attention. The praise is delivered randomly and is given without regard to the effort expended or the meaning of the accomplishment. In example #3, Mr. Mulder's praise is effective. He specifies the particulars of the accomplishments, rewards the attainment of specified performance

FIGURE 2.9
Guidelines for Praise

	Effective Praise	Ineffective Praise
1.	Is delivered contingently.	Is delivered randomly or unsystematically.
2.	Specifies the particulars of the accomplishment.	Is restricted to global positive reactions.
3.	Shows spontaneity, variety, and other signs of credibility, which suggests clear attention to the student's accomplishment.	Shows bland uniformity, which suggests conditioned response made with minimal attention.
4.	Rewards attainment of specified performance criteria, which can include effort criteria.	Rewards mere participation, without consideration of performance processes or outcomes.
5.	Provides information to students about their competence or the value of their accomplishments.	Provides students with information about their status, or gives no information at all.
6.	Orients students toward a better appreciation of their task-related behaviors and thoughts of problem solving.	Orients students toward comparisons with others and thoughts of competition.
7.	Uses students' prior accomplishments as the context for describing present accomplishments.	Uses the accomplishments of peers as the context for describing students' present accomplishments.
8.	Is given in recognition of noteworthy effort or success at difficult tasks.	Is given without regard to the effort expended or the meaning of the accomplishment.
9.	Attributes success to effort and ability, implying that similar successes can be expected in the future.	Attributes success to ability alone or to external factions such as luck or the ease of a task.
10.	Fosters endogenous attribution (i.e., students believe they expend effort on the task because they enjoy the task and/or want to develop task-relevant skills).	Fosters exogenous attributions (i.e., students believe they expend effort on the task for external reasons, such as to please the teacher or to win a competition or reward).
11.	Focuses students' attention on their own task-relevant behaviors.	Focuses students' attention on the teacher as an external authority who is manipulating them.
12.	Fosters appreciation of and desirable attributions about task-relevant behaviors after the process is completed.	Intrudes into the ongoing process, distracting attention from task-relevant behaviors.

Source: From "Teacher Praise: A Functional Analysis," by J. Brophy, 1981, *Review of Educational Research, 51*(1), p. 26. Copyright 1981 by the American Educational Research Association. Adapted with permission.

criteria—including effort—and fosters appreciation of task-related behaviors after the process is completed. In example #4, the praise given is restricted to global positive reactions, delivered randomly, and given without regard to the effort expended or the meaning of the accomplishment.

Though we call out specific guidelines for praise in the examples above, there are others that also may apply. Think about a recent time when you provided recognition to students. Describe what occurred in as much detail as possible. Analyze your experience, and see if you can identify why it was effective or ineffective.

Recommendation Three: Use concrete symbols of recognition.

Using rewards to recognize the quality of students' work and their progress toward the learning goal—rather than task participation or completion—can promote self-efficacy and improved performance (Alderman, 2008). Furthermore, tying rewards to accomplishments helps students understand that they are not completing a task merely for the reward. Rewards of this type can be helpful to develop initial interest in a skill whose value might not be apparent until students have used it for a while or until the student masters it. Teachers can use various concrete, symbolic tokens of recognition such as stickers, coupons, awards, treats, or other types of prizes. Such rewards are better used with routine tasks or ones that require rote learning (e.g., multiplication facts) rather than with those that require creativity or discovery (Brophy, 2004).

In the following vignette, see how Ms. Murphy uses concrete symbols—in this case, stickers and other trinkets—to help Blair and his classmates reenergize and focus on difficult material.

Blair was enrolled in advanced placement English for first and second semester. He loves to learn and is fairly successful in class. For some reason, though, he is feeling burned out as second semester progresses. His grades are slipping, and he finds it difficult to pay attention in class.

Ms. Murphy notices this about Blair and many of her other students. She decides things have been far too serious and she needs to help students lighten up. During the three weeks leading up to the final exam, she gives short, formative assessments. Every time students score between 90 and 100 percent, or every time they increase their score by 10 points above their previous score, students receive a prize. What are the prizes? They include silly party hats, funny balloons, and other inexpensive trinkets that lighten the mood.

Blair and his classmates really get into this new approach to recognition. They cheer and laugh at every award ceremony. More importantly, Ms. Murphy notices that students work hard for the small concrete symbols of recognition, and scores on the final exam have never been better.

Rubrics and Checklists

The teacher rubric provided in Figure 2.10 is intended to be a tool used for reflection on the way in which you currently provide recognition in your classroom. It is designed so that a 3 represents best practice as indicated by the research. A 4 indicates both teacher best practice as described in a 3 and how that practice transfers into student behaviors. You can also use this rubric as a growth tool, seeing where you are now and what the next level might look like. This will provide you with valuable information as you build your professional growth plan.

Using the teacher rubric will give you the chance to reflect on your practice. You can also ask your students how they perceive the way you provide recognition. Figure 2.11 provides a student checklist that you might want to use. Periodically give this checklist to your students, and ask them to react honestly to the statements. This checklist can help your students better understand how recognition helps them learn, and it can provide valuable feedback about how your students view your use of recognition.

Tools, Templates, and Protocols

If you are using this handbook as part of a school PLC or book study, Figure 2.12 provides statements that can serve as discussion prompts. Likewise, if you are using this book for individual growth, think about these prompts as they relate to your classroom practice. For example, if your answer to the first statement is a 0 or 1, then what steps should you take to move toward the other end of the spectrum, "to a great extent"? Use your individual or team results from Figure 2.12 to form the basis of a professional growth plan (see Figure 2.13).

FIGURE 2.10
Teacher Rubric: Providing Recognition

Promote a mastery-goal orientation. *When teachers adopt a mastery-goal orientation, they emphasize learning and meeting goals rather than comparing students' performances (i.e., performance orientation).*

4	3	2	1
I consistently differentiate instructional activities targeted to students with different learning abilities and provide my students with recognition for accomplishing those tasks. My students understand why they each receive recognition in different ways.	I consistently differentiate instructional activities targeted to students with different learning abilities and provide my students with recognition for accomplishing those tasks.	I occasionally differentiate instructional activities targeted to students with different learning abilities and provide my students with recognition for accomplishing those tasks.	I seldom differentiate instructional activities targeted to students with different learning abilities and provide my students with recognition for accomplishing those tasks.
I consistently scaffold my students' learning in ways that most ensure their potential for success. My students use strategies to support one another so that all can be successful.	I consistently scaffold my students' learning in ways that most ensure their potential for success	I occasionally scaffold my students' learning in ways that most ensure their potential for success	I seldom scaffold my students' learning in ways that most ensure their potential for success
I consistently establish learning activities that create an environment of support for all students. My students understand that they are most successful as a class when all students are individually successful.	I consistently establish learning activities that create an environment of support for all students.	I occasionally establish learning activities that create an environment of support for all students.	I seldom establish learning activities that create an environment of support for all students.

FIGURE 2.10
Teacher Rubric: Providing Recognition (continued)

Promote a mastery-goal orientation. *When teachers adopt a mastery-goal orientation, they emphasize learning and meeting goals rather than comparing students' performances (i.e., performance orientation).*

4	3	2	1
I consistently judge students against their own work and growth rather than against other students in the class. My students understand they are never competing against one another but only against themselves.	I consistently judge students against their own work and growth rather than against other students in the class.	I occasionally judge students against their own work and growth rather than against other students in the class.	I seldom judge students against their own work and growth rather than against other students in the class.

Provide praise that is specific and aligned with expected performance and behaviors. *Praise should be specific and focus on students' attainment of established goals for performance or behavior. It should also be aligned with the research on effective praise: it is delivered contingent on effort applied toward the objective, specifies particulars of the accomplishment, orients students to appreciate their own accomplishments, uses students' prior accomplishments as a basis for present accomplishments.*

4	3	2	1
I consistently praise my students using the research on effective praise. My students understand the criteria used for praise.	I consistently praise my students using the research on effective praise.	I occasionally praise my students using the research on effective praise.	I seldom praise my students using the research on effective praise.
I consistently praise my students with specific, personalized praise or recognition. My students provide specific and targeted praise to their peers.	I consistently praise my students with specific, personalized praise or recognition	I occasionally praise my students with specific, personalized praise or recognition	I seldom praise my students with specific, personalized praise or recognition

FIGURE 2.10

Teacher Rubric: Providing Recognition *(continued)*

Use concrete symbols of recognition. *It is appropriate to give verbal recognition for accomplishments as well as offer students concrete tokens of recognition.*

4	3	2	1
Verbal praise is consistently paired with concrete symbols of recognition when appropriate as a motivational tool. My students know why they receive verbal praise or recognition.	Verbal praise is consistently paired with concrete symbols of recognition when appropriate as a motivational tool.	Verbal praise is occasionally paired with concrete symbols of recognition when appropriate as a motivational tool.	Verbal praise is seldom paired with concrete symbols of recognition when appropriate as a motivational tool.

FIGURE 2.11
Student Checklist: Providing Recognition

		Always	Sometimes	Rarely	Never
MASTERY-GOAL ORIENTATION	My teacher helps me be successful in this class.				
	My teacher supports me when I have trouble.				
PERSONALIZED RECOGNITION	My teacher praises me when my work meets the expectations he/she established.				
	My teacher knows me well enough to know what kind of praise/recognition works best for me.				
SYMBOLS OF RECOGNITION	I understand that giving and receiving praise helps me accomplish more.				
	Because I understand that giving and receiving praise helps others accomplish more, I take time to praise my peers.				
	My teacher gives me specific praise that helps me recognize my past, present, and future accomplishments.				
	I have communicated my preferences for receiving recognition to my teacher, and he/she provides me with the type of recognition I like.				

FIGURE 2.12
Assessing Myself: Providing Recognition

I recognize students for their academic achievements based upon an established set of criteria or expected/desired level of achievement.

Not at all				To a great extent
0	1	2	3	4

I recognize students for how hard they work.

Not at all				To a great extent
0	1	2	3	4

I ask students how they would like to be recognized for their learning.

Not at all				To a great extent
0	1	2	3	4

I provide recognition that is genuine and specific to the individual.

Not at all				To a great extent
0	1	2	3	4

I understand the connections that exist among feedback, effort, and recognition.

Not at all				To a great extent
0	1	2	3	4

I help students understand the connections among feedback, effort, and recognition.

Not at all				To a great extent
0	1	2	3	4

FIGURE 2.12
Assessing Myself: Providing Recognition *(continued)*

I provide students with instruction that helps them recognize one another.

Not at all   To a great extent

| 0 | 1 | 2 | 3 | 4 |

I use concrete symbols of recognition appropriately.

Not at all   To a great extent

| 0 | 1 | 2 | 3 | 4 |

I provide recognition to entire groups of students even though some students in the group have not met the criteria of the learning objective.

Not at all   To a great extent

| 0 | 1 | 2 | 3 | 4 |

FIGURE 2.13
Professional Growth Plan: Providing Recognition

1. How will I recognize students for their academic achievements based upon an established set of criteria or expected/desired level of achievement?

2. How can I recognize students for how hard they work?

3. How can I get students thinking and talking about how they would like to be recognized for their learning?

4. How will I provide recognition that is genuine and specific to the individual?

5. How will I demonstrate the connections that exist among feedback, effort, and recognition?

6. How will I help students understand the connections among feedback, effort, and recognition?

FIGURE 2.13

Professional Growth Plan: Providing Recognition *(continued)*

7. How can I provide students with instruction that helps them recognize one another?

8. How will I use concrete symbols of recognition appropriately?

9. How can I provide recognition to entire groups of students even though some students in the group have not met the criteria of the learning objective?

Cooperative Learning

Cooperative Learning

Using cooperative learning helps teachers lay the foundation for student success in a world that depends on communication, collaboration, and cooperation. Few other instructional strategies are as theoretically grounded as cooperative learning (Johnson & Johnson, 2009), yet it is one of the most misunderstood instructional practices (Antil, Jenkins, Wayne, & Vadasy, 1998; Koutselini, 2009).

Some of the confusion about cooperative learning stems from the different ways people define it. For example, Drs. David Johnson and Roger Johnson (1999) use the following five elements to define cooperative learning:

- positive interdependence
- face-to-face promotive interaction
- individual and group accountability
- interpersonal and small-group skills
- group processing

Other researchers and practitioners define cooperative learning as a strategy that uses one or more of these elements, though generally not all five. For example, Kagan (1985, 1990) promotes the use of cooperative learning structures, highlighting positive interdependence and individual accountability. Another model of cooperative learning—known as complex instruction—addresses positive interdependence, individual accountability, and group processing (Cohen, 1994). (For additional information about the various models of cooperative learning, see Aronson, Stephan, Stikes, Blaney, & Snapp, 1978; DeVries & Edwards, 1973; Howard, 1996; Sharan & Sharan, 1992; Slavin, 1978, 1983, 1990.)

In this book, we define cooperative learning as small-group learning that incorporates at least two of Johnson and Johnson's five essential elements—positive interdependence and individual accountability.

Positive interdependence is a key element of cooperative learning because it emphasizes that everyone is in the effort together and that one person's success does not come at the expense of another's success. To foster positive interdependence, teachers must ensure that each individual's workload is reasonably equal to the workload of his or her team members. Teachers can accomplish this by clearly defining roles and responsibilities during the cooperative learning activity.

The second key element of cooperative learning, individual accountability, refers to each team member's need to receive feedback on how his or her personal efforts contribute toward achievement of the overall goal. To ensure individual accountability, teachers can use formative and summative assessments and determine students' contributions to the group goal. This practice discourages the tendency for a few individuals to carry the brunt of the entire group's workload. In addition, individual accountability establishes a means by which each group member can demonstrate proficiency with regard to the knowledge and skills embedded within the goals of the cooperative learning activity.

Why This Strategy?

The job outlook survey published by the National Association of Colleges and Employers (2009) identified the top five personal qualities/skills employers seek as they look at potential employees. They are

- communication skills (both verbal and written)
- strong work ethic
- teamwork skills
- initiative
- analytic skills

Having students work in cooperative learning groups, which emphasize positive interdependence and individual accountability, is certainly a way to help them learn the skills potential employers value. In addition, this strategy helps create an environment for learning because it emphasizes the social aspect of learning, an important part of a strong learning environment.

Cooperative learning is perhaps the most misunderstood instructional strategy in classrooms today. Many teachers say they regularly use cooperative learning when in fact they are engaging students in small-group work.

Small-group work is valuable, but cooperative learning, with elements of positive interdependence and individual responsibility, is the strategy that rises to the level of significance. The three recommendations that follow provide guidance for teachers as they use cooperative learning and create a learning environment for student success. Teachers are encouraged to

1. **Include elements of both positive interdependence and individual accountability.** By intentionally incorporating the elements of positive interdependence and individual accountability, teachers set the stage for students to be responsible for their own learning; the learning of those in their group; and the ability to demonstrate what they know, understand, and are able to do. Provide students with explicit guidance about what it means to expend effort.

2. **Keep group size small.** Studies show that as groups get larger, external and internal motivation tend to decrease, and members of larger groups tend to feel that their individual contributions will go unnoticed (Igel, 2010; Lou et al., 1996). A group size of two to five students is optimal.

3. **Use cooperative learning consistently and systematically.** Cooperative learning is itself a process. The component steps need to be taught to students independent of new content. Once students understand how to work in cooperative groups, cooperative learning should be used frequently enough that the steps of the process do not need to be retaught.

Teachers can use a variety of criteria to group students (e.g., by their interests, according to their birthdays, alphabetical by their first names, or by the color of their shirts). Students can also be grouped randomly by drawing names from a hat or bag. Varying the tactics you use to group students will ensure that different students have the opportunity to work together.

Research indicates that cooperative groups should be small (Igel, 2010). Many teachers follow the rule of thumb "the smaller, the better." Even though a particular task may seem to have enough work to occupy a large group, students may not have the skills needed to work effectively in larger groups. If resources allow, groups of two to five students are recommended (Igel, 2010; Lou et al., 1996).

Reflecting on My Current Practice

The questions listed in Figure 3.1 are provided as a means to assist you as you implement the instructional practices for cooperative learning.

FIGURE 3.1
Reflecting on Current Practice: Cooperative Learning

1. Does using cooperative learning enhance the outcome of the learning activity?

2. Have I provided a role or responsibility for each member of the group?

3. Have I built both individual and group accountability into the project?

4. Is group size five students or less?

5. Have I taught my students how to work within cooperative groups, or is this new learning?

6. Have I provided a rubric or checklist for both individual and small-group expectations?

Bringing the Strategy to Life in the Classroom

Recommendation One:
Include elements of both positive interdependence and individual accountability.

As you read the following vignette, notice how Ms. Frazee designs her cooperative learning project so every student has a distinct role and responsibility. In addition, the project includes both positive interdependence and individual accountability; every student has to contribute in order for the group to be successful.

Using her district curriculum and the Common Core State Standards for Language Arts, Ms. Frazee designs a series of lessons around the Declaration of Independence and the Declaration of Sentiments. She begins her first lesson by writing the following learning objective on the board: "We will compare the central themes in two primary documents and note the relationships among the key details and ideas."

After discussing the day's learning objective and allowing students time to personalize it for themselves, Ms. Frazee asks her students to move into cooperative groups and share with one another what they know about the Declaration of Independence and the Declaration of Sentiments. She then distributes a comparison matrix that serves as an advance organizer for the work that groups need to complete. She also provides a "Roles and Responsibilities" sheet so everyone understands the expectations for each member of the team.

"You can see from the comparison matrix that you are going to compare the Declaration of Independence and the Declaration of Sentiments, looking at five different characteristics," explains Ms. Frazee. Students review the comparison matrix and "Roles and Responsibilities" handout and then volunteer for the various group roles.

"I'll take the role of making sure that the key points from the Declaration of Independence are placed on the chart," says Ali.

"I'll do the same for the Declaration of Sentiments," says Jack.

"I want to write the summary statements. Chad, could you decide the similarities and differences for the comparison matrix?" asks Isabelle. Chad agrees.

The students go to work on their individual tasks, stopping often to share what they are learning with others in their group. Every few minutes, Ms. Frazee reminds the entire class to share the information they are gathering with their team.

As Ms. Frazee walks from group to group, she carries a large, plastic die. She rolls the die at each table and asks the student whose number matches the die roll to answer a specific question about the learning that is taking place in that group.

"Boy, I'm so glad we keep sharing what we're learning with one another," says Isabelle. "I don't want my grade to drop just because I don't know the information everyone else is adding as we do our work."

"Me too," says Chad. "The last group I was in didn't do a good job teaching one another. I lost individual points because I didn't know all of the information. I only knew my part."

Students continue to work together and teach one another. At the end of the period, Ms. Frazee says, "I really appreciate the way you got to work today and accomplished so much. You will have a portion of the period tomorrow to finish this first part. Before the bell rings, I want each of you to work independently and answer the question on the board so I can make sure each of you has learned what is expected." Students answer the question and place their papers in the basket by the door as they leave class.

Recommendation Two:
Keep group size small.

In the vignette above, Ms. Frazee not only emphasizes the responsibilities of positive interdependence and individual accountability but also designs the project so each group has four members. If there were seven or eight students in each group, it would be possible for some students to fade into the background and not be part of the positive interdependence. The project might be successful, but not every student will contribute. A true advantage to using cooperative learning is that every student is both necessary and valued. Therefore, keeping cooperative groups between two and five students is essential.

Recommendation Three:
Use cooperative learning consistently and systematically.

In the following vignette, notice how the staff identifies the importance of incorporating cooperative learning in a consistent and systematic manner.

The 6th grade team is meeting during its collaborative planning time. On the agenda is an issue Mr. Elliott raised about how poorly the students in his mathematics classes work together in small groups. He asserts, "I know it is a building goal to have our students working less in whole-group instruction and working more in small and cooperative groups, but frankly these kids can't be put into small groups without noise, disruptions, and fighting. It's just easier to keep them under control in whole-group settings."

Ms. Leland adds, "Every time I try to move into small groups, it seems like the noise level goes way up. Also, some kids just take over, while others sit there and don't participate."

Ms. Nagato joins in and says, "I have been taking a class and reading up on cooperative learning. Cooperative learning helps provide a structure so every student has a role and responsibility. That would probably also help with the discipline issues you are talking about, Mr. Elliott."

"I don't know about that," Mr. Conner interrupts. "I tried cooperative learning two years ago, and it was a mess. I spent the whole time just trying to get the kids to follow the process. I barely got any content covered."

"What we have been talking about in my class," replies Ms. Nagato, "is that cooperative learning is a process. Like any other kind of process, it needs to be taught and practiced repeatedly."

"I don't want to waste my time with repeated cooperative learning attempts and fall behind on content," answers Mr. Conner. "I'll just stick to whole-group instruction, regardless of the building goals."

"I think I have a suggestion that will help us out," says Ms. Leland. "I know that my kids have trouble when we begin a new procedure in science, and it takes a number of repetitions before they are really ready for independent practice. What if Ms. Nagato gives us the basics of what makes up the cooperative learning process, and we all agree to do one cooperative learning project within the next three weeks? That way, while each of us will be doing it one time, our students will be experiencing cooperative learning five times in a three-week period. The first couple of teachers who do it will probably have to spend a lot of time on the process part, but by the third time the kids see cooperative learning, they will be familiar enough with the process that content can take over."

Ms. Nagato says, "I really like that idea. I can come up with a two-page summary of what we have learned in my class and share it tomorrow during our planning time. I think that once we make this really intentional effort to teach the process to our students, it will be easy for each of us to bring in one or two cooperative learning lessons per grading period on an ongoing basis to keep the process in front of the kids."

Rubrics and Checklists

The teacher rubric provided in Figure 3.2 is intended to be a tool used for reflection on the way in which you currently use cooperative learning in your classroom. It is designed so that a 3 represents best practice as indicated by the research. A 4 indicates both teacher best practice as described in a 3 and how that practice transfers into student behaviors. You can also use this rubric as a growth tool, seeing where you are now and what the next level might look like. This will provide you with valuable information as you build your professional growth plan.

Using the teacher rubric will give you the chance to reflect on your practice. You can also ask your students how they perceive the way you teach them to use cooperative learning. Figure 3.3 provides a student checklist you might want to use. Periodically give this checklist to your students, and ask them to react honestly to the statements. This checklist can help your students better understand how cooperative learning helps them learn, and it can provide valuable feedback to you about how your students view the process of cooperative learning.

Tools, Templates, and Protocols

If you are using this handbook as part of a school PLC or book study, Figure 3.4 provides statements that can serve as discussion prompts. Likewise, if you are using this book for individual growth, think about these prompts as they relate to your classroom practice. For example, if your answer to the first statement is a 0 or 1, then what steps should you take to move toward the other end of the spectrum, "to a great extent"? Use your individual or team results from Figure 3.4 to form the basis of a professional growth plan (see Figure 3.5).

FIGURE 3.2
Teacher Rubric: Cooperative Learning

Include elements of both positive interdependence and individual accountability. *Groups should feel a sense of camaraderie and interdependence. Although group accountability encourages teamwork, individual accountability is also needed to encourage personal responsibility and motivate students to do their share of the work.*

4	3	2	1
I consistently encourage students to work together as a team, listen, negotiate, and lead. This may include modeling positive behaviors, student role-playing, and analyzing positive and negative cooperative learning scenarios. My students can set their own group norms when working in groups.	I consistently encourage students to work together as a team, listen, negotiate, and lead. This may include modeling positive behaviors, student role-playing, and analyzing positive and negative cooperative learning scenarios.	I occasionally encourage students to work together as a team. This may include modeling positive behaviors, student role-playing, and/or analyzing positive and negative cooperative learning scenarios.	I seldom teach students how to work together as a team.
I consistently plan cooperative learning projects and activities that require a group effort to be successful. My students understand that they produce a better product when they all contribute.	I consistently plan cooperative learning projects and activities that require a group effort to be successful.	I occasionally plan cooperative learning projects and activities that require a group effort to be successful.	I seldom plan cooperative learning projects and activities that require a group effort to be successful. Any individual student could accomplish the task working independently.
I consistently hold each student individually accountable to know the information and do his/her share of the work. My students demonstrate individual accountability.	I consistently hold each student individually accountable to know the information and do his/her share of the work.	I occasionally hold each student individually accountable to know the information and do his/her share of the work.	I seldom hold each student individually accountable to know the information and do his/her share of the work.

FIGURE 3.7
Teacher Rubric: Cooperative Learning *(continued)*

4	3	2	1
I consistently provide different roles and responsibilities for every student and try to make sure they are clear and reasonable. My students understand they individually contribute to the success of their groups.	I consistently provide different roles and responsibilities for every student and try to make sure they are clear and reasonable.	I occasionally provide different roles and responsibilities for every student and try to make sure they are clear and reasonable.	I seldom provide different roles and responsibilities for every student.
I consistently assign students to cooperative learning groups that are heterogeneous both academically and socially. My students can identify the individual strengths of their group members.	I consistently assign students to cooperative learning groups that are heterogeneous both academically and socially.	I occasionally assign students to cooperative learning groups that are heterogeneous both academically and socially.	I seldom assign students to cooperative learning groups that are heterogeneous both academically and socially.
I consistently provide a rubric or list for both the overall project goal and the roles/responsibilities of each student. My students take an active role in assessing the contributions of their peers toward the project goals.	I consistently provide a rubric or list for both the overall project goal and the roles/responsibilities of each student.	I occasionally provide a rubric or list for both the overall project goal and the roles/responsibilities of each student.	I seldom provide a rubric or list for both the overall project goal and the roles/responsibilities of each student.

FIGURE 3.2
Teacher Rubric: Cooperative Learning (*continued*)

Keep group size small. *If groups get too big, leadership opportunities are scarce, student input is diluted, and there are not enough meaningful responsibilities to go around.*

4	3	2	1
I consistently design cooperative learning groups with no more than 5 students to ensure that all students can have a voice. My students know they are all important to the group's success.	I consistently design cooperative learning groups with no more than 5 students to ensure that all students can have a voice.	I occasionally design cooperative learning groups with no more than 5 students to ensure that all students can have a voice.	I rarely design cooperative learning groups with no more than 5 students to ensure that all students can have a voice.
I consistently make sure group sizes and available resources match well enough so students have most of what they need to achieve their learning objectives. My students know how to obtain the resources they need.	I consistently make sure group sizes and available resources match well enough so students have most of what they need to achieve their learning objectives.	I occasionally make sure group sizes and available resources match well enough so students have most of what they need to achieve their learning objectives.	Group sizes and available resources seldom match well. Students often do not have what they need to achieve their learning objectives.

FIGURE 3.2
Teacher Rubric: Cooperative Learning *(continued)*

Use cooperative learning consistently and systematically. *Facilitating cooperative learning is a busy task that needs purposeful objectives, structure, clear directions, and continual progress monitoring to be successful.*

4	3	2	1
I consistently tell students about the objectives and success criteria of their cooperative learning projects and activities. My students can relate their work to the learning objectives and demonstrate the success criteria.	I consistently tell students about the objectives and success criteria of their cooperative learning projects and activities.	I occasionally tell students about the objectives and success criteria of their cooperative learning projects and activities.	The objectives and success criteria for cooperative learning projects and activities are seldom provided or understood by students.
I consistently provide methods and directions for cooperative learning projects and activities. All students can articulate the process and explain it to others.	I consistently provide methods and directions for cooperative learning projects and activities.	I occasionally provide methods and directions for cooperative learning projects and activities.	I seldom provide methods and directions for cooperative learning projects and activities.
I consistently monitor the cooperation of groups and the progress of each student's learning. My students use rubrics and lists to monitor their own learning.	I consistently monitor the cooperation of groups and the progress of each student's learning.	I occasionally monitor the cooperation of groups and/or the progress of each student's learning.	I seldom monitor the cooperation of groups and/or the progress of each student's learning.

FIGURE 3.3

Student Checklist: Cooperative Learning

		Always	Sometimes	Rarely	Never
POSITIVE INTERDEPENDENCE	My group understands that we must work together to succeed. We use negotiation and compromise to solve problems. We listen to and respect everyone's input.				
	Group members use teamwork to help one another succeed without unfairly burdening any particular members. Responsibilities are shared evenly. Everyone encourages one another to work hard.				
	Our cooperative learning projects and activities are not easily done by individuals. These projects and activities work best when we cooperate as a team.				
	My group and I feel accountable to one another for the group's overall success. My teacher encourages and evaluates the success of the overall group.				
	My group and I clearly understand the objectives of our cooperative learning projects and activities.				
	My teacher makes sure that my peers and I fully understand the methods and directions for cooperative learning projects and activities in writing and by modeling correct behavior.				
INDIVIDUAL ACCOUNTABILITY	My roles and responsibilities to the group are reasonable and clearly understood. I contribute my knowledge, opinions, and skills to the team effort.				
	I focus on my personal responsibilities to the group and complete tasks on time.				
	In addition to the assessment of the overall group's performance, my teacher assesses the individual performance of each person's responsibilities to the group.				

FIGURE 3.3
Student Checklist: Cooperative Learning *(continued)*

		Always	Sometimes	Rarely	Never
GROUP SIZE	The size of my cooperative group fits well with the purpose of the learning and the responsibilities of the group members (2–5 members per group).				
	My teacher makes certain that group sizes and available resources match well so we have what we need to be successful in our learning.				
	My teacher continually monitors the progress of my learning and my group's collaboration.				

FIGURE 3.4
Assessing Myself: Cooperative Learning

I teach students how to work together as a team, listen, negotiate, and lead.

Not at all   To a great extent

0   1   2   3   4

I plan cooperative learning projects and activities that require a group effort to be successful.

Not at all   To a great extent

0   1   2   3   4

I provide different roles and responsibilities for every student and try to make sure they are clear and reasonable.

Not at all   To a great extent

0   1   2   3   4

I assign students to cooperative learning groups that are heterogeneous both academically and socially.

Not at all   To a great extent

0   1   2   3   4

I provide rubrics for both the overall project goals and the roles/responsibilities of each student.

Not at all   To a great extent

0   1   2   3   4

FIGURE 3.4
Assessing Myself: Cooperative Learning (*continued*)

I design cooperative learning groups with no more than five students so all students can have a voice.

Not at all   To a great extent

| 0 | 1 | 2 | 3 | 4 |

I make certain that group sizes and available resources match well so students have what they need in order to achieve their learning objectives.

Not at all   To a great extent

| 0 | 1 | 2 | 3 | 4 |

I monitor the cooperation of groups and the progress of each student's learning.

Not at all   To a great extent

| 0 | 1 | 2 | 3 | 4 |

FIGURE 3.5
Professional Growth Plan: Cooperative Learning

1. How will I teach students how to work together as a team, listen, negotiate, and lead?

2. How will I plan cooperative learning projects and activities that require a group effort to be successful?

3. How will I provide different roles and responsibilities for every student and try to make sure they are clear and reasonable?

4. How will I assign students to cooperative learning groups that are heterogeneous both academically and socially?

5. How will I provide rubrics for both the overall project goals and the roles/responsibilities of each student?

6. What strategies will I use to design cooperative learning groups with no more than five students so all students can have a voice?

FIGURE 3.5
Professional Growth Plan: Cooperative Learning *(continued)*

7. How will I make certain that group sizes and available resources match well so students have what they need in order to achieve their learning objectives?

8. How will I monitor the cooperation of groups and the progress of each student's learning?

Part II

Helping Students Develop Understanding

Students come to the classroom with prior knowledge and must integrate new learning with what they already know. The strategies included in this section help teachers use students' prior knowledge as scaffolding for new learning, and they include

- Cues, Questions, and Advance Organizers
- Nonlinguistic Representations
- Summarizing and Note Taking
- Assigning Homework and Providing Practice

The process of acquiring and integrating knowledge requires students to construct meaning and then organize and store information. Strategies in this section acknowledge differences in the way students process and organize information. We often hear that teachers teach the way they were taught. Intentionally using the strategies in this section will help teachers reach a broader audience of students.

List of Figures

Chapter 4

4.1   Reflecting on Current Practice: Cues and Questions 101
4.2   Teacher Rubric: Cues and Questions 106
4.3   Student Checklist: Cues and Questions 109
4.4   Assessing Myself: Cues and Questions 110
4.5   Professional Growth Plan: Cues and Questions 111
4.6   Reflecting on Current Practice: Advance Organizers 114
4.7   SQ3R Protocol 117
4.8   Anticipation Guide 118
4.9   Episode Graphic Organizer 119
4.10   Anticipation Guide Template 120
4.11   Frayer Model 121
4.12   Teacher Rubric: Advance Organizers 122
4.13   Student Checklist: Advance Organizers 126
4.14   Assessing Myself: Advance Organizers 127
4.15   Professional Growth Plan: Advance Organizers 128

Chapter 5

5.1   Reflecting on Current Practice: Nonlinguistic Representations 132
5.2   Branches of Government 135
5.3   Teacher Rubric: Nonlinguistic Representations 143
5.4   Student Checklist: Nonlinguistic Representations 147
5.5   Assessing Myself: Nonlinguistic Representations 149
5.6   Professional Growth Plan: Nonlinguistic Representations 151

Chapter 6

6.1   Reflecting on Current Practice: Summarizing 156
6.2   Rule-based Summarizing Strategy 158
6.3   Rule-based Summarizing Example 159
6.4   Narrative Frame 162
6.5   Topic-Restriction-Illustration Frame 163
6.6   Definition Frame 165
6.7   Argumentation Frame 167
6.8   Problem–Solution Frame 168
6.9   Conversation Frame 171
6.10   Teacher Rubric: Summarizing 177

6.11   Student Checklist: Summarizing 180

6.12   Assessing Myself: Summarizing 181

6.13   Professional Growth Plan: Summarizing 183

6.14   Reflecting on Current Practice: Note Taking 188

6.15   Teacher-Prepared Notes 190

6.16   Webbing Example 192

6.17   Mitosis Lesson Plan 194

6.18   Rubric for Assessing Combination Notes 196

6.19   Student-Created Combination Notes 197

6.20   Teacher Rubric: Note Taking 198

6.21   Student Checklist: Note Taking 201

6.22   Assessing Myself: Note Taking 202

6.23   Professional Growth Plan: Note Taking 204

Chapter 7

7.1   Reflecting on Current Practice: Assigning Homework 210

7.2   Sample District Homework Policy 212

7.3   Teacher Rubric: Assigning Homework 217

7.4   Student Checklist: Assigning Homework 219

7.5   Assessing Myself: Assigning Homework 220

7.6   Professional Growth Plan: Assigning Homework 221

7.7   Learning Line 224

7.8   Reflecting on Current Practice: Providing Practice 225

7.9   Massed and Distributed Practice 227

7.10   Teacher Rubric: Providing Practice 231

7.11   Student Checklist: Providing Practice 234

7.12   Assessing Myself: Providing Practice 235

7.13   Professional Growth Plan: Providing Practice 236

Cues, Questions, and Advance Organizers

Cues and Questions

The strategies in this section help students access their prior knowledge and make connections to new knowledge. These strategies present opportunities for teachers to differentiate instruction and provide multiple venues for sense-making and skill-building.

Data from over 151,000 classroom observations (conducted using McREL's Power Walkthrough® software, which allows observers to use hand-held devices to gather data on teachers' use of instructional strategies) indicate cueing and questioning were identified as the primary instructional strategy in 19 percent of all classroom observations. Practice was the primary instructional strategy in 20 percent of all observations. It is clear from both research and classroom observations that the use of cues and questions is one of the main instructional strategies in a teacher's tool belt.

We group cues and questions together in this category because each functions in a similar manner: both activate students' prior knowledge and give them an idea of what they will learn. Cues are hints about the content of an upcoming lesson; in addition, they both reinforce information that students already know and provide some new information on the topic. Similarly, questions allow students to access previously learned information and assess what they do not already know.

Using cues and questions at the beginning of a lesson or unit focuses learning on the important content to come. Such an approach can motivate students by tapping into their innate curiosity and interest in the topic. In addition, using higher-order questions helps students deepen their knowledge by requiring the use of critical-thinking skills (e.g., making inferences, analyzing perspectives). Effective cues and questions help students access their prior knowledge and put that knowledge to use learning new information.

Why This Strategy?

Since cues and questions account for approximately 80 percent of what occurs in a classroom on a given day, it is essential for teachers to be well vetted in the appropriate use of the strategies and intentional in their use (Fillippone, 1998). Since cues and questions are vehicles frequently used to deliver instruction, teachers need to reflect upon their use of this strategy and always strive toward best practice.

Walk into any classroom and you will probably not have to wait very long before the teacher asks a question. Although cues and questions are usually thought of as impromptu strategies, teachers can plan for and align them to be used in class with the content and skills listed in the learning objectives. This means that attention must be given to which cues and questions are used in the classroom, how they are used, and the effect of their use upon student learning. This information should be kept in the daily lesson plans.

Cues are explicit reminders or hints about what students are about to experience. They help students activate what they already know about a topic and let them know what they should expect. In the classroom, teachers who know their content often fail to understand that students need explicit cueing as an aid to learning. Although the reading assignment is somewhat contrived, consider how you would react as a learner in each of the following classrooms.

Classroom One. Ms. Franklin is always in a hurry to get students started with the learning. After she briefly describes the objective, she immediately begins her lesson. As she passes out papers, she says, "Okay, I have a short piece for you to read before we break into your learning team groups. Please take a few minutes and read the information on the paper." Students get right to work and read.

The process often involves drilling and extracting. The work can be expensive and time consuming. Silver and gold are two minerals recovered from the operation by skilled operators who perform the necessary tasks. As with any procedure that involves instruments and machinery, there is some level of risk. In fact, some have died during the extraction process. Other dilemmas that can arise are due to poor resurfacing. If the surface area is not returned to its original contour after the drilling and extracting process, erosion of surrounding materials can and often does occur.

When students finish, she asks them to discuss the following question: How does the process you read about relate to what we were discussing yesterday? Confusion erupts as students attempt to answer the question.

Travis says, "I was at the dentist yesterday, and I know this is about having cavities filled. How can learning about cavities tie in to what we talked about yesterday?"

"It's about mining, not the dentist," says Tabota.

"No, it's not," replies Travis.

"Let's ask Ms. Franklin," offers Beth.

Classroom Two. Even though she is a third-year teacher, Ms. Foster spends a lot of time thinking about how her lessons are perceived by her students. She knows that she is only successful if her students understand information and apply activities from the lesson to the bigger picture. As she plans her lesson about mining, she keeps in mind that her students might have only very limited background knowledge relevant to her unit on nonrenewable resources. Ms. Foster begins by asking students to follow along as she reads aloud the lesson objectives that discuss the effect of primary economic activities in a geographic context. She then asks students what they know about the terms *nonrenewable* and *strip mining*. Ms. Foster has her students discuss what they want to learn with their study partners. As she passes out the short reading assignment, she cues students into the learning by explaining that they should read the paragraph with a focus on being able to share three important points about mining with their partners. She also asks them to think about how the reading connects to the previous day's discussion of precious metals.

The process often involves drilling and extracting. The work can be expensive and time-consuming. Silver and gold are two minerals recovered from the operation by skilled operators who perform the necessary tasks. As with any procedure that involves instruments and machinery, there is some level of risk. In fact, some have died during the extraction process. Other dilemmas that can arise are due to poor resurfacing. If the surface area is not returned to its original contour after the drilling and extracting process, erosion of surrounding materials can and often does occur.

As you can see, teachers who take the time to explicitly cue their students into the lesson's content provide a valuable service in focusing student attention on what is important, and they provide their students with the opportunity to use prior knowledge as an anchor point for new learning. Cueing students also helps reduce confusion and expedite the process of sense-making.

As you introduce a unit or lesson, there is no need to be subtle or ambiguous with students about what you want them to learn. Use explicit cues to tell students what they are about to learn, and help them identify and discuss what they already know about the topic.

The more students know about a topic, the more interested they will be in it. Asking questions that help students access their prior knowledge about a topic brings that knowledge to the conscious level and increases the likelihood that students will pay attention to or engage in new information related to the topic.

The following four recommendations provide guidance for teachers as they create a learning environment for student success. Teachers are encouraged to

1. **Focus on what is important.** Focusing on the important aspects of a topic helps students recognize the point of a lesson and helps them integrate what they are learning with their relevant prior knowledge.

2. **Use explicit cues.** Explicit cues activate students' prior knowledge by bringing to mind their relevant personal experiences or situations they encounter on a regular basis.

3. **Ask inferential questions.** When teachers ask questions that require students to make inferences, students draw upon what they already know to "fill in the blanks" and address missing information in the presented material.

4. **Ask analytic questions.** Analytic questions prompt students to think more deeply and critically about the information presented. Teachers can frame questions around the skills of analyzing errors, constructing support, and analyzing perspectives.

Reflecting on My Current Practice

The questions listed in Figure 4.1 are provided as a means to assist you as you implement the instructional practices for using cues and questions.

| FIGURE 4.1 |
| **Reflecting on Current Practice: Cues and Questions** |

1. Do I help students develop an understanding of how their background and prior knowledge connect with what they are about to learn?

2. Do I focus on what is important as I provide information, share examples, and engage students in activities that tightly align with the learning objective?

3. Do I use explicit cues at the beginning of a lesson or unit to focus students on the important content to come?

4. Do I use explicit cues throughout the lesson or unit to focus students on the important content to come?

5. Do I intentionally ask questions that require students to make inferences, draw upon what they already know to "fill in the blanks," and address missing information in the presented material?

6. Do I intentionally ask analytic questions to prompt students to think more deeply and critically about the information presented?

Bringing the Strategy to Life in the Classroom

Recommendation One:
Focus on what is important.

Using research as a backdrop for our discussion of cues and questions provides an avenue to reflect upon current practice and establish standards of performance for growth and improvement. Ideally, cues and questions trigger student thinking and memories of prior experiences and learning. Teachers who use this information to their advantage in lesson design and delivery understand the importance of focusing students on significant—not trivial—information. When teachers use an unusual or odd piece of information as a hook, students are very likely to pay attention. However, the downside is that this type of learning experience often results in student confusion and distracts from the core content. For example, a 6th grade teacher beginning a unit on space and the solar system may engage and draw many comments from students if they are asked to describe what they have heard or read about UFOs and alien life. The discussion may even turn lively, with much speculative information shared. The unfortunate outcome of this discussion is that students might draw the conclusion that UFOs and space creatures occupy a definite place in our solar system. Teachers who instead use video clips of a Mars landing to stimulate thinking help students draw upon their previous knowledge and set the stage for additional learning without sensationalizing the examples.

Recommendation Two:
Use explicit cues.

Students are more likely to learn if they connect new information to what they already know—their prior knowledge. Be clear and concise as you prepare them for a unit or lesson; using a direct approach is most effective. Simply tell students what they are about to learn, and then help them identify and discuss what they already know about the topic and predict what they think they will learn.

A well-known structured approach to eliciting prior knowledge is the KWL. In this model, the *K* reminds the students to answer the question "What do I already know about this topic?" For example, when students are learning about westward expansion in the United States, they might recall that they know about Lewis and Clark and that their expedition involved something about charting new territories. The *W* cues them to answer "What do I want to know?" Students might want to know about the role Sacagawea played in assisting Lewis and Clark. Finally, after the learning experience, students answer the question "What did I learn?" Students might answer the questions they had and record any other important information they learned. Teachers have reported that when they use explicit cues such as those in the KWL strategy, students begin to use the strategy when they work in small groups or even when they study alone.

Recommendation Three:
Ask inferential questions.

Students are asked to engage in thinking at three levels: literal, inferential, and analytical. Although well-intentioned teachers may provide questions and instruction at various levels, the truth is that most questions are asked at the literal level. This means that the teacher provides information, and students are asked to repeat that information in the same form. It is much like storing a product in a warehouse, which is wheeled out in exactly the same form when it is needed again.

Inferential thinking is much like a factory. Raw materials are taken in, and new products are created. Many of the questions that comprise state assessments require students to think inferentially as they identify missing information. Inferring is a processing skill that students and adults use on a daily basis. For instance, one evening a teacher walks into a local grocery store to buy balloons and cups for a Saturday science seminar. While she is in the store, she decides to purchase some ice cream. When she places the three items on the counter, the young clerk asks, "Are you having a birthday party?" The inference made by the clerk—with the information available—is logical and can be defended.

One of the tipping points for inferential thinking is the ability to differentiate between predicting and inferring. A prediction is made from the present to the future. It must be logical, it can be defended based upon available information, and the results are almost always known. Predicting the outcome of a baseball game prior to the game or predicting if it will rain on Sunday fit this definition. On the other hand, an inference is made from past to present. It too must be logical, it too can be defended based upon available information, but the results are almost never known. Many textbooks require teachers to read a passage and have students infer what will occur next. In reality, these situations ask students to predict because they will know the outcome as soon as they read the next section. If a story ends in such a way that students must create their own ending and never know if it was really what the author intended, then they have inferred.

Recommendation Four:
Ask analytic questions.

Analytical thinking is a critical 21st-century skill. At this level, new uses are developed for the product that was manufactured. Students use what they have learned to produce original or creative ideas. They judge the accuracy of materials, distinguish between fact and opinion, identify propaganda techniques, and ask, "What can I do with the information I have?" Conceptual understanding is apparent. Although there are those who believe this type of processing is only possible as students enter secondary school, we provide arguments to the contrary. All students are capable of thinking at a higher level. It is the obligation of the teacher to provide opportunities for students to apply their thinking at various levels. Joyce Valenza (2000) offers some wonderful examples of how teachers can take what appears to be a generic and uninspiring event and turn it into a higher-level experience. For example, instead of asking students to write a report on pollution, ask them to propose a solution to an environmental problem where they live. Instead of asking students to write a report on Philadelphia, ask them to decide which city in the Mid-Atlantic region is the best place to live. Instead of asking students to identify the main characters in a story, ask them how it would change the story if one of those characters weren't in the book or if the story had taken place at a different point in history.

In addition to thinking at a higher level, we can help students think analytically by having them analyze errors and construct support. Students know that in many places during winter, salt is used on icy roads. They may make the assumption that salt melts ice. The teacher needs to help students use accurate information from the science curriculum to help them learn that salt does not melt ice; it in fact lowers the freezing temperature of water, allowing water to remain in a liquid state below 32° Fahrenheit. Although it certainly appears that applying salt to an icy road surface "melts" the ice, this isn't the case. Students can construct support for this fact by conducting an experiment in which they put a temperature probe into a glass of ice water and keep adding ice until the probe indicates 32° Fahrenheit. They can then begin adding salt, a little at a time, while adding more ice. They will see that the temperature begins to drop into the 20s and the water is still in a liquid state.

Rubrics and Checklists

The teacher rubric provided in Figure 4.2 is intended to be a tool used for reflection on the way in which you currently use cues and questions in your classroom. It is designed so that a 3 represents best practice as indicated by the research. A 4 indicates both teacher best practice as described in a 3 and how that practice transfers into student behaviors. You can also use this rubric as a growth tool, seeing where you are now and what the next level might look like. This will provide you with valuable information as you build your professional growth plan.

Using the teacher rubric will give you the chance to reflect on your practice. You can also ask your students how they perceive the way you teach them to use cues and questions. Figure 4.3 provides a student checklist you might want to use. Periodically give this checklist to your students, and ask them to react honestly to the statements. This checklist can help your students better understand how cues and questions help them learn, and it can provide valuable feedback to you about how your students view the process of using cues and questions.

Tools, Templates, and Protocols

If you are using this handbook as part of a school PLC or book study, Figure 4.4 provides statements that can serve as discussion prompts. Likewise, if you are using this book for individual growth, think about these prompts as they relate to your classroom practice. For example, if your answer to the first statement is a 0 or 1, then what steps should you take to move toward the other end of the spectrum, "to a great extent"? Use your individual or team results from Figure 4.4 to form the basis of a professional growth plan (see Figure 4.5).

FIGURE 4.2
Teacher Rubric: Cues and Questions

Focus on what is important. *Focusing on the important aspects of a topic helps students garner the point of the lesson and helps them to integrate what they are learning with their relevant prior knowledge.*

4	3	2	1
I continually focus on what is important and do not stray with the examples, questions, or activities I use. My students can identify and apply their background knowledge as they use the important information.	I continually focus on what is important and do not stray with the examples, questions, or activities I use.	I occasionally focus on what is important and sometimes stray with the examples, questions, or activities I use.	I seldom focus on what is important and frequently stray with the examples, questions, or activities I use.

Use explicit cues. *Explicit cues activate students' prior knowledge by bringing to mind their relevant personal experiences or situations they encounter on a regular basis.*

4	3	2	1
I continually use explicit cues to present students with a preview of to-be-learned information. My students use cues to focus their thinking around the topic.	I continually use explicit cues to present students with a preview of to-be-learned information.	I occasionally use explicit cues to present students with a preview of to-be-learned information.	I seldom use explicit cues to present students with a preview of to-be-learned information.
I continually use explicit cues to help my students connect new learning to personal experience or prior knowledge. My students use a variety of tools to help them elicit prior knowledge and connect it to new learning.	I continually use explicit cues to help my students connect new learning to personal experiences or prior knowledge.	I occasionally use explicit cues to help my students connect new learning to personal experience or prior knowledge.	I seldom use explicit cues to help my students connect new learning to personal experience or prior knowledge.

FIGURE 4.2
Teacher Rubric: Cues and Questions (continued)

Ask inferential questions. *When teachers ask questions that require students to make inferences, students draw upon what they already know to "fill in the blanks" and add information that is missing in the presented material.*

4	3	2	1
I continually provide opportunities for my students to think inferentially. My students can defend their inferences to ensure they are logical and use available information.	I continually provide opportunities for my students to think inferentially.	I occasionally provide opportunities for my students to think inferentially.	I seldom provide opportunities for my student to think inferentially.
I continually place key inferential questions in my lesson plans. My students can identify and craft inferential questions to deepen their thinking.	I continually place key inferential questions in my lesson plans.	I occasionally place key inferential questions in my lesson plans.	I seldom or never place key inferential questions in my lesson plans.

Ask analytic questions. *Analytic questions prompt students to think more deeply and critically about the information presented. Teachers can frame questions around the skills of analyzing errors, constructing support, and analyzing perspectives.*

4	3	2	1
I continually provide opportunities for my students to think analytically. My students can explain their thinking as they analyze errors, construct support, and analyze perspectives.	I continually provide opportunities for my students to think analytically.	I occasionally provide opportunities for my students to think analytically.	I seldom provide opportunities for my students to think analytically.

FIGURE 4.2

Teacher Rubric: Cues and Questions (continued)

4	3	2	1
I continually place key analytic questions in my lesson plans. My students can identify and craft analytic questions to deepen their thinking.	I continually place key analytic questions in my lesson plans.	I occasionally place key analytic questions in my lesson plans.	I seldom or never place key analytic questions in my lesson plans.
I continually provide opportunities for students to analyze their errors and construct support for their thinking. My students often challenge one another to justify their statements.	I continually provide opportunities for students to analyze their errors and construct support for their thinking.	I occasionally provide opportunities for students to analyze their errors and construct support for their thinking.	I seldom provide opportunities for students to analyze their errors and construct support for their thinking.

FIGURE 4.3					
Student Checklist: Cues and Questions					
		Always	Sometimes	Rarely	Never
FOCUS	I understand why my teacher focuses me on the important information we are about to learn.				
	I can relate my personal experiences and background knowledge directly to the content we are studying.				
EXPLICIT CUES	I understand how the cues my teacher provides help me focus on the topic we are learning.				
	I understand how the graphic organizers my teacher provides help me focus on the topic we are learning.				
INFERENTIAL QUESTIONS	I understand how to make logical connections and inferences based on the information provided.				
	I understand the difference between predicting and inferring.				
	I understand how to create my own inferential questions to deepen my and my peers' understanding of the topic.				
ANALYTIC QUESTIONS	I understand how to analyze information for errors.				
	I understand how to construct supporting evidence for my thinking.				
	I understand how to craft analytic questions.				
	I understand how to challenge my peers to justify their assumptions.				

FIGURE 4.4
Assessing Myself: Cues and Questions

I help students develop an understanding of how what they are about to learn connects to what they already know.

Not at all   To a great extent

0   1   2   3   4

I focus on what is important as I provide information, share examples, and engage students in activities that tightly align with the learning objective.

Not at all   To a great extent

0   1   2   3   4

I use explicit cues at the beginning of a lesson or unit to focus students on the important content to come.

Not at all   To a great extent

0   1   2   3   4

I use explicit cues throughout a lesson or unit to focus students on the important content to come.

Not at all   To a great extent

0   1   2   3   4

I continually ask questions that require students to make inferences, draw upon what they already know to "fill in the blanks," and address missing information in the presented material.

Not at all   To a great extent

0   1   2   3   4

I continually ask analytic questions to prompt students to think more deeply and critically about the information presented.

Not at all   To a great extent

0   1   2   3   4

FIGURE 4.5
Professional Growth Plan: Cues and Questions

1. How can I help students develop an understanding of how what they are about to learn connects to what they already know?

2. How can I focus on what is important as I provide information, share examples, and engage students in activities that tightly align with the learning objective?

3. How can I use explicit cues at the beginning of a lesson or unit to focus students on the important content to come?

4. How can I use explicit cues throughout a lesson or unit to focus students on the important content to come?

5. How can I continually ask questions that require students to make inferences, draw upon what they already know to "fill in the blanks," and address missing information in the presented material?

6. How can I continually ask analytic questions to prompt students to think more deeply and critically about the information presented?

Advance Organizers

We also include advance organizers in this category because they help students use their background knowledge to learn new information. Advance organizers are introduced before a lesson to draw attention to important points, identify relationships within the material, and connect material to students' prior knowledge (Lefrancois, 1997; Woolfolk, 2004). The most effective advance organizers provide an organized conceptual framework that is meaningful to the learner and allows the learner to relate concepts in the instructional material to elements of that framework (Martorella, 1991; White & Tisher, 1986).

The remaining portion of this chapter emphasizes specific practices that will help you make the most effective use of advance organizers to increase student understanding and achievement. Students should use a variety of different types of advance organizers to help them access their prior knowledge, but keep in mind that the purpose of an advance organizer is to clarify what students will be learning with regard to a particular topic. Ensure that the connection between the advance organizer and the focus of the lesson is clear.

Why This Strategy?

Teachers who understand how students learn are well aware that it is imperative to be as transparent as possible about what is to be learned, the expectations for learning, the outcomes for which students should aim, and the activities and tools that will be made available to students as they are learning, making sense of the materials, and preparing to transfer their learning to other situations. In order for teachers to prepare themselves and their students for the instructional journey, attention must be paid to the strategies that best fit the various segments of the instruction.

Advance organizers help students frame their learning by providing a vehicle for retrieving prior knowledge, anticipating the information that lies ahead, and providing a structure for learning. Because an advance organizer is presented at the onset of instruction, students have a chance to begin the lesson or unit with a stable and well-defined framework for learning. Teachers who employ advance organizers provide an invaluable service to their students by enticing them into the learning, allowing them to see what they already know and are going to learn, and helping them progress through the selected content. Graphic organizers, anticipation guides, stories, and video clips are good examples of the four types of advance organizers, which we discuss below.

As with cues and questions, advance organizers should focus on essential information, especially when unusual or trivial aspects of the topic might distract students. Advance organizers can, of course, help students get ready to learn facts and details about a topic, but you can use them more effectively as a tool to help your students prepare to use various reading strategies. For example, if students are getting ready to read informational text, an advance graphic organizer could focus them as they look for examples of main ideas and concepts the teacher knows to be important to the understanding of the concept. Alternatively, you could read a short article on the topic to be studied to students—which could serve as a narrative advance organizer—and model the strategy of skimming for students, looking at headings, pictures, charts, boldface words, and unfamiliar vocabulary. Advance organizers help teachers prepare students for upcoming learning and take the mystery out of what is to come. They help students retrieve what they already know about a topic and prepare them to connect with and make sense of new information.

The following four recommendations provide guidance for teachers as they create a learning environment for student success. Teachers are encouraged to

1. **Use expository advance organizers.** Expository advance organizers describe or explain in written or verbal form the new content students are about to learn. They emphasize the important content and help students build a framework for learning by providing the meaning and purpose of what is to follow.
2. **Use narrative advance organizers.** Narrative advance organizers present information to students in a story format and serve to engage students' interest while activating their prior knowledge on a topic.
3. **Use skimming as an advance organizer.** Skimming is the process of quickly looking over material to get a general impression before reading it fully. Done appropriately, it helps students create a picture of what the material addresses, and it helps organize new information.
4. **Use graphic advance organizers.** Teachers provide students with graphic advance organizers in advance of the learning to introduce them to new material. To be effective, graphic advance organizers must clearly communicate what students are expected to learn.

Reflecting on My Current Practice

The questions listed in Figure 4.6 are provided as a means to assist you as you implement the instructional practices for using advance organizers.

FIGURE 4.6

Reflecting on Current Practice: Advance Organizers

1. Do I help students develop an understanding of how their background and prior knowledge connect with what they are about to learn?

2. Do I focus on what is important as I provide information, share examples, and engage students in activities that tightly align with the learning objective?

3. Do I use advance organizers at the beginning of a lesson or unit to focus students on the important content to come?

4. Do I use a variety of advance organizers appropriately to focus students on the important content to come and assist them in elaborating on their learning?

5. Do I use the advance organizers throughout the instruction as a means to align learning with the intended learning objective?

Bringing the Strategy to Life in the Classroom

Recommendation One:
Use expository advance organizers.

Advance organizers, whether they prepare students to learn details or process information at a higher level, can take on many formats. Some teachers mistakenly use the term *advanced organizers*, giving the impression that they are more complex organizers or should be used with more complex topics. In reality, the term *advance* only refers to the timing of the delivery. In this chapter, we discuss several examples of and approaches to each of the four recommendations.

Expository advance organizers are straightforward descriptions of new content that students will learn. These descriptions can be provided orally or in written form, but as with all advance organizers, you should emphasize the important content—not the unusual or trivial. In some cases, an expository advance organizer may include text or pictures as a means to clarify complex information. For example, a teacher is designing a lesson about health and nutrition. As an expository advance organizer, she provides the key vocabulary words that students will encounter, the trend data on childhood obesity, and sample menus from the school cafeteria. She asks students to review the data and menus prior to beginning instruction.

Recommendation Two:
Use narrative advance organizers.

Stories are a form of narrative advance organizers. They are an effective way to help students make personal or real-world connections with new content. Since stories do not always come to mind easily, it is important that examples are placed in lesson plans prior to lesson delivery. Stories can make unfamiliar content—such as a time in history, a scientific discovery, or a complex concept—seem more personal and familiar. For example, students in a social studies class are studying the women's suffrage movement. Simply reading about the 19th Amendment does not help students connect to the difficulties that arose, the years it took to secure the right for women to vote, and the changes that swept through the nation because of this amendment. Their teacher realizes that a good way to spark interest and establish key vocabulary is to share a story about Susan B. Anthony's suffrage trial.

Recommendation Three:
Use skimming as an advance organizer.

Skimming information before reading can be a powerful advance organizer. Skimming allows students to preview important information they will encounter by focusing on and noting what is contained within the headings, subheadings, and other highlighted information. Expository texts are particularly suited for skimming because the organizational schema of information in textbooks, articles, and other informational texts commonly includes major headings, boldface terms, pictures with captions, inset quotations, and other assistive clues.

Skimming is a strategy that teachers must model and provide time for students to practice. Teachers who fail to do so miss opportunities to set the stage for learning in advance of instruction. Tools such as an SQ3R protocol (Survey, Question, Read, Recite, Reflect) (Figure 4.7) or anticipation guide (Figure 4.8) increase the probability of positively influencing student achievement. Teachers who model skimming through think alouds and reflective discussions find that their students tend to gravitate toward these previewing strategies.

Recommendation Four:
Use graphic advance organizers.

When graphic organizers are used to set the stage for learning, they are referred to as advance graphic organizers. Graphic organizers used at the onset of a lesson are not necessarily different from other types of graphic organizers; they are simply given to students in advance of the instruction and learning. Students must be made aware of the fact that a graphic organizer such as a Venn diagram can be used before a lesson as an advance organizer or during a lesson to compare the similarities and differences of specific information.

Graphic organizers are useful tools that are embedded within several categories of strategies outlined in both this book and *Classroom Instruction That Works*. They are a vital component of cues, questions, and advance organizers; nonlinguistic representations; summarizing and note taking; identifying similarities and differences; and generating and testing hypothesis. Because of the diverse application of graphic organizers, it is imperative that teachers provide explicit instruction in their use and appropriately employ the vast array of graphic organizers available for specified learning.

When information is unfamiliar to students, and when the relationships among pieces of information are complex, teachers should present that information using a graphic organizer.

FIGURE 4.7 SQ3R Protocol		
Stage	**What It Means**	**Notes**
Survey (what you are about to read)	• Think about the title. What do I know about this subject? What do I want to know? • Glance over the heading and/or skim the first sentences of paragraphs. • Look at illustrations and graphic aids. • Read the first paragraph. • Read the last paragraph or summary.	
Question	• Turn the title into a question. This becomes the major purpose for your reading. • Write down any questions that come to mind during the survey. • Turn headings into questions. • Turn subheadings, illustrations, and graphic aids into questions. • Write down unfamiliar vocabulary and determine the meaning.	
Read (actively)	• Read to search for answers to questions. • Respond to questions and use the context clues for unfamiliar words. • React to unclear passages, confusing terms, and questionable statements by generating additional questions.	
Recite	• Look away from the answers and the book to recall what was read. • Recite answers to questions aloud or in writing. • Reread text for unanswered questions.	
Review	• Answer the major purpose questions. • Look over answers and all parts of the chapter to organize information. • Summarize the information learned by creating a graphic organizer that depicts the main ideas, drawing a flowchart, writing a summary, participating in a group discussion, or writing an explanation of how this material has changed your perceptions or applies to your life.	

FIGURE 4.8
Anticipation Guide

Directions: Read each statement below. In the column labeled *Me*, place a *T* if you believe the statement is true and an *F* if you believe the statement is false. Tell why you think it is true or false in the section labeled *Explanation*. Then read pages 21 through 28 in your text. In the column labeled *Text*, place a *T* by the statements the text considers true and an *F* by the statements the text considers false. Compare your opinions about those statements with information contained in the text.

Me	Text	
_____	_____	1. Heat can move three ways: conduction, convection, and radiation. *Explanation:*
_____	_____	2. In liquids and gases, heat moves most often by convection. *Explanation:*
_____	_____	3. As warmer, less densely packed molecules rise through cooler surroundings, they gain energy. *Explanation:*
_____	_____	4. The third type of movement of heat does not deal with molecules; instead, radiation exists as waves of energy. *Explanation:*

The episode graphic organizer (Figure 4.9) would be a great way for students to organize their learning, retrieve prior knowledge, check for understanding, process information to ensure that what they learned makes sense, and apply learning to other situations.

Another useful advance graphic organizer is the anticipation guide (Figure 4.10). The purpose of an anticipation guide is twofold. It allows students to activate and use their prior knowledge on the topic, and it provides a focus for the salient points of the lesson or unit.

The Frayer Model (Figure 4.11) is often used as an advance graphic organizer to help students understand vocabulary words that are critical to the

FIGURE 4.9
Episode Graphic Organizer

(Organizes a large amount of diverse information about a specific event.)

Questions to guide the use of this graphic organizer:

1. What event is explained or described?
2. What is the setting where the event occurs?
3. When did this event occur?
4. Who are the major figures or characters that play a part in this event?
5. List, in the order they occur, the specific incidents involved with this event.
6. What caused this event?
7. What effects has this event had on the people involved?
8. What effects has this event had on society in general?

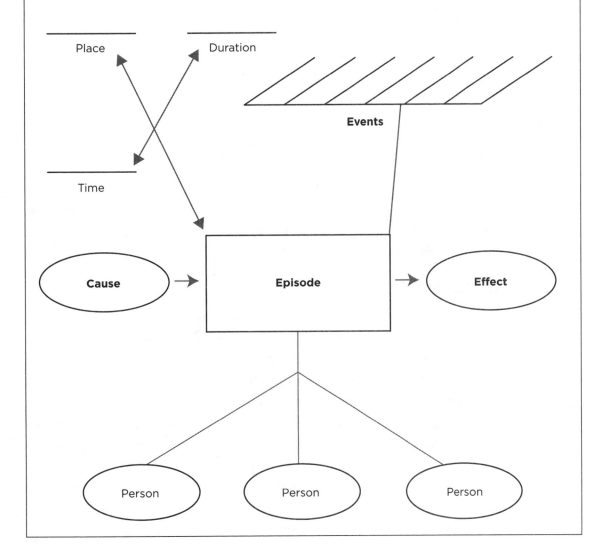

FIGURE 4.10
Anticipation Guide Template

Directions: Read each statement below. In the column labeled "Me," place a *T* if you believe the statement is true and an *F* if you believe the statement is false. Explain why you think the statement is true or false in the section labeled "Explanation." Then read pages 17–21 in your text. In the column labeled "Text," place a *T* by the statement the text considers true and an *F* by the statement the text considers false. Compare your opinion about those statements with the information contained in the text.

Me	Text	Statement
_____	_____	1. _____
_____	_____	2. _____
_____	_____	3. _____
_____	_____	4. _____

Explanation:

---

understanding of a topic. When they use this advance organizer, students have an opportunity to deepen their understanding of a word and apply their new knowledge in a graphic form.

Rubrics and Checklists

The teacher rubric provided in Figure 4.12 is intended to be a tool used for reflection on the way in which you currently use advance organizers in your classroom. It is designed so that a 3 represents best practice as indicated by the research. A 4 indicates both teacher best practice as described in a 3 and how that practice transfers into student behaviors. You can also use this rubric as a growth tool, seeing where you are now and what the next level might look like. This will provide you with valuable information as you build your professional growth plan.

Using the teacher rubric will give you the chance to reflect on your practice. You can also ask your students how they perceive the way you teach them to use advance organizers. Figure 4.13 provides a student checklist you might want to use. Periodically give this checklist to your students, and ask them to react honestly to the statements. This checklist can help your students better understand how advance organizers help them learn, and it can provide valuable feedback to you about how your students view the process of using advance organizers.

Tools, Templates, and Protocols

If you are using this handbook as part of a school PLC or book study, Figure 4.14 provides statements that can serve as discussion prompts. Likewise, if you are using this book for individual growth, think about these prompts as they relate to your classroom practice. For example, if your answer to the first statement is a 0 or 1, then what steps should you take to move toward the other end of the spectrum, "to a great extent"? Use your individual or team results from Figure 4.14 to form the basis of a professional growth plan (see Figure 4.15).

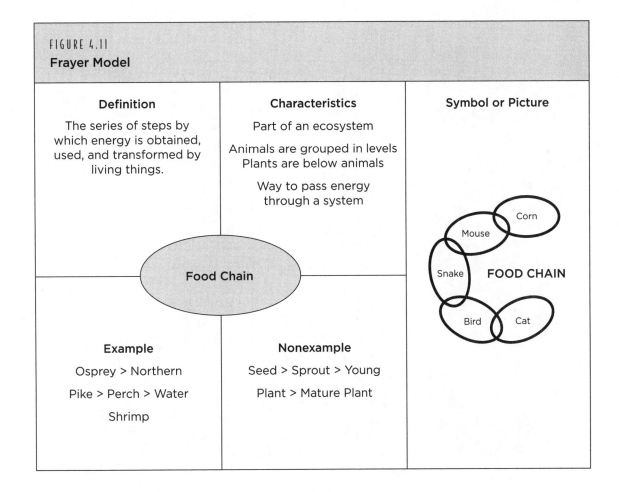

FIGURE 4.11
Frayer Model

Definition	Characteristics	Symbol or Picture
The series of steps by which energy is obtained, used, and transformed by living things.	Part of an ecosystem Animals are grouped in levels Plants are below animals Way to pass energy through a system	

Food Chain

Example	Nonexample	
Osprey > Northern Pike > Perch > Water Shrimp	Seed > Sprout > Young Plant > Mature Plant	

FIGURE 4.12
Teacher Rubric: Advance Organizers

Use expository advance organizers. *Expository advance organizers describe or explain in written or verbal form the new content students are about to learn. They emphasize the important content and help students build a framework for learning by providing the meaning and purpose of what is to follow.*

4	3	2	1
I consistently provide expository advance organizers to describe or explain in written or oral form the new content to be learned. My students can articulate how the expository organizer helps them connect prior learning to new learning.	I consistently provide expository advance organizers to describe or explain in written or oral form the new content to be learned.	I occasionally provide expository advance organizers to describe or explain in written or oral form the new content to be learned.	I seldom provide expository advance organizers to describe or explain in written or oral form the new content to be learned.
I consistently provide expository advance organizers to emphasize important content and provide my students with a framework for their learning. My students understand the purpose of using an expository advance organizer to frame their learning.	I consistently provide expository advance organizers to emphasize important content and provide my students with a framework for their learning.	I occasionally provide expository advance organizers to emphasize important content and provide my students with a framework for their learning.	I seldom provide expository advance organizers to emphasize important content and provide my students with a framework for their learning.

FIGURE 4.12
Teacher Rubric: Advance Organizers (continued)

Use narrative advance organizers. *Narrative advance organizers present information to students in a story format and serve to engage students' interest while at the same time activating their prior knowledge on a topic.*

4	3	2	1
I consistently use narrative advance organizers to engage students' interest. My students are able to create their own stories that connect with new learning.	I consistently use narrative advance organizers to engage students' interest.	I occasionally use narrative advance organizers to engage students' interest.	I seldom use narrative advance organizers to engage students' interest.
I consistently use narrative advance organizers to activate students' prior knowledge. My students can articulate how the narrative helps them connect prior learning to new learning.	I consistently use narrative advance organizers to activate students' prior knowledge.	I occasionally use narrative advance organizers to activate students' prior knowledge.	I seldom use narrative advance organizers to activate students' prior knowledge.

Use skimming as an advance organizer. *Skimming is the process of quickly looking over material to get a general impression before reading it fully. Done appropriately, it helps students create a picture of what the material addresses, and it helps organize new information.*

4	3	2	1
I consistently use skimming to help my students create a picture of what the upcoming material addresses. My students apply skimming techniques to different types of materials.	I consistently use skimming to help my students create a picture of what the upcoming material addresses.	I occasionally use skimming to help my students create a picture of what the upcoming material addresses.	I seldom use skimming to help my students create a picture of what the upcoming material addresses.

FIGURE 4.12
Teacher Rubric: Advance Organizers (continued)

4	3	2	1
I consistently use skimming to help my students organize new information. My students are able to use skimming to identify the main points or ideas.	I consistently use skimming to help my students organize new information.	I occasionally use skimming to help my students organize new information.	I seldom use skimming to help my students organize new information.

Use graphic advance organizers. *Teachers provide students with graphic advance organizers in advance of the learning to introduce them to new material. To be effective, graphic advance organizers must clearly communicate what students are expected to learn.*

4	3	2	1
I consistently use graphic advance organizers to introduce new material. My students can articulate how a graphic advance organizer helps them connect prior learning to new learning.	I consistently use graphic advance organizers to introduce new material.	I occasionally use graphic advance organizers to introduce new material.	I seldom use graphic advance organizers to introduce new material.
I consistently use graphic advance organizers to clearly communicate what students are expected to know, understand, and be able to do. My students can articulate what is expected of them.	I consistently use graphic advance organizers to clearly communicate what students are expected to know, understand, and be able to do.	I occasionally use graphic advance organizers to clearly communicate what students are expected to know, understand, and be able to do.	I seldom use graphic advance organizers to clearly communicate what students are expected to know, understand, and be able to do.

FIGURE 4.12
Teacher Rubric: Advance Organizers *(continued)*

4	3	2	1
I consistently select the appropriate graphic organizer for the intended learning. I allow students to make choices about which graphic organizer they will use.	I consistently select the appropriate graphic organizer for the intended learning.	I occasionally select the appropriate graphic organizer for the intended learning.	I seldom select the appropriate graphic organizer for the intended learning.

FIGURE 4.13

Student Checklist: Advance Organizers

		Always	Sometimes	Rarely	Never
EXPOSITORY	I understand how expository advance organizers connect my prior knowledge to new learning.				
	I understand how using an expository advance organizer frames my learning.				
NARRATIVE	I am able to create my own stories that connect to new learning.				
	I can explain how stories help me connect prior learning to new learning.				
SKIMMING	I understand how to skim different types of materials.				
	I understand how to identify main ideas when I skim.				
GRAPHIC	I understand how graphic advance organizers help me connect prior learning to new learning.				
	I understand how graphic advance organizers help me know what is expected of me.				
	I can select the correct graphic advance organizer for the material I am about to learn.				

FIGURE 4.14

Assessing Myself: Advance Organizers

I help students develop an understanding of how their background and prior knowledge connect with what they are about to learn.

Not at all   To a great extent

0   1   2   3   4

I focus on what is important as I provide information, share examples, and engage students in activities that tightly align with the learning objective.

Not at all   To a great extent

0   1   2   3   4

I use advance organizers at the beginning of a lesson or unit to focus students on the important content to come.

Not at all   To a great extent

0   1   2   3   4

I use a variety of advance organizers appropriately to focus students on the important content to come and help them elaborate on their learning.

Not at all   To a great extent

0   1   2   3   4

I use advance organizers throughout the instruction as a means to align learning with the intended learning objective.

Not at all   To a great extent

0   1   2   3   4

FIGURE 4.15
Professional Growth Plan: Advance Organizers

1. How can I help students develop an understanding of how their background and prior knowledge connect with what they are about to learn?

2. How can I focus on what is important as I provide information, share examples, and engage students in activities that tightly align with the learning objective?

3. How can I use advance organizers at the beginning of a lesson or unit to focus students on the important content to come?

4. How can I use a variety of advance organizers appropriately to focus students on the important content to come and help them elaborate on their learning?

5. How can I use advance organizers throughout the instruction as a means to align learning with the intended learning objective?

Nonlinguistic Representations

Nonlinguistic Representations

Psychologists believe that information is stored in memory in two ways: as words (linguistic) and as images (nonlinguistic). This chapter focuses on the imagery form (Clark & Paivio, 1991; Paivio, 2006). Imagery can be expressed as mental pictures or as physical sensations, such as smell, taste, touch, kinesthetic association, and sound (Richardson, 1983). Nonlinguistic representations provide students with useful tools that merge knowledge presented in the classroom with mechanisms for understanding and remembering that knowledge (Jewitt, 2008; Kress, 1997).

Why This Strategy?

When teachers use nonlinguistic representation strategies, they help students represent knowledge as mental imagery. These strategies are powerful because they tap into students' natural tendency for visual image processing, which helps them construct meaning from relevant content and skills and have a better capacity to recall it later (Medina, 2008). For example, diagrams and models are used in science and mathematics to help represent phenomena that students cannot observe, such as the arrangement of atoms in a molecule and how that arrangement changes during a chemical reaction (Michalchik, Rosenquist, Kozma, Kreikemeier, & Schank, 2008). In other subjects, students can use nonlinguistic representations such as graphic organizers to organize information into a conceptual framework. This type of representation increases transfer of knowledge because it allows students to see how the information connects in new situations (Bransford, Brown, & Cocking, 1999). The ultimate goal for using these strategies is to produce nonlinguistic representations of knowledge in the minds of students so they are better able to process, organize, and retrieve information from memory. Consider the following classroom example.

Ms. Elias and her 6th grade students are studying the roles that Lewis and Clark played in westward expansion. Ms. Elias gives each student a black-line master of a Conestoga wagon and asks them to place information about Meriwether Lewis on the front wheel of the wagon and information about William Clark on the back wheel. She also provides information about the Corps of Discovery Expedition, which students place on the wagon's canopy. Information about Sacagawea is placed on the wagon's frame. After the final assessment, students report to Ms. Elias that, as they answered questions, they pictured the wagon in their minds to help them remember the information.

This scenario provides insight into what occurs when a teacher intentionally plans for instruction. Ms. Elias used a graphic to help her students organize their learning and transfer that information into a mental image. Students were successful on the exam because they were able to employ a powerful combination—linking linguistic knowledge to a nonlinguistic representation—and create an enduring understanding.

The more we use nonlinguistic representations while learning, the better we can think about and recall our knowledge. This is particularly relevant to the classroom, since teachers primarily present new knowledge to students linguistically—by talking to students about new content or by having them read about the new content. As a result, students are commonly left to their own devices to generate nonlinguistic representations for new knowledge. However, when teachers help students in this endeavor, the effects on achievement are strong. Explicitly engaging students in the creation of nonlinguistic representations actually stimulates and increases activity in the brain (Gerlic & Jausovec, 1999). Although students may not initially create nonlinguistic representations on their own, you can create opportunities for them to use this strategy.

Asking students to generate nonlinguistic representations of the knowledge they are learning is a straightforward way of representing information. Although using a nonlinguistic representation may not come naturally to many students, the process of assisting students need not be complicated. It is important, however, to explicitly teach students how to use the tools. Modeling the use of strategies through think alouds or demonstrations can help students understand how to use different types of nonlinguistic representations. For example, to demonstrate the use of a graphic organizer, you might give students a completed organizer that summarizes a familiar film or set of information you discussed in class. You might also give students a blank organizer and walk them through the process of organizing information in different ways. This approach lets students focus on learning to use the graphic organizer without also having to worry about learning new content (Anderson, 1995; Karpicke & Roediger, 2008; Newell & Rosenbloom, 1981).

The following five recommendations provide guidance for teachers as they create a learning environment for student success. Teachers are encouraged to

1. **Use graphic organizers.** Students combine words and phrases with symbols, arrows, and shapes to represent relationships in the knowledge being learned. Graphic organizers include representations for descriptive patterns, time-sequence patterns, process patterns, episode patterns, generalization patterns, and concept patterns.

2. **Make physical models or manipulatives.** Students are involved in hands-on tasks to build concrete representations of the knowledge being learned.

3. **Generate mental pictures.** Students visualize the knowledge being learned. Mental pictures incorporate senses, physical sensations, and emotions.

4. **Create pictures, illustrations, and pictographs.** Students draw, paint, or use technology to create symbolic pictures that represent knowledge being learned.

5. **Engage in kinesthetic activities.** Students engage in physical movement associated with specific knowledge to generate a mental image of content and skills being learned.

Reflecting on My Current Practice

The questions listed in Figure 5.1 are provided as a means to assist you as you implement the instructional practices for using nonlinguistic representations.

FIGURE 5.1

Reflecting on Current Practice: Nonlinguistic Representations

1. Do I intentionally engage students in using nonlinguistic representations?

2. Do I help students use the six types of graphic organizers (descriptive patterns, time-sequence patterns, process/cause-effect patterns, episode patterns, generalization/principle patterns, concept patterns)?

3. Do I ask students to create mental images of their thinking and help them add details, including emotions and the five senses?

4. Do I use physical models to help students deepen their understanding of abstract concepts or items difficult to interact with in person?

5. Do I use kinesthetic movement to help students elaborate on their learning?

6. Do I use pictures, illustrations, and pictographs to help students represent their ideas and deepen their understanding?

7. Do I explain, model, and practice nonlinguistic representations within familiar contexts?

Bringing the Strategy to Life in the Classroom

Using nonlinguistic representations is one of the strongest ways to teach vocabulary. Ongoing use will lead to students "owning" words instead of relying on the age-old strategy of rote memorization. Vocabulary is known as a gatekeeper to student success since the more familiar students are with the vocabulary of a given topic, the more interested they are, the easier it is for them to learn, the more willing they are to push themselves to learn, and the more motivated they are to continue reading and writing. Knowing this, it is imperative for teachers to pay attention to the types of instruction they provide to help students develop a robust vocabulary. One important feature of using nonlinguistic representations is that the five recommendations are employed to help students improve their bank of words.

Capitalizing on the relationship that exists between learning vocabulary and elaborating on student understanding through the inclusion of nonlinguistic representations is a point not to be lost. The following vignette illustrates how easily and efficiently a teacher can incorporate multiple nonlinguistic representations into a lesson and assist students as they learn the critical words for a unit of study.

Mr. Kissler is helping his 6th grade students learn the concepts and associated vocabulary words for a unit on ecology. Today, Mr. Kissler is teaching the term *food chain*. He has learned from his past experience teaching vocabulary, which revealed that simply asking students to look up new words in the glossary had little impact on their ability to remember and correctly use those words. He also knows that students need multiple opportunities to learn the critical words associated with a unit of study. Therefore, he first provides students with a conversational definition of the word and then says, "Close your eyes and picture a food chain as I describe each portion in detail [mental imagery]. Working in your cooperative groups, let's act out the term by hooking arms and forming a food chain [kinesthetic]." Students organize themselves into groups and follow the directions given.

"Now I want each of you to take turns and explain your role in the chain," instructs Mr. Kissler. Finally, he asks students to place the term, its definition, and an appropriate picture [pictograph] that will help them remember the meaning of *food chain* into the vocabulary section of their science notebooks. The following day, Mr. Kissler begins class by asking students to work in pairs and use the material on their tables to create a model of a food chain. Students are to demonstrate the flow of energy through the food chain and identify the various plants and animals that make up the chain. Over the course of two class periods, each strategy Mr. Kissler employs allows his students the opportunity to rehearse their learning, deepen their understanding, and provide an anchor for future application of the new term.

Recommendation One:
Use graphic organizers.

Graphic organizers are typically used to organize declarative knowledge, or information. Declarative knowledge can be organized into patterns that help students recognize different relationships and connections among pieces of information. Six common patterns used to organize information are descriptions, time sequences, process/cause-effect relationships, episodes, generalizations/principles, and concepts. Although there are many ways to construct graphic organizers, these organizational patterns provide a consistent structure for teachers and students.

Descriptive. Descriptive graphic organizers represent facts about specific people, places, things, and events. The information organized into a descriptive pattern does not need to be in any particular order.

Time-sequence. Time-sequence graphic organizers help students put events in a specific chronological order.

Process/Cause-effect. Process/cause-effect graphic organizers help students put information into a causal network that leads to a specific outcome or into a sequence of steps that lead to a specific product.

Episode. Episode graphic organizers help students organize information about specific events, including

- a setting (time and place)
- specific people
- a specific duration
- a specific sequence of events
- a particular cause and effect

Generalization/Principle. Generalization/principle graphic organizers help students organize information into general statements with supporting examples.

Concept. Concept graphic organizers, the most general of all graphic organizers, organize information around a word or phrase that represents an entire class or category of people, places, things, and events. The characteristics or attributes of the concept, along with examples of each, should be included in this pattern.

In the following vignette, see how the teacher uses a descriptive pattern graphic organizer as both an advance graphic organizer and a nonlinguistic graphic organizer to help his students better understand the branches of the U.S. government.

Mr. Cooper is beginning a unit on the U.S. government with his 5th grade class. To help his students activate their prior knowledge, he provides an advance graphic organizer and asks them to fill the ovals with the branches of government they know (Figure 5.2). He tells his students that it is OK if they only remember one or two, or even none at all, since they are just beginning the unit.

As an opening activity for the lesson, Mr. Cooper divides the class into groups of three students. He explains they are going to use a jigsaw cooperative learning activity to help them all learn together. He reminds them that when they work in cooperative learning groups, it is important for everyone to work hard and do their part so that everyone in the group learns the information.

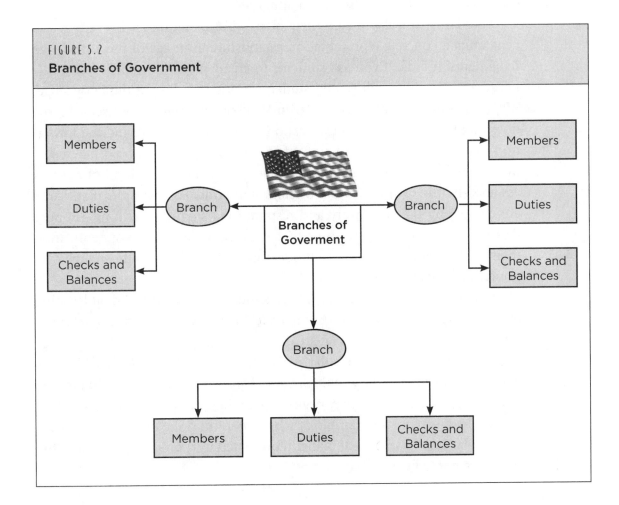

FIGURE 5.2
Branches of Government

Each member of the group is asked to pick one branch of government in which he or she wants to become an "expert". When students join their expert groups, they complete their respective section of the graphic organizer and rehearse the way they are going to present the information to the group. When the original groups reconvene, their task is to teach about their branch to the entire group and make sure every student completes the graphic organizer. Students are also told they should use the graphic organizer as a study guide for the upcoming formative assessment.

Recommendation Two:
Make physical models or manipulatives.

As the name implies, physical models are representations or concrete depictions of the knowledge students are learning. Mathematics and science teachers commonly refer to concrete representations as *manipulatives*. Young students might use math manipulatives to learn the processes of addition and subtraction. Older students might use geometric models to study a variety of attributes of three-dimensional figures.

Students can also create their own physical models. The very act of generating a concrete representation establishes an image of the knowledge in students' minds. If you ask students to create physical models, make certain that the activity will extend students' understanding of the knowledge. What purpose does building a Berlin Wall out of sugar cubes serve? How does building a papier-mâché volcano help students understand the formation of magma? The construction of the physical model should be closely tied to the content students are learning and maintain the level of rigor as assigned by the Common Core or state standards. For example, if students are comparing the circulatory and respiratory systems by creating a model that shows the interrelationships that exist between the two systems, then their teacher should not accept a model that merely identifies the major components of each system.

Physical models and manipulatives must elaborate on student learning by providing opportunities for students to interact with concrete representations of concepts and items that are difficult to see or understand. Ms. Lamping is teaching a unit on the solar system to her 6th grade students. She tells them they are going to be working in small groups to create a physical model of the solar system. Before they begin to plan their models, however, she says, "I want to show you an example of what *not* to do." She brings out a model of the solar system with each planet represented by a ping-pong ball and the sun represented by a softball.

"This is supposed to represent what we have learned about the solar system. What is wrong with this?" she asks.

Alex begins, "Well, it shows that all the planets are the same size, for one thing."

Julie adds, "Each of the planets is the same distance from one another. We know that the space between the planets is different."

Cassidy observes, "This model has all of the planets in one long line. I don't think the planets would ever line up like that. If they did, I am sure something bad would happen."

Ms. Lamping stops the conversation and says, "You are all right. There are just so many things wrong with this physical model. When you start your design, remember that your model has to represent what we have learned. It should help other students understand the solar system as well."

Recommendation Three:
Generate mental pictures.

Of the five strategies housed in the category of nonlinguistic representations, none serves a more important role than generating mental pictures, since each of these strategies ultimately leads to the formation of a mental image. When teaching students this strategy, teachers should keep in mind that not all students understand what they are supposed to do when they are tasked with creating mental images. Many students fail to include the senses and their emotions as components of mental pictures. Leaving these critical components out of a mental image lessens the effectiveness of the learning. Mental images eventually become the end result of student learning. These images are the stored pieces of information that serve to form students' prior knowledge onto which new information is attached. The more proficient students become at generating mental images and using this strategy as an intentional learning tool, the more completely their understanding allows for the transfer of learning to other situations.

Teachers should also be cognizant of the fact that, although information is shared with students who are asked to create a mental image, not every learner will create the same picture. This means that if it is important for students to develop understanding by constructing a replica of what is in the teacher's head, then a considerable amount of detail and guidance must be provided. The following vignette illustrates how a teacher can help his or her students understand the importance of creating mental images and the roles that senses and emotions play in providing detail to those images.

Ms. Wiedeman's 4th grade students have been reading short stories and describing the mental images they form as they read. Ms. Wiedeman realizes that many of her students do not fully understand how to create detailed mental pictures of what they read by incorporating senses, sensations, and emotions. She decides that, during the next reading block, she will dedicate time to helping students understand the importance of mental images and help them develop the skills necessary to create those images in detail.

The following day, she places a short paragraph on the interactive whiteboard:

> I stood on the top of a grassy rise watching a young girl and her dog. The dog had been swimming in a muddy pond, and upon seeing the girl ran at full speed to greet her. He placed his muddy paws on her shoulders and vigorously licked her face. The girl laughed with glee and stroked the dog's fur. I imagined how the fur must smell from the water in the muddy pond and realized that the girl must now smell the same. I could almost feel how gritty her hands had become from petting the dog. My thoughts traveled to the fact that her face must be sticky from the "dog kisses." The two ran off together. I continued to hear her laugh and the dog bark even after they were well out of sight. *I smiled as I walked back home.*

Ms. Wiedeman reads the paragraph as her students follow along. When she is finished, she asks students to identify where senses, sensations, and emotions appear.

Jake says, "Right in the beginning, the person is watching. He is using his sense of sight."

Sara chimes in and says, "Well, the girl would be able to feel the dog's paws on her shoulders, so that is touch."

"You are both right," says Ms. Wiedeman. "What else are you discovering?"

Rojelio says, "The smell of a wet dog. Yuck! And the gritty fur and the girl being smelly and gritty."

"Don't forget her sticky face," adds Tom. "My dog gives those kinds of kisses, too."

Ms. Wiedeman tells her students that she is pleased they found so many senses in the story. "You have missed a couple," she says.

"The dog is barking, and the girl is laughing," says Ti.

"What else?" asks Ms. Wiedeman.

"Well, you told us that emotion was part of building our mental pictures, and I think the person watching is happy and so are the girl and her dog. So happiness is what we should feel when we build our mental images," says Tom.

"You all worked very hard to find the correct answers," says Ms. Wiedeman. "Now let's be sure to put all the pieces in place as we create our mental pictures. First, *see* the dog and the girl. Next, *feel* the weight of the paws on your shoulders. And, I want you to *smell* wet fur and *feel* the grittiness on your hands. Is it working?" she asks.

Students state that they are creating better mental images for themselves. Ms. Wiedeman continues and helps students use their so-called mental senses to feel, hear, see, touch, and smell the sensations in the story. She also asks them to work with partners, share details about the images they created, and decide what is necessary to build happiness into a mental image. Ms. Wiedeman realizes that she will need to repeat this type of exercise several more times with her students to help them solidify what mental imaging entails and how useful the strategy is to help them learn and remember.

Recommendation Four:
Create pictures, illustrations, and pictographs.

Drawing pictures or pictographs (e.g., symbolic pictures) to represent knowledge is another way to generate nonlinguistic representations. For example, many students have drawn or colored the human skeletal system or have seen a picture of one. Similarly, many students have drawn or colored a representation of our solar system. A variation of a picture is a pictograph—a drawing that uses symbols, symbolic images, or key words to represent information. When helping students create pictures, illustrations, and pictographs, it is important to stress that the work being done represents learning and is not an abstract art project. In other words, students should not focus on the artistic quality of their drawings but rather on what the drawings help them remember. Ultimately, students should share their thinking with partners in order to rehearse their learning, use the associated vocabulary, and, ultimately, elaborate on their thinking and knowledge base.

Ms. VanderWegen is midway through a unit on the Civil War, and her students are learning about the Battle of Gettysburg. As the class begins, she plays an audio reenactment of the battle as told by two brothers, one a Confederate soldier and the other a Union soldier. The actors describe what it was like on the battlefield, sometimes in fairly graphic detail. Before she starts the audio, she instructs her students to pay close attention to the visuals the actors create with their words. She tells her students that their task will be to create pictographs that represent their mental images of the Gettysburg battlefield.

After students create their pictographs, they are asked to share their drawings with partners and explain why they included various details.

Recommendation Five:
Engage in kinesthetic activities.

Kinesthetic activities involve physical movement. Physical movement associated with specific content or information helps generate a mental image of knowledge. Many students find this to be an enjoyable way to express their understanding of a concept. Students can role-play many processes or events, such as the inner working of an electric circuit, the revolution of planets around the sun, the exchange of oxygen and carbon dioxide molecules in the human body, the mathematical operations of addition and subtraction, or the operation of a computer network. Students need time to debrief a kinesthetic activity to ensure that they have formed a correct understanding of the concept or principle. This provides the teacher with an opportunity to help students clarify their understanding and to address any misconceptions students may have formed.

Elementary teachers (possibly because of the age of their students) frequently incorporate kinesthetic activities into their lessons. Secondary teachers often shy away from this strategy for fear of students seeing such activities as silly or childish. The following vignette illustrates how a middle school teacher appropriately includes kinesthetic movement as part of a lesson on positive and negative numbers.

Mr. Peterson uses lots of different activities to help his students learn. Hannah had never really liked math before joining Mr. Peterson's class, but she finds his 7th grade math class to be interesting and easier than she expected. Today, she walked into class and noticed that all of the desks had been pushed into a large circle on the perimeter of the room. Long strips of masking tape were placed on the floor where the desks used to be, creating a number line.

When the bell rings, students take their seats, and Mr. Peterson points to the learning objective on the board. "Today we are going to add and subtract integers," Mr. Peterson begins. "What have we been learning about integers?"

"Well," says Troy, "They can be positive and negative."

"That's correct," replies Mr. Peterson. After a little more discussion, students are asked to work within small groups to complete a KWL about adding and subtracting integers. When they finish, they are asked to stand as a group along one of the strips of masking tape. For the next ten minutes, Mr. Peterson gives students math problems that require them to physically move along the number line of positive and negative numbers, thus demonstrating an understanding of adding and subtracting integers.

After students take their seats, Mr. Peterson asks, "Why do you think I had you walk along the strips of tape instead of just working the problems at your desks?" Students erupt with answers, telling him how much easier it was to "see" the problem because they were physically and mentally engaged.

"I caught on so quickly," says Hannah.

"Yeah, it was fun, and I learned a lot," says Kathleen.

Mr. Peterson asks, "How can you now use what you learned?"

Joe answers, "Well, I can think back to how we moved along the number line and use that information to change the movement into a mental picture of what my group did." Mr. Peterson is pleased that his students learned the information so quickly and that they now have new strategies they can use in other situations.

Rubrics and Checklists

The teacher rubric provided in Figure 5.3 is intended to be a tool used for reflection on the way in which you currently use nonlinguistic representations in your classroom. It is designed so that a 3 represents best practice as indicated by the research. A 4 indicates both teacher best practice as described in a 3 and how that practice transfers into student behaviors. You can also use this rubric as a growth tool, seeing where you are now and what the next level might look like. This will provide you with valuable information as you build your professional growth plan.

Using the teacher rubric will give you the chance to reflect on your practice. You can also ask your students how they perceive the way you teach them to use nonlinguistic representations. Figure 5.4 provides a student checklist you might want to use. Periodically give this checklist to your students, and ask them to react honestly to the statements. This checklist can help your students better understand how nonlinguistic representations help them to learn, and it can also provide valuable feedback to you as to how your students view the process of using nonlinguistic representations.

Tools, Templates, and Protocols

If you are using this handbook as part of a school PLC or book study, Figure 5.5 provides statements that can serve as discussion prompts. Likewise, if you are using this book for individual growth, think about these prompts as they relate to your classroom practice. For example, if your answer to the first statement is a 0 or 1, then what steps should you take to move toward the other end of the spectrum, "to a great extent"? Use your individual or team results from Figure 5.5 to form the basis of a professional growth plan (see Figure 5.6).

FIGURE 5.3
Teacher Rubric: Nonlinguistic Representations

Use graphic organizers. *Students combine words and phrases with symbols, arrows, and shapes to represent relationships in the knowledge being learned. Graphic organizers include representations for descriptive patterns, time-sequence patterns, process/cause-effect patterns, episode patterns, generalization/principle patterns, and concept patterns.*

4	3	2	1
I consistently use a variety of graphic organizers with my students. My students can select the appropriate graphic organizer to fit the learning situation.	I consistently use a variety of graphic organizers with my students.	I occasionally use a variety of graphic organizers with my students.	I seldom use a variety of graphic organizers with my students.
I consistently provide opportunities for students to transfer their learning from graphic organizers into mental images. My students can describe the mental images they create based on the graphic organizers used.	I consistently provide opportunities for students to transfer their learning from graphic organizers into mental images.	I occasionally provide opportunities for students to transfer their learning from graphic organizers into mental images.	I seldom provide opportunities for students to transfer their learning from graphic organizers into mental images.

FIGURE 5.3

Teacher Rubric: Nonlinguistic Representations (continued)

Make physical models or manipulatives. *Students are involved in hands-on tasks to create concrete representations of the knowledge being learned.*

4	3	2	1
I consistently use physical models and manipulatives to help students develop an understanding of abstract concepts. My students can create physical models and use manipulatives to show their understanding of ideas and concepts.	I consistently use physical models and manipulatives to help students develop an understanding of abstract concepts.	I occasionally use physical models and manipulatives to help students develop an understanding of abstract concepts.	I seldom use physical models and manipulatives to help students develop an understanding of abstract concepts.
I consistently provide opportunities for students to transfer their physical models into mental images. My students can describe the mental images they create based on the physical models created.	I consistently provide opportunities for students to transfer their physical models into mental images.	I occasionally provide opportunities for students to transfer their physical models into mental images.	I seldom provide opportunities for students to transfer their physical models into mental images.

FIGURE 5.3

Teacher Rubric: Nonlinguistic Representations *(continued)*

Generate mental pictures. *Students visualize the knowledge being learned. Mental pictures incorporate senses, physical sensations, and emotions.*

4	3	2	1
I consistently provide opportunities for students to develop mental images of the concepts and content they are learning. My students can create mental images that incorporate senses, physical sensations, and emotions.	I consistently provide opportunities for students to develop mental pictures of the concepts and content they are learning.	I occasionally provide opportunities for students to develop mental pictures of the concepts and content they are learning.	I seldom provide opportunities for students to develop mental pictures of the concepts and content they are learning.

Create pictures, illustrations, and pictographs. *Students draw, paint, or use technology to create symbolic pictures that represent knowledge being learned.*

4	3	2	1
I consistently provide opportunities for students to represent their learning through pictures and pictographs. My students can create pictures and pictographs and connect them to their learning.	I consistently provide opportunities for students to represent their learning through pictures and pictographs.	I occasionally provide opportunities for students to represent their learning through pictures and pictographs.	I seldom provide opportunities for students to represent their learning through pictures and pictographs.

FIGURE 5.3
Teacher Rubric: Nonlinguistic Representations (continued)

4	3	2	1
I consistently provide opportunities for students to transfer their learning from pictures, illustrations, and pictographs into mental images. My students can describe the mental images they create based on the pictures, illustrations, and pictographs used.	I consistently provide opportunities for students to transfer their learning from pictures, illustrations, and pictographs into mental images.	I occasionally provide opportunities for students to transfer their learning from pictures, illustrations, and pictographs into mental images.	I seldom provide opportunities for students to transfer their learning from pictures, illustrations, and pictographs into mental images.

Engage in kinesthetic activities. *Students engage in physical movement associated with specific knowledge to generate a mental image of content and skills being learned.*

4	3	2	1
I consistently engage students in representing their learning through physical movement. My students can demonstrate their learning through movements.	I consistently engage students in representing their learning through physical movement.	I occasionally engage students in representing their learning through physical movement.	I seldom engage students in representing their learning through physical movement.
I consistently provide opportunities for students to transfer their kinesthetic activity into mental images. My students can describe the mental images they create based on their kinesthetic movement.	I consistently provide opportunities for students to transfer their kinesthetic activity into mental images.	I occasionally provide opportunities for students to transfer their kinesthetic activity into mental images.	I seldom provide opportunities for students to transfer their kinesthetic activity into mental images.

FIGURE 5.4

Student Checklist: Nonlinguistic Representations

		Always	Sometimes	Rarely	Never
GRAPHIC ORGANIZERS	I understand the purpose of using graphic organizers to organize my thinking and learning.				
	I can explain the content and skills I am learning through the use of a graphic organizer.				
	I can select an appropriate graphic organizer to fit a learning situation.				
	I can describe how I use the information from graphic organizers to create mental images of my learning.				
PHYSICAL MODELS/MANIPULATIVES	I understand the purpose of using physical models and manipulatives to represent abstract concepts.				
	I can explain the content and skills I am learning through the use of physical models and manipulatives.				
	I can use or create a variety of physical models and manipulatives to represent the content I am learning.				
	I can describe how I use the information from physical models and manipulatives to create mental images of my learning.				
MENTAL PICTURES	I understand the purpose of using mental pictures to represent my learning, incorporating senses, physical sensations, and emotions.				
	I can explain the content and skills I am learning through the use of mental images.				

FIGURE 5.4

Student Checklist: Nonlinguistic Representations *(continued)*

		Always	Sometimes	Rarely	Never
PICTURES, ILLUSTRATIONS, AND PICTOGRAPHS	I understand the purpose of using pictures, illustrations, and pictographs to represent my learning.				
	I can explain the content and skills I am learning through the use of pictures, illustrations, and pictographs.				
	I can use or create a variety of pictures, illustrations, and pictographs to represent the content I am learning.				
	I can describe how I use the information from pictures, illustrations, and pictographs to create mental images of my learning.				
KINESTHETIC ACTIVITY	I understand the purpose of using kinesthetic activities to represent my learning.				
	I can explain the content and skills I am learning through the use of kinesthetic movement.				
	I can use or create a variety of kinesthetic activities to represent the content I am learning.				
	I can describe how I use the information from kinesthetic activities to create mental images of my learning.				

FIGURE 5.5
Assessing Myself: Nonlinguistic Representations

I intentionally engage students in using nonlinguistic representations.

Not at all   To a great extent

0   1   2   3   4

I help students use the six types of graphic organizers (descriptive patterns, time-sequence patterns, process/cause-effect patterns, episode patterns, generalization/principle patterns, concept patterns).

Not at all   To a great extent

0   1   2   3   4

I ask students to create mental images of their thinking and help them add details, including emotions and the five senses.

Not at all   To a great extent

0   1   2   3   4

I use physical models to help students deepen their understanding of abstract concepts or items difficult to interact with in person.

Not at all   To a great extent

0   1   2   3   4

I use kinesthetic movement to help students elaborate on their learning.

Not at all   To a great extent

0   1   2   3   4

FIGURE 5.5

Assessing Myself: Nonlinguistic Representations *(continued)*

I use pictures, illustrations, and pictographs to help students represent their ideas and deepen their understanding.

Not at all   To a great extent

0   1   2   3   4

I explain, model, and practice nonlinguistic representations within familiar contexts.

Not at all   To a great extent

0   1   2   3   4

FIGURE 5.6
Professional Growth Plan: Nonlinguistic Representations

1. How can I intentionally engage students in using nonlinguistic representations?

2. How can I help students use the six types of graphic organizers (descriptive patterns, time-sequence patterns, process/cause-effect patterns, episode patterns, generalization/ principle patterns, concept patterns)?

3. How can I ask students to create mental images of their thinking and help them add details, including emotions and the five senses?

4. How can I use physical models to help students deepen their understanding of abstract concepts or items difficult to interact with in person?

5. How can I use kinesthetic movement to help students elaborate on their learning?

6. How can I use pictures, illustrations, and pictographs to help students represent their ideas and deepen their understanding?

7. How can I explain, model, and practice nonlinguistic representations within familiar contexts?

6

Summarizing and Note Taking

Summarizing

Imagine you have just watched a movie with a friend and are walking out of the theater together. As you discuss the movie, it is likely that you have different views about what happened and why. You might not remember the movie scene for scene, but you probably remember the parts that were most important to you. As you discuss the movie with your friend, you begin to wonder if you were even watching the same movie. You bring up a scene you felt was pivotal to the story, and your friend responds, "Wow, I don't even remember that happening." Without a structure for summarizing, you each focused on the elements that interested you personally and paid less attention to those that didn't. Perhaps you were so focused on the actors, costumes, or locations that the plot eluded you at times. Likewise, students do this in class all too frequently. Without clear guidelines, they might miss important details from a text or video and leave critical gaps in their understanding.

The act of summarizing facilitates learning by providing opportunities for students to capture, organize, and reflect on important facts, concepts, ideas, and processes they will need to access at a later time (Piolat, Olive, & Kellogg, 2005). When students summarize, they must sort, select, and combine information, which can lead to increased comprehension (Boch & Piolat, 2005). Summarizing also requires students to distill information. The process may seem straightforward, but it is quite complex. To summarize information, we must decide which parts are important, which parts are trivial, and which parts are repetitive. We must delete some information, reword some ideas, and reorganize information. Summarizing involves many mental processes. We include summarizing and note taking in the same category because they both require students to distill information into a parsimonious and synthesized form.

In his book *Brain Rules* (2008), Medina talks about the relationship among summarizing, note taking, and higher-order thinking skills. He identifies 12 principles that characterize how the human brain works. Many of these principles have connections to summarizing and note taking, including the importance of repeating information (by summarizing or rereading notes) and recording information with pictures (a form of note taking).

Unfortunately, summarizing is also a strategy that we tell our students to use without explicitly teaching them how to do so. Where in your school or district curriculum is a grade level identified as being responsible for teaching students to summarize and take notes? In many districts, it is a very hit-or-miss proposition.

Why This Strategy?

Summarizing is a process we do almost automatically. When we read, hear, or see information, we don't take it in exactly as we experience it. We pick and choose what is most important and then restate that information in a brief, synthesized fashion. In a sense, we find the main pattern running through a story or event and make connections among important pieces of information. Summarizing involves at least two highly related elements: filling in missing parts and translating information into a synthesized form. The first aspect of summarizing (filling in the missing information) can be illustrated with the following scenario.

Two card players stare at each other across a table. Both appear tense, although the man smoking a cigar seems to have a slight smile on his face. He lays down his cards in a fanning motion that displays one card at a time. When each new card is shown, his opponent in the silk shirt seems to sink lower and lower into his chair. When the cigar-smoking antagonist finally shows all of his cards, the silk-shirted man gets up and leaves the table without showing his cards and without saying a word.

As you read these sentences, your mind naturally fills in many unstated elements. For example, you probably inferred that both men had bet substantial amounts of money on the hand, that the cigar-smoking man knew he had a winning hand, and that the silk-shirted man lost the hand. Inferences such as these might be thought of as default inferences. Unless explicitly stated otherwise, we expect certain things to occur in certain situations.

A few hours from now, if you were asked to retell what you had read in the passage, you would most likely engage in the second aspect of summarizing—translating information into a synthesized form. In your retelling, you probably would not give a verbatim account of the passage. Rather, you might provide a brief, synthesized version such as the following.

Two men had a large bet on a single hand of poker. As soon as the cards were dealt, one of the men knew he had won the hand. After he showed his hand, his opponent silently got up and left, knowing he had lost.

Students do this automatically when they watch a video, listen to a lecture, or even read the textbook. Providing them with structure as they summarize will enhance their ability to glean the most important information from the material and make sense of what they are learning. Compared to retelling, summarizing requires a higher level of cognition. By equipping students with the skills to summarize successfully, we help them distill large amounts of information into manageable parcels. This aids in understanding, memorizing, and learning the relevant material. To effectively summarize, students need to use higher-order thinking skills and analyze information at a deep level as they decide which information to keep, which to delete, and which to replace with more general terms (Anderson & Hidi, 1988/1989; Broer, Aarnoutse, Kieviet, & van Leeuwe, 2002; Hidi & Anderson, 1987). For example, an elementary student watching a video about mammals might see a section on different types of dogs, including a collie, beagle, poodle, and pug. In her summary, though, she would simply use the term *dogs* as she writes about the subject of the movie.

The following recommendations provide guidance for teachers as they help students understand and master the process of summarizing. Teachers are encouraged to help students by providing structures that guide them through the process.

1. **Teach students the rule-based summarizing strategy.** The rule-based summarizing strategy helps demystify the process of summarizing by providing explicit, concrete steps for students to follow. It provides guidance that helps students decide which information to keep and which to omit when they summarize.

2. **Use summary frames.** Using summary frames is one way that teachers can help students understand and use the structure of different kinds of text to summarize information.

3. **Engage students in reciprocal teaching.** Reciprocal teaching is used primarily with expository text. The teacher models how to use the four comprehension strategies that constitute reciprocal teaching—summarizing, questioning, clarifying, and predicting—gradually releasing students to lead the process.

Reflecting on My Current Practice

The questions listed in Figure 6.1 are provided as a means to assist you as you implement the instructional practices for summarizing.

FIGURE 6.1

Reflecting on Current Practice: Summarizing

1. Do I teach my students rule-based summarizing?

2. Do I model rule-based summarizing for my students?

3. Do I reference the steps for rule-based summarizing as my students summarize information?

4. Do I provide opportunities for students to practice summarizing familiar information before they are expected to summarize new material?

5. Do I provide an appropriate summary frame as an advance organizer to aid in my students' summarization?

FIGURE 6.1
Reflecting on Current Practice: Summarizing *(continued)*

6. Do I engage students in reciprocal teaching?

7. Do I model the roles in reciprocal teaching for my students?

8. Do I scaffold the learning for my students as they engage in reciprocal teaching?

Bringing the Strategy to Life in the Classroom

Recommendation One:
Teach students the rule-based summarizing strategy.

Many students understand the basic idea of summarizing: you take a large amount of information, pick out the main points, and make it shorter. Drawing from this understanding of the summarizing process, you can teach students to effectively summarize with the rule-based summarizing strategy (Brown, Campione, & Day, 1981). This strategy involves a set of rules or steps that students use to construct a summary (Figure 6.2).

FIGURE 6.2
Rule-based Summarizing Strategy

1. Take out material that is not important to understanding.

2. Take out words that repeat information.

3. Replace a list of things with one word that describes them (e.g., replace "oak, elm, and maple" with "trees").

4. Find a topic sentence or create one if it is missing.

Mr. Edmonson is concerned that his 7th grade students don't seem to have an idea of how to summarize. He notices that some students use nearly verbatim paragraphs from the text in their summaries, whereas others seem to select random factoids. He hears about the rule-based summarizing strategy and decides to model the process for his class. He puts a selection about civil wars from Wikipedia (Figure 6.3) on the screen, and they read it together as a class. He then tells the students they will be learning to summarize together using established rules. He provides copies of the rules to each student and then tells them they will be going sentence by sentence through the article and deciding as a group what will stay in and what will be left out of the summary. Mr. Edmonson points out to his students that if they decide something should be omitted from the summary, then they need to identify which rule they used to make that decision.

Katrina says, "I think everything between the commas in the first sentence needs to come out of our summary."

"Which rule are you using to remove it?" Mr. Edmonson asks.

FIGURE 6.3
Rule-based Summarizing Example

Civil wars since the end of World War II have lasted on average just over four years, ~~a dramatic rise from the one and a half year average of the 1900–1944 period. While the rate of emergence of new civil wars has been relatively steady since the mid 19th century,~~ the increasing length of those wars resulted in increasing numbers of wars ongoing at any one time. ~~For example, there were no more than five civil wars underway simultaneously in the first half of the 20th century, while over 20 concurrent civil wars were occurring at the end of the Cold War, before a significant decrease as conflicts strongly associated with the superpower rivalry came to an end.~~ Since 1945, civil wars have resulted in the deaths of over 25 million people, as well as the forced displacement of millions more. Civil wars have further resulted in economic collapse; ~~Burma (Myanmar), Uganda and Angola are examples of nations that were considered to have promising futures before being engulfed in civil wars~~ <u>of a number of countries engulfed in civil wars.</u>

"It's rule #1: take out material that's not important to the understanding," Katrina replies.

"Good job, Katrina. Who wants to tackle the next sentence?" Mr. Edmonson asks.

Billy volunteers, "I think the whole second sentence should come out."

"Which rule do you think applies?" asks the teacher.

Billy answers, "I think it's #2. It is just an example."

"Class, thumbs up or thumbs down if you agree," the teacher says. Almost everyone in the room gives the thumbs-up signal. "Good job, Billy," Mr. Edmonson replies. "Our textbooks and articles have lots of supporting detail. The supporting detail helps you get a clearer picture of what the author is trying to say, but in a summary we usually omit supporting details."

The class continues summarizing the selection until they come up with the summary—"Civil wars since the end of World War II have lasted on average just over four years. The increasing length of those wars resulted in increasing numbers of wars going on at any one time. Since 1945, civil wars have resulted in the deaths of more than 25 million people, as well as the forced displacement of millions more. Civil wars have further resulted in economic collapse."

Mr. Edmonson ends the lesson by saying, "Rule-based summarization provides you with a way to look at text and really decide what is important and what can be omitted as you summarize. Tomorrow we will use this process again, but you will be doing the summaries as small groups. After a few more practice sessions, we will try it individually. I want you to see that summarizing is a process, and there are rules to help you do it well."

Using a think-aloud process as described above gives students a model for the rule-based summarizing strategy and helps them understand how each step in the process works. Modeling the process in this way also prepares students to practice the rule-based strategy in less structured situations. Moving from whole group to small group and then to individual practice also gives students the repetitions that are necessary to learn a skill or process. We will discuss this further in the next chapter on providing practice.

To maximize this strategy in an entire school, it would be helpful if every teacher used the same process and taught students the same rules. When all of the teachers in a school agree to use the rule-based summarizing strategy on a consistent basis, it enhances the overall learning environment for students. Students do not have to alter their thinking about how to summarize as they move from classroom to classroom or grade level to grade level. For example, if a 7th grade class is taught to use the rule-based summarizing strategy, then students feel more confident and less confused at the beginning of 8th grade when the teacher asks them to summarize a poem about summer. Teachers know that students are already familiar with the rule-based summarizing strategy; therefore, they are able to use the relevant academic language to prompt a familiar task.

Recommendation Two:
Use summary frames.

A summary frame is another powerful tool that students can use to help them summarize information. A summary frame is a series of questions designed to highlight the important elements of specific patterns commonly found in text. Although the questions may look like something you would ask students on a quiz, they are actually forms of advance organizers. Students should be given the appropriate summary frame before they read or watch the material. As they read or watch an assigned section, the questions in the summary frame remind them of the important things they should be paying attention to. Common patterns and their accompanying summary frames include

- narrative frame
- topic-restriction-illustration frame
- definition frame
- argumentation frame
- problem–solution frame
- conversation frame

You are probably familiar with the basic structure of all of these patterns because they commonly occur in a variety of texts, including fiction, textbooks, and editorial pieces. A summary frame requires us to consider the specific elements found in each pattern and create a set of questions that guides students as they summarize a text. In other words, you build the summary frame around the pattern of the text students are reading. As you look at the following six examples, keep in mind that summary frames are advance organizers that give students a framework for learning—hence the term *summary frame*.

The first example shows the use of the narrative frame (Figure 6.4). The complete narrative frame that follows summarizes the classic story *Jack and the Beanstalk*.

Frame Questions

1. Who are the main characters? What distinguishes them from the other characters?

   a little boy named Jack, his mother who is a widow, the tricky butcher, the mean giant, and the giant's wife

2. When and where does the story take place? What are the circumstances?

   a long time ago in a little cottage; Jack and his mother suffered through a long winter, and they are very poor. Jack's mother is sick.

3. What prompts the action in the story?

   Jack's mother asks him to take their cow to the market to sell it.

4. How do the characters express their feelings?

   Jack is worried about not having any money, so he knows he has to sell the cow.

5. What do the main characters decide to do? Do they set a goal? What is it?

   Jack takes the cow to the market to get money so they can buy food.

6. How do the main characters try to accomplish their goals?

   Jack trades the cow for the magic beans. Jack goes home and shows the beans to his mother. She gets very angry and throws the beans out the door. The next morning, Jack finds that the beans grew overnight into a thick, tall beanstalk. Jack climbs the beanstalk and finds himself in front of a big castle owned by a rich giant.

7. What are the consequences?

   On different trips to the castle, the giant's wife lets Jack in and helps him take some gold coins, a hen that lays golden eggs, and a harp that plays beautiful music. On the last trip, the giant chases Jack. When Jack gets to the bottom of the beanstalk, he chops it down and kills the giant.

FIGURE 6.4
Narrative Frame

1. Who are the main characters? What distinguishes them from the other characters?

2. When and where does the story take place? What are the circumstances?

3. What prompts the action in the story?

4. How do the characters express their feelings?

5. What do the main characters decide to do? Do they set a goal? What is it?

6. How do the main characters try to accomplish their goals?

7. What are the consequences?

Summary:

Jack and his mother lived a long time ago in a little cottage. They were very poor, and Jack's mother was very sick. Jack's mother asked him to take their cow to market to sell it for money. Jack traded their cow for some magic beans, which grew into a giant beanstalk. Jack climbed the beanstalk and found a big castle owned by a mean giant and his wife. The giant's wife helped Jack take some gold coins, a hen that laid golden eggs, and a harp that played music from the giant. Jack chopped down the beanstalk and killed the giant. Then Jack and his mother returned to the cottage where they once lived.

FIGURE 6.5

Topic-Restriction-Illustration Frame

1. What is the general statement or topic?

2. What information narrows or restricts the general statement or topic?

3. What examples illustrate the topic or restriction?

The second example illustrates the topic-restriction-illustration frame (Figure 6.5). The passage that follows is about mammals:

Mammals are a group of vertebrate animals—animals with backbones. Mothers nourish baby mammals with milk. Mammals are warm-blooded, which means they keep their body temperature within a narrow range despite changes in the environment. One subgroup of mammals is the marsupial group. Marsupials give birth to live young, but the babies are still undeveloped when they are born. Baby marsupials live inside a special pouch on the mother's underside and feed on milk supplied by her nipples. Kangaroos are one type of marsupial. They live in Australia and on nearby islands. Kangaroos use their large back legs and tails for hopping. Another marsupial is the opossum. The Virginia opossum is the only marsupial that lives in North America. Long, shiny, white hair and an undercoat of soft, woolly fur cover the Virginia opossum. An opossum has 50 teeth. It sleeps during the day and hunts food at night.

Frame Questions

Topic: *Mammals are warm-blooded animals with backbones who nourish their babies with milk.*

Restriction: *Marsupials are one subgroup of mammals.*

Illustration: *Kangaroos are one kind of marsupial that live in Australia. The Virginia opossum is the only marsupial that lives in North America.*

Summary: *Mammals are warm-blooded animals with backbones. Mothers feed their young with milk. Marsupials are a category of mammals. Two examples of marsupials are the kangaroo and opossum.*

The third example illustrates the definition frame (Figure 6.6). The passage that follows is about sonnets.

Sonnets are lyric poems with 14 lines that follow a formal rhyme scheme. The two major types of sonnets are the Petrarchan (Italian) and the Shakespearean (English).

The Petrarchan sonnet, named for the Italian poet Petrarch, consists of an octave, or eight-line stanza, with two quatrains that rhyme *a b b a, a b b a*. The first quatrain introduces the theme of the sonnet, and the second quatrain develops the theme. The last six lines form a sestet and rhyme *c d e c d e, c d c d c d,* or *c d e d c e*. The first three lines of the sestet illustrate the theme; the last three lines bring closure to the whole poem. Sir Philip Sidney's "Astrophel and Stella" (1591) exemplifies the Petrarchan sonnet written in English. In the 17th century, John Milton also wrote sonnets based on the Petrarchan form in both English and Italian.

The Shakespearean sonnet, named for the English poet and playwright William Shakespeare, consists of three quatrains, each rhymed differently—*a b a b, c d c d, e f e f*—and a closing couplet rhymed *g g*. English sonnets written in the 16th century dealt primarily with love, but in the 17th century, writers such as John Donne wrote sonnets that dealt with other subjects. In the 18th century, Romantic poets such as William Wordsworth, Samuel Taylor Coleridge, and Percy Bryce Shelley revitalized the form. Elizabeth Barrett Browning and Dante Gabriel Rossetti wrote sonnets during the Victorian period.

FIGURE 6.6
Definition Frame

1. What is being defined?

2. To which general category does the item belong?

3. What characteristics separate the item from the other things in the general category?

4. What are some different types or classes of the item being defined?

Frame Questions

1. What is being defined?

   The sonnet

2. To which general category does the item belong?

   The genre of lyric poems

3. What characteristics separate the item from the other things in the general category?
   Sonnets consist of 14 lines and follow rhyming schemes.

4. What are some types or classes of the item being defined?
   Petrarchan and Shakespearean sonnets have three quatrains and a couplet.

Summary:

A sonnet is a lyric poem with 14 lines that follows a rhyming scheme. The Petrarchan or Italian sonnet consists of an octave and a sestet. The Shakespearean or English sonnet consists of three quatrains and a couplet.

The fourth illustration refers to the argumentation frame (Figure 6.7).

Mr. Frost uses the argumentation frame as a way to help students summarize an article they are assigned to read about Mark Twain. He provides his students with an advance organizer that lists the questions contained in the argumentation frame. He tells his students to think about these questions as they work in pairs to read the article and discuss it.

When all students have read the article and had a chance to discuss it, they answer the questions collaboratively. Mr. Frost then asks pairs of students to join with other pairs, compare answers, and construct a group summary of the article.

Finally, each group of four presents its summary as Mr. Frost takes notes on the board. Students look for consistencies and outliers, and they eventually build a final class summary.

Frame Questions

1. What is the basic claim or focus of the information?
   The author of the article presents Mark Twain as the "quintessential" American author of the 20th century.

2. What information is presented that leads to a claim?
   The author of the article argues that a true American author should exhibit the key characteristics of American culture in the 20th century. These include a pioneering spirit, a rebellious nature, a humorous viewpoint, and a clear use of American language.

3. What examples or explanations support the claim?
   The article highlights various works by Mark Twain along with literary criticisms of his works, exemplifying the four characteristics presented in the article.

4. What restricts the claim? What evidence counters the claim?

The author also mentions the works of other 20th-century authors. Each of those authors exhibits some or even all of the characteristics, though not as profoundly as Twain, in the author's opinion.

Summary:

There are a number of great 20th-century American authors, each exhibiting some or all of the characteristics of a great American author: a pioneering spirit, a rebellious nature, a humorous viewpoint, and a clear use of American language. Twain, however, rises to the top of the list as his work exemplifies each of those characteristics. Mark Twain is therefore the quintessential 20th-century American author.

FIGURE 6.7
Argumentation Frame

1. What is the basic claim or focus of the information?

2. What information is presented that leads to a claim?

3. What examples or explanations support the claim?

4. What restricts the claim? What evidence counters the claim?

FIGURE 6.8
Problem–Solution Frame

1. What is the problem?

2. What is a possible solution?

3. What is another possible solution?

4. Which solution has the best chance of succeeding, and why?

Using the topic of fossil fuels, the next example employs the problem-solution frame (Figure 6.8). The passage that follows is about fossil fuels:

Humans are consuming fossil fuels at much faster rates than they are produced in Earth's crust. Eventually, we will use up these nonrenewable resources. We don't know for certain when Earth's fossil fuels will be depleted, but we have already seen evidence that certain fossil fuels are being depleted in some regions. For example, the United States' production of crude petroleum was at its highest in 1970. Since that time, the United States has begun importing a higher percentage of petroleum.

Reducing the world's dependence on fossil fuels is problematic. However, there are several alternative energy sources, including nuclear energy, hydroelectric energy, solar energy, and wind energy. These energy sources currently account only for about 14 percent of the world's energy consumption; therefore, we need to focus efforts on developing these viable alternatives.

Different types of nuclear reactors that use different types of fuel, moderators, and coolants have been built throughout the world to produce electric power. However, public concerns about the safety of nuclear power, risks of accidents, high construction costs, high waste-disposal costs, and strict regulations have hindered the growth of nuclear power as an energy source. In fact, many countries have opted to phase out nuclear power plants altogether.

Falling water is another source of energy used to generate electric power. Hydroelectric power is renewable because of the recurring nature of the hydrologic cycle, and it produces neither thermal nor particulate pollution; however, geography limits the use of hydroelectricity. Large dams are typically used to take advantage of falling water to create hydroelectric power. Countries with mountains that lie close to industrial areas and experience heavy rainfall, such as Norway, Sweden, Canada, and Switzerland, can rely heavily on hydroelectricity. A number of other countries, including the United States, Russia, China, India, and Brazil, also use hydroelectricity, but on a much smaller scale.

Solar energy has enormous potential. Each day, Earth receives solar energy that is almost 200,000 times the total world electrical-generating capacity. Solar energy itself is free, but collecting, converting, and storing it has limited its use.

Wind energy can be converted into mechanical energy to perform work such as pumping water or grinding grain. Modern wind turbines convert wind energy into electrical energy. Wind is a clean and renewable source of energy, so many countries, such as Germany, Denmark, India, China, and the United States, are expanding their use of modern wind turbines. Clusters of individual wind turbines are grouped to form wind power plants, sometimes called "wind farms." Typically the electricity produced from these "wind farms" supplements more traditional sources of electric power, such as burning coal. Wind energy technology has improved so that modern wind turbines produce electric power as efficiently as other power-generating technologies. Widespread use of wind energy faces obstacles such as suitable terrain, wind conditions, and environmental concerns such as the visual alteration of the landscape, noise from spinning turbine rotors, and impact on wildlife.

There is no clear answer to the diminishing supply of fossil fuels available for energy production. Given the intricacies and limitations of alternative energy sources, the solution for each nation depends on a variety of factors, including geography, citizen concerns, and environmental issues.

Frame Questions

1. What is the problem?

   Fossil fuels are being depleted at a faster rate than they are being replenished.

2. What is a possible solution?

   alternative energy sources, such as nuclear energy

3. What is another possible solution?

   hydroelectric energy; solar energy; wind energy

4. Which solution has the best chance of succeeding, and why?

   There is not one right answer to the problem. The best solution in any one situation depends on a number of factors, such as geography, resource availability, and environmental concerns.

Summary:

Humans are consuming fossil fuels at much faster rates than they are produced in Earth's crust. We need to find ways to use alternative energy sources more efficiently. Nuclear energy, hydroelectric energy, solar energy, and wind energy are all possible sources for supplementing and eventually replacing the use of fossil fuels. Development of any of these alternatives faces obstacles and concerns. There is not one correct answer; rather, the solution will be different for different countries.

The last example uses questions in the conversation frame (Figure 6.9). The passage that follows is excerpted from *Bailey's Café* (Naylor, 1992):

> We've got no menus.
> All right, give me a hamburger. Hold the fries.
> Hamburgers only on Tuesday.
> Some roast beef, then. Make it lean. And...
> No roast beef till the weekend.
> So what can I get today?
> What everybody else is having.
> I don't eat corned-beef hash.
> That's what we got. And warm peach cobbler.
> I'm not eating no hash. How's the peach cobbler?
> Divine.

Frame Questions

1. How did the members of the conversation greet one another?

   A worker in a restaurant told a customer they had no menus.

2. What question or topic was insinuated, revealed, or referred to?

   The customer wanted a hamburger without fries.

3. How did the conversation progress?

The restaurant worker said hamburgers were available only on Tuesday, roast beef was only available on the weekend, and the customer could have what everyone else was eating.

4. How did the conversation conclude?

The restaurant worker implied that if the customer did not want corned-beef hash, he or she could go somewhere else to eat. The restaurant worker said that they were serving corned-beef hash and warm peach cobbler. The customer didn't want corned-beef hash and asked about the peach cobbler, suggesting that he or she might want to order some. The restaurant worker told the customer the peach cobbler was "divine."

FIGURE 6.9
Conversation Frame

1. How did the members of the conversation greet one another?

2. What question or topic was insinuated, revealed, or referred to?

3. How did the conversation progress?

4. How did the conversation conclude?

Summary:

A worker in a restaurant tells a customer that the restaurant has no menus. The restaurant apparently serves only specific foods on certain days of the week. The customer tries to order a hamburger and then roast beef but is told he or she can only have what everyone else is eating and today that was corned-beef hash or warm peach cobbler. Finally, the customer asks about the warm peach cobbler.

As you can see, these frames, used as advance organizers, provide students with a clear focus to help them synthesize and distill information into a concise summary. Consider the following two approaches to summarizing and how they likely will yield different results in the classroom.

Ms. Burger and Ms. Donaldson both teach 9th grade current events. They find an article from the local newspaper about a controversy caused when a "big box" store filed a request with the zoning commission to change the status of a large parcel of land near an elementary school from residential to commercial. The company claimed there would be an enormous economic benefit to the community, including an increase in tax revenues that would directly help the local schools. A community group countered that the increase in vehicular traffic would pose an unnecessary danger to the students walking to school, would create traffic flow issues at school dismissal, and would probably increase litter and crime in the area. Both teachers agree that the article will provide a perfect topic for debate in their classes.

Ms. Burger copies the article and hands it out to her students. She tells them to read the article for homework, summarize it, and be ready to debate the topic in class. The next day, Ms. Burger begins class by asking for a volunteer to take each side of the debate. Sarah, representing the anti-commercial position, starts the debate by saying, "I talked to my parents, and they think it would be a bad idea. We have plenty of stores around here, and we can always drive 20 minutes to Springfield if we can't get what we want here."

Adam, representing the pro-commercial position, counters, "I think they should be allowed to build a store here. We really need a place to get hunting and fishing equipment at a good price, and I will be looking for a summer job soon." Ms. Burger tries to focus the discussion on the facts presented in the article, but her students have too many gaps in their understanding.

Ms. Donaldson also copies the article for her students, but in addition, she reviews the argumentation summary frame they had used the previous week on a similar article. She says, "Remember, as you read the article you want to remember the four questions we used in the argumentation frame. As you read the article tonight for homework, use the argumentation frame to sift through the claims presented by both sides. Try to distinguish facts from opinions. Tomorrow we will debate this topic."

The next day in class, Ms. Donaldson asks Darcie to take the pro-commercial position and Cody to represent the counter position. Darcie begins, "We believe that our store in this area will increase the tax base in the community and provide both hundreds of jobs and almost double the taxes collected and paid to the school district. We know our store will increase traffic in the area and have agreed to a special assessment from the commission to widen the roads and install traffic lights."

Cody counters, "Our biggest concern is for the safety of the elementary school children. The traffic flow before and after school is already an issue with 16 school buses and dozens of cars dropping off and picking up kids. The problem is much worse on bad weather days. In addition to the traffic concern, we worry about the increase of strangers in the area." As the discussion progresses, Ms. Donaldson sees how the summary frame allows her students to focus on the key points from the article and engage in a meaningful debate.

In this example, it was important that students had some understanding of the topic before attempting to summarize. Using the summary frame, Ms. Donaldson helped her students focus on what was important, which allowed them to gain a better understanding of the real issues.

Recommendation Three:
Engage students in reciprocal teaching.

A common strategy for teaching students how to summarize is reciprocal teaching, which is used primarily with expository text (Palincsar & Brown, 1985). During reciprocal teaching, students assume four roles (summarizer, questioner, clarifier, and predictor) and take turns leading the discussion. One student can play all four roles, or different students can assume each role. When students first learn how to use reciprocal teaching, the teacher should model all four roles that constitute reciprocal teaching: summarizing, questioning, clarifying, and predicting. After the process has been modeled a few times, one student can be assigned to be the summarizer, while the teacher continues with the other three roles. After a repetition or two, the scaffolding process can continue, and other students can be assigned the roles of summarizer and clarifier. Gradually, the teacher should release implementation of all four roles to student control. Each of the four roles in reciprocal teaching is defined below.

1. **Summarizing:** After students have silently or orally read a short section of a passage, a single student acting as the student leader

summarizes what has been read, heard, or seen. Other students, with guidance from the student leader, may add to the summary. If students have difficulty summarizing, the teacher might point out clues (e.g., important items or obvious topic sentences) that aid in the construction of good summaries.

2. **Questioning:** The student leader poses questions to the class. The questions are designed to help students identify important information in the passage. For example, the student leader might look back over the selection and ask questions about specific pieces of information. The other students then try to answer these questions based on their recollection of the information.

3. **Clarifying:** Next, the student leader tries to clarify confusing points in the passage. She or he might point these out or ask other students to point them out. For example, the student leader might say, "The part about the baseball player who was really an alien was confusing to me. Can anyone explain this?" The student leader might also have students ask clarification questions. The group then attempts to clear up the confusing parts. This process might involve rereading parts of the passage.

4. **Predicting:** The student leader asks for predictions about what will happen in the next section of the text. The leader can write the predictions on the board or a projection, or all students can write them in their notebooks.

The summary statement that begins the reciprocal teaching strategy might be considered a first draft of a summary. The summarizer might use a summary frame or rule-based summarization to build that initial summary. The other phases of reciprocal teaching—questioning, clarifying, and predicting—help students analyze the information, which provides for a group-enhanced summary. As shown in the following vignette, reciprocal teaching works well because the process involves multiple analyses and interactions with the summary.

Students in Ms. Hood's class are studying how computers work. After students read a long passage about computers, Ms. Hood asks several students to serve as student leaders for a reciprocal teaching task. Ms. Hood had previously taught her students the steps for reciprocal teaching, and they had practiced them, so they knew their roles and what each step required. After reading the passage, Chantelle, one of the student leaders, summarizes the first passage:

The operating system is the software that makes a computer work. It does three big things. Number one, it tells the computer hardware, like the mouse, printers, monitor, and computer memory, what to do. Two, it deals with hardware errors and data loss. And three, it organizes the files you store on the hard drive, a CD, or a flash drive. Today's operating systems, like Windows or Mac or UNIX, can do several things at one time. That's called multitasking.

Finn adds, "Windows and Mac operating systems use a GUI—a graphical user interface—with pictures called icons that represent various commands. Examples of icons are folders and the trash can."

To begin the questioning phase of the process, Chantelle asks questions about specific information: (1) When an operating system is multitasking, what is it actually doing? (2) What is virtual memory?

After students answer the questions, Chantelle asks if anyone has questions they want to ask to clarify confusions they have. Craig says he is confused about how a multitasking operating system creates the illusion of processes running simultaneously. Lissa answers, "On computers with only one CPU, a multitasking operating system runs each process individually for a set period of time. If the process doesn't finish in the given time, the OS puts it on hold and runs another process according to its schedule. Short processes run quickly and our sense of time is much slower, so processes appear to be running simultaneously."

Finally, Chantelle asks students to predict the content of the next section of text, which is titled "Computer Memory." Kara says, "I think the next section will talk about how a computer stores data. And it will probably explain RAM and ROM."

Rubrics and Checklists

The teacher rubric provided in Figure 6.10 is intended to be a tool used for reflection on the way in which you currently summarize in your classroom. It is designed so that a 3 represents best practice as indicated by the research. A 4 indicates both teacher best practice as described in a 3 and how that practice transfers into student behaviors. You can also use this rubric as a growth tool, seeing where you are now and what the next level might look like. This will provide you with valuable information as you build your professional growth plan.

Using the teacher rubric will give you the chance to reflect on your practice. You can also ask your students how they perceive the way you teach them to summarize. Figure 6.11 provides a student checklist you might want to use. Periodically give this checklist to your students, and ask them to react honestly to the statements. This checklist can help your students better understand how summarizing helps them learn, and it can provide valuable feedback to you about how your students view the process of summarizing.

Tools, Templates, and Protocols

If you are using this handbook as part of a school PLC or book study, Figure 6.12 provides statements that can serve as discussion prompts. Likewise, if you are using this book for individual growth, think about these prompts as they relate to your classroom practice. For example, if your answer to the first statement is a 0 or 1, then what steps should you take to move toward the other end of the spectrum, "to a great extent"? Use your individual or team results from Figure 6.12 to form the basis of a professional growth plan (see Figure 6.13).

FIGURE 6.10
Teacher Rubric: Summarizing

Teach students the rule-based summarizing strategy. *The rule-based summarizing strategy helps demystify the process of summarizing by providing explicit, concrete steps to follow. It provides guidance that helps students decide which information to keep and which to omit when summarizing information.*

4	3	2	1
I consistently model rule-based summarizing for my students to ensure they are applying the rules correctly. My students are able to use rule-based summarizing independently.	I consistently model rule-based summarizing for my students to ensure they are applying the rules correctly.	I occasionally model rule-based summarizing for my students to ensure they are applying the rules correctly.	I seldom model rule-based summarizing for my students to ensure they are applying the rules correctly.
I consistently use the same wording for rule-based summarizing as the other teachers in my building. My students see the consistency of rule-based summarizing throughout their classes.	I consistently use the same wording for rule-based summarizing as the other teachers in my building.	I occasionally use the same wording for rule-based summarizing as the other teachers in my building.	I seldom use the same wording for rule-based summarizing as the other teachers in my building.
I consistently post the rules for rule-based summarizing in my classroom. My students independently reference the rules when they summarize.	I consistently post the rules for rule-based summarizing in my classroom.	I occasionally post the rules for rule-based summarizing in my classroom.	I seldom post the rules for rule-based summarizing in my classroom.

FIGURE 6.10

Teacher Rubric: Summarizing (continued)

Use summary frames. *Using summary frames is one way that teachers can help students understand and use the structure of different kinds of text to summarize information.*

4	3	2	1
I consistently use summary frames as a type of advance organizer to help my students set the stage for learning and summarizing. My students use summary frames to guide their thinking as they read, listen to, or watch instructional material.	I consistently use summary frames as a type of advance organizer to help my students set the stage for learning and summarizing.	I occasionally use summary frames as a type of advance organizer to help my students set the stage for learning and summarizing.	I seldom use summary frames as a type of advance organizer to help my students set the stage for learning and summarizing.
I consistently provide summary frames appropriate to the type of text, lecture, or video with which my students are working. My students can identify which summary frame is best suited for the material they are reading, hearing, or watching.	I consistently provide summary frames appropriate to the type of text, lecture, or video with which my students are working.	I occasionally provide summary frames appropriate to the type of text, lecture, or video with which my students are working.	I seldom provide summary frames appropriate to the type of text, lecture, or video with which my students are working.

FIGURE 6.10

Teacher Rubric: Summarizing *(continued)*

Engage students in reciprocal teaching. *Reciprocal teaching is used primarily with expository text. The teacher models how to use the four comprehension strategies that constitute reciprocal teaching—summarizing, questioning, clarifying, and predicting—and then gradually releases students to lead the process.*

4	3	2	1
I continually have students participate in reciprocal teaching as a means to summarize material. My students are comfortable with using reciprocal teaching from the perspective of both learner and teacher.	I continually have students participate in reciprocal teaching as a means to summarize material.	I occasionally have students participate in reciprocal teaching as a means to summarize material.	I seldom have students participate in reciprocal teaching as a means to summarize material.
I consistently model reciprocal teaching for my students to ensure they understand and demonstrate the roles. My students are able to use reciprocal teaching independently.	I consistently model reciprocal teaching for my students to ensure they understand and demonstrate the roles.	I occasionally model reciprocal teaching for my students to ensure they understand and demonstrate the roles.	I seldom model reciprocal teaching for my students to ensure they understand and demonstrate the roles.

FIGURE 6.11
Student Checklist: Summarizing

		Always	Sometimes	Rarely	Never
RULE-BASED SUMMARIZING	My teacher shows me how to use rule-based summarizing to help me summarize information in class.				
	I know each of the four rules for rule-based summarizing and know what they mean.				
	Rule-based summarizing helps me do a better job of summarizing.				
SUMMARY FRAMES	My teacher gives me a summary frame before I read or watch things I need to summarize.				
	My teacher helps me use summary frames to summarize material I read or watch in class.				
	I know which summary frame is best for the information I need to summarize.				
RECIPROCAL TEACHING	I understand the four roles of reciprocal teaching				
	I can lead my class in summarizing by taking on one of the roles in reciprocal teaching.				
	When students in my class lead us in reciprocal teaching, it helps me better understand the material.				

FIGURE 6.12
Assessing Myself: Summarizing

I teach my students rule-based summarizing.

Not at all   To a great extent

| 0 | 1 | 2 | 3 | 4 |

I model rule-based summarizing for my students.

Not at all   To a great extent

| 0 | 1 | 2 | 3 | 4 |

I reference the steps for rule-based summarizing as my students summarize information.

Not at all   To a great extent

| 0 | 1 | 2 | 3 | 4 |

I provide opportunities for students to practice summarizing using familiar information before they are expected to do so with new material.

Not at all   To a great extent

| 0 | 1 | 2 | 3 | 4 |

I provide an appropriate summary frame to my students as an advance organizer to aid in their summarization.

Not at all   To a great extent

| 0 | 1 | 2 | 3 | 4 |

FIGURE 6.12
Assessing Myself: Summarizing *(continued)*

I engage students in reciprocal teaching.

Not at all   To a great extent
0   1   2   3   4

I model the roles in reciprocal teaching for my students.

Not at all   To a great extent
0   1   2   3   4

I scaffold my students as they engage in reciprocal teaching.

Not at all   To a great extent
0   1   2   3   4

FIGURE 6.13
Professional Growth Plan: Summarizing

1. How will I teach my students rule-based summarizing?

2. How will I model rule-based summarizing for my students?

3. How will I reference the steps for rule-based summarizing as my students summarize information?

4. How will I provide opportunities for students to practice summarizing using familiar information before they are expected to do so with new material?

5. How will I provide an appropriate summary frame to my students as an advance organizer to aid in their summarization?

FIGURE 6.13
Professional Growth Plan: Summarizing *(continued)*

6. How will I engage students in reciprocal teaching?

7. How will I model the roles in reciprocal teaching for my students?

8. How will I scaffold my students as they engage in reciprocal teaching?

Note Taking

Note taking and summarizing are closely related. Both processes require students to identify what is most important about the content they are learning and then state that information in their own words. Maybe you have never thought about specifically teaching students to take notes. Many teachers assume it is a strategy that has been or will be taught somewhere else in the system. Although note taking is one of the most useful study skills a student can cultivate, teachers often do not explicitly teach note-taking strategies in the classroom. We all have our own personal style for taking notes. We may use arrows and bullets, capitals and indentations, underlines and double underlines, flowcharts and doodles. Ultimately, students construct their own personal note-taking systems.

Why This Strategy?

Note taking (and its partner strategy, summarizing) are both used to help students capture, organize, and reflect on important facts, concepts, ideas, and processes they will need to access at a later time. We want to reiterate the importance of teaching students these processes rather than assuming they already know how to do them. How did you learn to take notes? Who taught you? Were you provided with a number of note-taking strategies? Were the notes you took helpful as you studied for tests?

Note taking, like summarizing, requires students to identify essential information. When students take notes, they must access, sort, and code information, which can help them memorize information and conceptualize new ideas. They must also synthesize material, prioritize pieces of data, restate some information, and organize concepts, topics, and details.

Students often struggle with this strategy because note-taking strategies are not intuitive. Like any other process, teachers need to intentionally take time to teach note taking to students. In addition, note taking is idiosyncratic to the user. Bulleted lists may work for one student, whereas a web or concept map might help another. Therefore, teachers should take the time to teach a variety of note-taking strategies so students can choose the specific strategies that work for them.

Note taking does not mean simply copying everything you read or hear. Verbatim notes are not effective. When students are asked to capture word-for-word representations of a lecture, conversation, or video, they pay so much attention to the physical act of writing that they neglect to focus on what is being said. This leads to a lack of content understanding.

In the following vignette, notice the difference in how Leah and Jamie were taught to take notes and the results.

Leah and Jamie get together after school to study for an upcoming test on copyright law in their graphic design class. The girls take out their notes and begin to study. Leah looks over at Jamie's notes and asks, "What's with all of the bubbles and pictures? Ms. Cook told us to take notes using an outline."

"I know," replies Jamie, "but outlines just don't work well for me. Last year, Mr. Sauer showed us lots of different ways to take notes in language arts. I tried outlines, Cornell notes, bulleted lists, and bubble maps. I learned that for me, bubble maps help me understand what I am supposed to be learning better."

"I haven't even heard of all of those things," says Leah. "I had Ms. Brown last year for language arts, and she said outlines were the best way to take notes. She showed us how to do a formal outline and even graded our notes to make sure we were doing the outlines properly."

"I had to learn outlining too with Mr. Sauer, but they just don't make as much sense for me. I spent more time thinking about the rules for outlining than I did about what I was supposed to be learning in the video or lecture," says Jamie.

"Yeah, that happens to me sometimes too, but outlining is the only way I know to take notes," explains Leah. "Sometimes the outline helps me, and sometimes I look at the outline and think, 'What was that even about?' I wish I had Mr. Sauer last year. Maybe I would have found a way to take notes that actually helped me learn."

The following recommendations provide guidance for teachers as they help students develop understanding of the note-taking process:

1. **Give students teacher-prepared notes.** Teacher-prepared notes can be in the form of a template that the teacher prepares and distributes to students. They should give the student guidance as to what is important in the unit, chapter, or video.

2. **Teach students a variety of note-taking formats.** It is important to teach students a variety of models for note taking, including formal and informal outlines, webbing, and combination notes. When students know a variety of formats, they can choose the format that works best for them for a particular project.

3. **Provide opportunities for students to revise their notes and use them for review.** The practice of providing time for students to review and revise their notes underscores the point that notes are a work in progress and a valuable tool for learning.

Reflecting on My Current Practice

The questions listed in Figure 6.14 are provided as a means to assist you as you implement the instructional practices for note taking.

FIGURE 6.14

Reflecting on Current Practice: Note Taking

1. Do I teach my students a variety of note-taking formats?

2. Do I provide students with opportunities to practice note-taking techniques using familiar information before they are expected to use them with new material?

3. Do I model the note-taking process several times before students are expected to demonstrate an understanding of and appropriately use the various formats?

4. Do I provide explicit corrective feedback that helps students elaborate on their understanding and improve their note-taking skills?

5. Do I instruct students to leave space between each note they take so they have room to add to their notes as they continue learning about the topic?

6. Do I intentionally build time into my lesson plans for students to review and edit their notes?

7. Do I provide time for students to share their thinking about their notes with other students?

Bringing the Strategy to Life in the Classroom

Recommendation One:
Give students teacher-prepared notes.

Providing students with teacher-prepared notes before introducing new content is a powerful way to give them a clear understanding of what they are expected to know and understand. They give students a clear idea of what you think is important and help students focus their learning. Teacher-prepared notes also give students a good model for how they can organize content. Teachers should provide notes in a variety of formats throughout the year to help students identify the note-taking structure that works best for them.

In Chapter 4, we talked about advance organizers. Teacher-prepared notes can be another form of advance organizer. When a teacher provides students with a bulleted list or bubble map prior to instruction, he or she gives students both the major points they should focus on and an example of how to organize and take their notes.

In the following vignette, notice how Ms. Cho provides her students with two different formats of teacher-prepared notes to use as an advance organizer prior to starting a unit on checks and balances. In addition, note that she includes the learning objective on the teacher-prepared notes to help keep her students focused.

Ms. Cho provides her 5th grade social studies students with teacher-prepared notes before they begin their unit on checks and balances (Figure 6.15). After creating her notes in two different formats, she gives both examples to her class. She explains that if they want to use the bubble map version, they should add bubbles attached to "members," "duties," and "checks and balances" for each branch of the government. If they decide to use the outline version, then they need to add their notes under "members," "duties," and "checks and balances" in the spaces provided. Ms. Cho tells her students to look at both formats and pick the one they think will work best for them.

Recommendation Two:
Teach students a variety of note-taking formats.

This recommendation makes sense when you consider learning styles. Some students are primarily linguistic learners, and informal outlines and bulleted lists might make the most sense to them. Other students are primarily nonlinguistic learners, and webbing might resonate best with them. Thinking back to what we discussed in the previous chapter on nonlinguistic learning, it is important to combine linguistic and nonlinguistic learning to

FIGURE 6.15
Teacher-Prepared Notes

Bubble Map Example

Branches of Government

We will understand how the three branches of the U.S. government are designed to provide checks and balances so that no one branch is in total control.

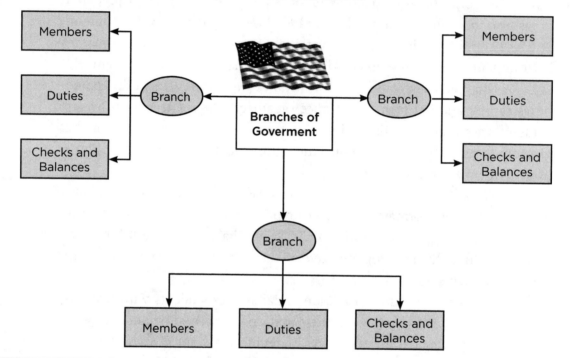

Outline Example

Branches of Government

We will understand how the three branches of the U.S. government are designed to provide checks and balances so that no one branch is in total control.

I. Branch
   1. Members
   2. Duties
   3. Checks and Balances

II. Branch
   1. Members
   2. Duties
   3. Checks and Balances

III. Branch
   1. Members
   2. Duties
   3. Checks and Balances

help students build enduring understanding. Three formats that have been found to be useful are webbing, informal outlining, and combination notes. A form of note taking called combination notes can address a variety of learning styles. When students know a variety of formats, they can choose the format that works best for them for a particular project.

Webbing is nonlinear and uses shapes, colors, and arrows to show relationships between and among ideas. When students use webbing as a note-taking strategy, they build a mental image of learning as they construct their notes. This mental image can then trigger their memory as they retrieve the knowledge for a test or quiz.

In the following vignette, see how Jamie uses both teacher-prepared notes and webbing to help her organize her thinking as she learns about the grey wolf.

Ms. Velasquez is teaching her 3rd grade students about mammals. Ms. Velasquez gives them teacher-prepared notes to guide their thinking (Figure 6.16). She explains to the class, "In this science unit, we are learning about mammals, fish, and reptiles. We are going to see how they are the same and how they are different. Before we can do that though, we have to learn about each species. Today you each will get to pick a mammal from these pictures on the front table. Pick one you are interested in studying further. As you research your mammal, take notes on the graphic organizer I just handed out. You need to focus on where your mammal lives, what it eats, how it gives birth, and how it moves about. I want you to use some of the reference books in the room and the sites I posted on our class website. If you need to add additional boxes to any of the areas, feel free to do so. Make sure your notes are in sentence form. It will help you remember what you were thinking, and it will also be a good start for the report you are going to write for your mammal."

Each student selects a picture of a mammal from the table in the front of the room. Jamie picks the grey wolf because her family recently visited a wolf sanctuary in Colorado, and she thinks they are really interesting. Though there are many things she wants to know about the grey wolf, she looks at Ms. Velasquez's handout and remembers that she really needs to focus on where it lives, what it eats, how it has babies, and how it moves. She is pretty sure she knows how it moves, but she needs to research the other things. She goes to the class website and begins looking at the resources Ms. Velasquez provided. The first link takes her to a website about habitats. It says that grey wolves are endangered in some areas because of man's development of the land. She looks on the handout and sees that, even though this is an interesting fact, it really isn't part of what she needs to know for this unit. As she reads further, she learns that female wolves give birth to live baby wolves and then feed them with mother's milk, just like humans do. She takes notes on the handout under the "babies" label. In one box, she writes, "The grey wolf mother delivers live baby wolves just like mother humans do." In the other box, she writes, "Mother wolves feed their baby wolves milk just like my mom feeds my baby sister."

Having Ms. Velasquez's teacher-prepared notes helps Jamie organize her thoughts and keeps her focused on the important things she needs to know and understand. Although there are some other things Jamie finds interesting in her research about wolves, she had a clear understanding and focus on the learning objective. In addition, Jamie is able to take her notes in a webbing format as a way to help her organize her thinking. When it is time to use the information to write a report or do a presentation, Jamie already has her information organized and ready to use.

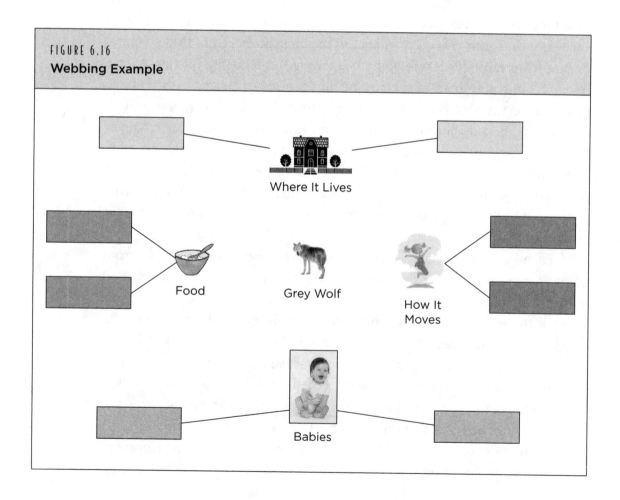

FIGURE 6.16
Webbing Example

Where It Lives

Food   Grey Wolf   How It Moves

Babies

A very flexible note-taking strategy that uses both informal outlines and pictures or graphic representations is referred to as combination notes. Each page of notes is divided into two parts by a line running down the middle of the page. On the left-hand side of the page, students take notes using some variation of informal outlining. On the right-hand side of the page, students use graphic representations to organize the new information. Finally, in a strip across the bottom of the page, students write a summary statement for the notes.

This note-taking method takes extra time, but it is useful because students review the information several times—first, as they summarize their notes into a few main points; second, as they create nonlinguistic representations for each of the major points; third, as they construct summary statements of what they learned from the information.

The lesson plan in Figure 6.17 illustrates how a teacher can plan for and use combination notes to help his or her students better understand mitosis. The rubric referenced in the lesson plan is shown in Figure 6.18. An example of student-created combination notes is shown in Figure 6.19.

Recommendation Three:
Provide opportunities for students to revise their notes and use them for review.

Allowing time for students to share their thinking with other students provides opportunities for them to rehearse their learning, use relevant vocabulary, and deepen their understanding. As students share their thinking, they learn from their peers and may see a need to return to their webs and make corrections or additions. In the following vignette, notice how Alex revises his notes as his understanding of the topic deepens.

Alex is supposed to read the chapter on the solar system in his 6th grade science textbook. He has been taught how to use webbing and informal outlining to take notes, and he is most comfortable using an informal outline. For homework, he reads the solar system chapter and takes notes as he reads:

- Solar System
  - Planets revolve around the sun, which is really a star
  - Made up of nine planets
    - Mercury
      - Smallest planet
      - Closest to sun
    - Venus
      - Second planet
      - Surrounded by a poisonous cloud

FIGURE 6.17
Mitosis Lesson Plan

Subject area: Life Science   **Grade level:** 7th Grade   **Lesson title:** Mitosis Combination Notes

Brief Lesson Description
Students will use their books, the Internet, outside resources, and their notes to gather background knowledge about the process of mitosis. After students become informed about mitosis, they will use PowerPoint® to present information in a multimedia style (using movie clips, animations, sounds, voice, and pictures). These presentations will then be presented to the class by each student.

District Content Standard Addressed
1. (C) Use appropriate tools, mathematics, technology, and techniques to gather, analyze, and interpret data.
2. (B) Conduct research.
   (E) Possess technical skills: read/write/present; Use technology (PowerPoint, Internet, search tools).
4. Understand that the cell is the basic unit of life.
   (C) Understand the role of cell division, reproduction, and heredity for all living things.
   (D) Differentiate between asexual and sexual reproduction in plants and animals.

NET*S Technology Standard Addressed
1. Basic operations and concepts
3. Technology productivity tools
5. Technology research tools

Technology Resources Needed
- computer
- Internet
- PowerPoint software
- microphone
- speakers/headphones
- multimedia software

Procedure
Introduction: Students were introduced to the unit of cells and cell parts prior to starting this project. They also had a background in the use of combination notes because it is incorporated into our building improvement plan.
Activity: Students were to use outside resources, along with their notes and textbook, to find information about mitosis and cell division. The information had to be presented in written, voice, picture, and movie/animation format. Students then prepared the information, in the form of combination notes, into a PowerPoint presentation.
Technology integration: Students used a teacher-designed template to present the information. Students found the information using the Internet, search engines, and more traditional resources (books and notes). This allowed different information to be presented to the class. Students also used a microphone to record their voice for the presentation, explaining a particular picture or fact. Headphones were used to listen to their voices and find other sounds they might want to use to help explain the information.

Assessment Method
Students were assessed using a rubric based on a 10/5/1 point scale. The rubric was based on the following: use of color/formatting, quality of the content of information presented, use of pictures/movies/animations, participation/correct use of technology, and sketched-out written rough draft.

◆ Earth
  ~ Where we live
  ~ Atmosphere we can breathe
◆ Mars
  ~ Known as the "red planet"
  ~ About the same size as Earth
◆ Jupiter
  ~ Largest planet
  ~ Many moons
◆ Saturn
  ~ The ringed planet
  ~ The rings around Saturn are not solid like it looks in some
    pictures but made up of asteroids
◆ Neptune
◆ Uranus
◆ Pluto
  ~ Farthest planet from the sun
  ~ Takes about 248 Earth years to make one revolution around
    the sun

The next day in class, Alex's teacher Ms. Hess asks students to share their notes with their table partners. Alex notes that his partner, Angela, has about the same information as he does, but she used a web to take her notes. After they have time to share their notes, Ms. Hess says, "I know you all read in the book that there were nine planets in our solar system, but our book was written a few years ago. Since our textbook was published, scientists have decided that Pluto isn't really a planet; rather, it is a dwarf planet."

Alex says, "What? Does that mean our book is wrong?"

"Yes," answers Ms. Hess. "Pluto was literally voted out of the solar system. It is still out there, but we no longer consider it a planet."

Angela asks, "Does that mean there are only eight planets in the solar system now? I mean, if that question was on the test, is the answer eight or nine like the book says?"

"The correct and accurate answer would be eight. That's probably something that you really need to correct in your notes. When you study for the test on the solar system, I am pretty sure you will want to know that one," Ms. Hess says as she smiles.

Alex goes back to his notes and makes two changes. First, where he originally wrote "Made up of nine planets," he writes, "Made up of ~~nine~~ eight planets." He decides to leave Pluto in his notes, but he crosses out "Farthest

FIGURE 6.18
Rubric for Assessing Combination Notes

	10	5	1
Use of Color and Format	Eye catching, attractive, and easy to read; lots of color used.	Some color; hard to read information, plain background.	Little color.
Quality of the Content of Information	Well-defined information, explained process in detail, more that just textbook info.	Only used textbook for info, vague explanation.	Not enough detail, no explaining of processes.
Pictures, Movie, Animations	Media was used in a creative way to help explain info.	Media was random; movies were copied and not inserted.	No movie; not enough pictures.
Participation and Using Technology Correctly.	Student worked well and tried new things; student asked questions and went above technology comfort zone.	Student worked well, but did what student already knew how to do.	Student didn't try something new.
Sketched and Written Rough Draft	Rough draft was detailed and had a well-thought-out plan.	Rough draft was vague and covered a broad area of concentration.	Rough draft was quickly thrown together without detail.

planet from the sun" and instead writes, "Originally considered a planet, Pluto is now called a dwarf planet."

Rubrics and Checklists

The teacher rubric provided in Figure 6.20 is intended to be a tool used for reflection on the way in which you currently use note taking in your classroom. It is designed so that a 3 represents best practice as indicated by the research. A 4 indicates both teacher best practice as described in a 3 and how that practice transfers into student behaviors. You can also use this rubric as a growth tool, seeing where you are now and what the next level might look like. This will provide you with valuable information as you build your professional growth plan.

Using the teacher rubric will give you the chance to reflect on your practice. You can also ask your students how they perceive the way you teach them to take notes. Figure 6.21 provides a student checklist you might want to use. Periodically give this checklist to your students, and ask them to react honestly to the statements. This checklist can help your students better understand how note taking helps them learn, and it can also provide valuable feedback to you about how your students view the process of note taking.

FIGURE 6.19
Student-Created Combination Notes

Mitosis

1. Mitosis is the process by which a cell divides into two identical nuclei. 2. Mitosis occurs in plants and animals. 3. Mitosis occurs in five different phases. 4. The threadlike DNA structures are called chromosomes. 5. The five phases are Anaphase, Telophase, Metaphase, Interphase, and Prophase.	

Mitosis is something that happens in both plant and animal cells that happens in five different phases. Mitosis is also the process by which a cell divides into two identical nuclei.

Tools, Templates, and Protocols

If you are using this handbook as part of a school PLC or book study, Figure 6.22 provides statements that can serve as discussion prompts. Likewise, if you are using this book for individual growth, think about these prompts as they relate to your classroom practice. For example, if your answer to the first statement is a 0 or 1, then what steps should you take to move toward the other end of the spectrum, "to a great extent"? Use your individual or team results from Figure 6.22 to form the basis of a professional growth plan (see Figure 6.23).

FIGURE 6.20

Teacher Rubric: Note Taking

Give students teacher-prepared notes. *Teacher-prepared notes can be in the form of a template that the teacher prepares and distributes to students. They should give the student guidance as to what is important in the unit, chapter, or video.*

4	3	2	1
I consistently provide teacher-prepared notes for my students that identify the key points they should focus and take notes on. My students understand how to use teacher-prepared notes to guide their note taking.	I consistently provide teacher-prepared notes for my students that identify the key points they should focus and take notes on.	I occasionally provide teacher-prepared notes for my students that identify the key points they should focus and take notes on.	I seldom provide teacher-prepared notes for my students that identify the key points they should focus and take notes on.

Teach students a variety of note-taking formats. *It is important to teach students a variety of modes for note taking, including formal and informal outlines, webbing, and combination notes. When students know a variety of formats, they can choose the format that works best for them for a particular project.*

4	3	2	1
I consistently provide my students with guidance in using webbing and informal outlines. My students can create webs and informal outlines on their own.	I consistently provide my students with guidance in using webbing and informal outlines.	I occasionally provide my students with guidance in using webbing and informal outlines.	I seldom provide my students with guidance in using webbing and informal outlines.

FIGURE 6.20
Teacher Rubric: Note Taking (continued)

4	3	2	1
I consistently have my students use combination notes when it is important for them to develop enduring understanding of the topic. My students can create combination notes on their own.	I consistently have my students use combination notes when it is important for them to develop enduring understanding of the topic.	I occasionally have my students use combination notes when it is important for them to develop enduring understanding of the topic.	I seldom have my students use combination notes when it is important for them to develop enduring understanding of the topic.
I consistently encourage my students to use the note-taking format that works best for them. My students can explain why they chose the format they are using.	I consistently encourage my students to use the note-taking format that works best for them.	I occasionally encourage my students to use the note-taking format that works best for them.	I seldom encourage my students to use the note-taking format that works best for them.

Provide opportunities for students to revise their notes and use them for review. *The practice of providing time for students to review and revise their notes underscores the point that notes are a work in progress and a valuable tool for learning.*

4	3	2	1
I consistently provide opportunities for my students to revise their notes throughout a unit of instruction. My students understand how to make revisions based on new understanding of a topic.	I consistently provide opportunities for my students to revise their notes throughout a unit of instruction.	I occasionally provide opportunities for my students to revise their notes throughout a unit of instruction.	I seldom provide opportunities for my students to revise their notes throughout a unit of instruction.

FIGURE 6.20
Teacher Rubric: Note Taking (continued)

4	3	2	1
I consistently encourage my students to use their notes to review for assessments. My students regularly use their notes as study guides.	I consistently encourage my students to use their notes to review for assessments.	I occasionally encourage my students to use their notes to review for assessments.	I seldom encourage my students to use their notes to review for assessments.
I consistently give my students opportunities to share and discuss their notes with peers. My students discuss and revise their notes with peers.	I consistently give my students opportunities to share and discuss their notes with peers.	I occasionally give my students opportunities to share and discuss their notes with peers.	I seldom give my students opportunities to share and discuss their notes with peers.

FIGURE 6.21

Student Checklist: Note Taking

		Always	Sometimes	Rarely	Never
TEACHER-PREPARED NOTES	My teacher provides me with notes before he or she begins a lesson or unit.				
	My teacher prepares notes to help me focus on what is important in the lesson.				
VARIETY OF NOTE-TAKING STRATEGIES	I understand how to create webs as a form of note taking.				
	I understand how to create informal outlines as a form of note taking.				
	I understand how to create and use combination notes as a form of note taking.				
	I know which note-taking format best helps me understand what we are learning.				
REVISING NOTES	I revise my notes during a lesson or unit as I learn new information.				
	It helps me learn when I can discuss my notes with my peers.				

FIGURE 6.22

Assessing Myself: Note Taking

I teach my students a variety of note-taking formats.

Not at all   To a great extent

0   1   2   3   4

I provide students with opportunities to practice note-taking techniques using familiar information before they are expected to use them with new material.

Not at all   To a great extent

0   1   2   3   4

I model the note-taking process several times before students are expected to demonstrate an understanding of and appropriately use the various formats.

Not at all   To a great extent

0   1   2   3   4

I provide explicit corrective feedback that helps students elaborate on their understanding and improve their note-taking skills.

Not at all   To a great extent

0   1   2   3   4

I instruct students to leave space between each note they take so they have room to add to their notes as they continue learning about the topic.

Not at all   To a great extent

0   1   2   3   4

FIGURE 6.22
Assessing Myself: Note Taking *(continued)*

I intentionally build time into my lesson plans for students to review and edit their notes.

Not at all   To a great extent

0   1   2   3   4

I provide time for students to share their thinking about their notes with other students.

Not at all   To a great extent

0   1   2   3   4

FIGURE 6.23

Professional Growth Plan: Note Taking

1. What steps will I take to teach my students a variety of note-taking formats?

2. How will I provide students with opportunities to practice note-taking techniques using familiar information before they are expected to use them with new material?

3. How will I plan to model the note-taking process several times before students are expected to demonstrate an understanding of and appropriately use the various formats?

4. How will I provide explicit corrective feedback that helps students elaborate on their understanding and improve their note-taking skills?

5. How will I intentionally instruct students to leave space between each note so they have room to add to their notes as they continue learning about the topic?

6. How will I intentionally build time into my lesson plans for students to review and edit their notes?

7. How will I provide time for students to share their thinking about their notes with other students?

7

Assigning Homework and Providing Practice

Assigning Homework

Homework and practice are staples of the K–12 classroom. Both give students opportunities to deepen their understanding of and proficiency with content they are learning. Homework can even be thought of as a place-based activity that provides time for students to practice their skills (although students still practice apart from homework).

Research on homework reveals a few things. First, in general, homework is more effective for older students than for younger students (Cooper, Lindsay, Nye, & Greathouse, 1998). Second, when learning a skill, students need a great deal of practice in order to achieve mastery (Karpicke & Roediger, 2008). Third, teachers should communicate the purpose of homework and comment on it (Pashler, Rohrer, Cepeda, & Carpenter, 2007). Students also need time to shape and adapt a skill as they practice so they can use it effectively and correctly. In this section, we offer suggestions for using what research tells us works in the classroom. We encourage you to use these and other approaches for assigning homework to enhance students' learning.

Why This Strategy?

"When seven classes worth of homework is piled on us nightly, we're up until midnight studying for things that, at that hour, don't even make sense. In the morning, we stumble into class, sometimes unshowered, and then the teacher complains. Let's think about this: We do homework but get nothing out of it. Then we get into trouble, plus we stink. To me, there's no benefit here."

—Katie, age 15

By the time students reach the middle grades, homework has become part of their lives. The usual reason for giving homework makes good sense: homework extends learning opportunities beyond the confines of the school day. Studies show that students are in school a relatively short amount of time (Fraser, Walberg, Welch, & Hattie, 1987); thus, homework seems to be a good idea. Although assigning homework can be a great asset, it can also be a liability, depending on how teachers approach it. Consider the following quotes from two high school seniors:

"Sometimes, when teachers explain something, it's not enough. I have to do it by myself at home."

—Wilbert, age 17

"All homework is busywork and a waste of time. For me, it's more beneficial to talk to friends, relax, and explore personal interests like lasers."

—Jose, age 17

In the first case, Wilbert saw his homework as an extension of the class's activity and an opportunity to deepen his understanding of the skill or process he had learned. Jose, on the other hand, saw little or no connection between his homework assignments and what he was learning in the classroom, viewing it as busywork rather than an opportunity to deepen his understanding of a skill or process.

In the last few years, there have been mixed research reviews on the effectiveness and importance of homework, yet most teachers continue to assign homework and believe there is a good reason to do so (e.g., Kohn, 2006; Marzano & Pickering, 2007). Teachers often feel pressure from parents when they receive comments such as, "I had a lot of homework when I was a student, and I turned out just fine. It must have helped me." In this chapter, we provide information that will help you think carefully about the purpose and effects of assigning homework.

We use the word *homework* to refer to opportunities for students to learn or review content and skills outside of the regular school day. Homework can also be used as an opportunity to connect background knowledge to an upcoming unit by providing advance organizers, engaging students in making observations, watching videos, initiating conversations, and reading assignments. In the following example, see how the teacher uses homework to prepare his students for new material they will soon study about ecosystems.

Mr. Cottrell wants his ecology class to understand that ecosystems are interdependent. Before he begins the unit, he gives them a homework assignment and asks them to create a graphic organizer that depicts the knowledge they already have about various ecosystems and their relationships to one another. He then uses these organizers to help him identify additional information students need to learn.

Assigning homework is a highly charged and emotional strategy for many schools and districts. When we have discussions about homework with colleagues, friends, and our own children, the conversations quickly turn to statements about punishment, unfairness, and inequalities. The real purpose of homework should be to give students opportunities to review content and skills outside of the classroom. In some schools, however, this is simply not the case.

In a western state, teachers working in a rural district with approximately 2,500 students were asked how much weight homework had on their students' final grades. The number ranged from 5 percent all the way up to 50 percent. Teachers were also asked if it would be possible for a student to pass or fail their class solely on the basis of the amount of homework completed. A startling 60 percent of secondary school teachers replied in the affirmative. The data indicate that it is possible for students to complete the educational objectives of a course and still fail because they did not complete and/or turn in their homework.

This scenario clearly shows some of the abundant misperceptions about homework that exist. Homework, when applied correctly, is not punitive or a rite of passage. It should be assigned solely for the purposes of deepening a student's understanding of the curriculum, introducing new material at a surface level (as a cue or advance organizer), and to increase speed and accuracy of a skill.

The following recommendations provide guidance for teachers as they help students develop an understanding of homework. Teachers are encouraged to

1. **Develop and communicate a district or school homework policy.** An established homework policy communicates and clarifies the purpose of homework in your district or school.

2. **Design homework assignments that support academic learning and communicate their purpose.** Homework should support rather than discourage student learning. It should be assigned to help students prepare for instruction, to review or practice, or to extend learning opportunities.

3. **Provide feedback on assigned homework.** Homework should be aligned to a learning objective, and the feedback should be tied to that objective.

The staff at JFK Middle School is grappling with the perennial issue of homework. Ms. Scoville begins the conversation by saying, "My kids just don't bother doing homework. I assign it every day, and most kids don't turn in anything. I have 32 students who are likely to fail my language arts class because of missing homework assignments."

Mr. Oltman adds, "Not only that, but their parents just don't care. How are we supposed to teach our students to be responsible if we can't even get them to do their homework?"

The new principal, Dr. Lasker, listens to the continuing conversation and finally asks, "Have we taken the time to look at root causes for the issue? Why is it that our kids aren't doing their homework?"

Ms. Shipman, the school social worker, answers, "I have conducted numerous home visits over the past two months, and I have a view on that. Most of our students come from low-income homes, and many of the adults are working one or even two jobs just to make ends meet. I don't think it's at all accurate to say that parents don't care. I think it is more like parents are overwhelmed."

Mr. Oltman replies, "That may be, but these kids need to take responsibility."

Dr. Lasker intervenes. She says she has read research that indicates that when homework is assigned, it needs to be commented on. "When you give homework, how many of you provide comments on the work that is returned to the students?"

Ms. Scoville replies, "I have 137 kids through my language arts room every day. You don't expect me to provide feedback on the 80 or 90 papers that are returned to me, do you?"

Dr. Lasker answers, "I can only tell you what research identifies as best practice. If homework is assigned, it needs to be commented upon. If you can't provide feedback, it might be that you are assigning too much homework. Maybe if you gave one homework assignment a week that was very clearly aligned with your learning objective, then you would be better able to provide meaningful feedback to your students. In addition, your students wouldn't feel overwhelmed by the quantity of homework they receive from you and the other six teachers they see every day. I also have a concern that we are considering failing students in our classes solely based on their inability to turn in their homework. Understand that, as Ms. Shipman indicated, some of our students just don't have an environment at home that is conducive to doing homework."

This hypothetical conversation likely echoes conversations we have all heard in our own schools. Some teachers consider homework to be a rite of passage. What the research indicates, however, is that homework should be assigned to support academic learning and to give students opportunities to practice and apply their learning. If your students come from homes in which there isn't a suitable environment for them to complete homework, then it might be best to consider providing time after school for a homework club or space in the library or classroom for students to do their work. If we want students to demonstrate mastery of the content, should it really be possible for a student to pass in-class assessments and still fail the class due to missing or late homework? Our view is a resounding *no*.

Parents do have a clear supporting role in the completion of their children's homework assignments. However, their role is not to do the homework or serve as a tutor. Rather, their role is to establish routines related to study times and study habits, provide a suitable environment and study area, reduce distractions, provide encouragement, and communicate with the school/teacher if difficulties arise. It is important to note that parents should have their children stop working on their homework if they become overly frustrated. Parents should then communicate with the teacher, saying, "I had my child stop doing the homework because he/she reached the frustration level." Teachers and parents don't want to see students staying up late at night upset or discouraged because they can't do the assignment.

Reflecting on My Current Practice

The questions listed in Figure 7.1 are provided as a means to assist you as you implement the instructional practice of assigning homework.

FIGURE 7.1
Reflecting on Current Practice: Assigning Homework

1. Do I have a classroom homework policy aligned to the district/school policy?

2. Do I communicate the purpose of homework assignments to both students and parents?

3. Do I ensure the homework I assign clearly aligns with the learning objectives I am teaching?

4. Do I maintain open communications with parents or guardians related to homework?

5. Do I provide corrective feedback on all homework assignments?

6. Do I help my students provide self- and peer feedback on homework assignments?

Bringing the Strategy to Life in the Classroom

Recommendation One:
Develop and communicate a district or school homework policy.

Students and their parents need to understand expectations for homework. What is the purpose of homework? How much homework will be assigned? What are the consequences for missing or late homework assignments? How should parents be involved in their child's homework? A district, school, or teacher can establish and communicate a homework policy to answer such questions and to set feasible and defensible expectations of students and their parents. A clearly articulated homework policy can decrease tensions about homework that might arise among parents, teachers, and students. Further, following explicit homework policies can enhance student achievement.

To help parents better understand how they can support their children's efforts to complete homework, teachers can share information on different structures and monitoring techniques that parents can use to create conditions at home that match a child's learning preferences. Providing such information during parent workshops and encouraging dialogue about schoolwork between parents and their children have demonstrated positive effects on student achievement in reading (Bailey, Silvern, Brabham, & Ross, 2004).

A note of caution is needed here. Research indicates that when parents help their children with homework, they can interfere with students' learning (Balli, 1998; Balli, Demo, & Wedman, 1998). Parents should know what homework their children are responsible for completing, and they certainly can facilitate the homework process, but they should not directly solve problems for their children. You can clarify these issues with parents in your written homework policy and at parent–teacher conferences.

We recommend that a homework policy address district/school responsibilities, parent responsibilities, and student responsibilities. The sample homework policy in Figure 7.2 can serve as a useful template as your district/school reviews its current homework policy. You will see how all three of the recommendations from the research play out in this policy. If your district/school doesn't have a unified homework policy, then this can at least serve as a model for your classroom policy. Once your school board has approved a homework policy at the district level, each school and teacher should create a policy that is congruent with the district guidelines.

FIGURE 7.2
Sample District Homework Policy

The ABC School District Board of Education believes homework is an important instructional tool and should be a part of the educational experience that supports students' efforts toward reaching proficiency related to the content standards. Homework should not be a substitute for classroom instruction, nor should it be used for disciplinary purposes or as a measure of rigor. Instead, homework is a continuation of school assignments that will reinforce the content and skills learned in the classroom. The amount of homework assigned to students should be different from elementary to high school.

Homework should be assigned to meet one or more of the following purposes:

• Prepare for new learning.
• Practice skills to increase speed and/or accuracy.
• Deepen understanding of concepts learned.

The Board believes that homework is an extension of the school day and therefore should be completed by the student. The Board encourages teachers at the elementary level to work closely with parents/guardians to enhance students' academic success. The Board encourages teachers at the secondary level to structure homework assignments so that students are able to independently complete the work.

The Board recognizes that when assigning homework, teachers should be cognizant of the age and ability of the student and conditions that exist within the community that may hamper the homework process. The effective use of homework should not require an unnecessary commitment of time on the part of the student or the student's family.

The Board is committed to using research-based information to support the district work related to homework. To this end, homework must be given for a specific purpose and commented on by the teacher. Though we are not regulating the type of feedback teachers should provide, the Board expects teachers to offer specific feedback to students in a timely manner.

The Board believes that student performance should be assessed against curriculum that is aligned with the content standards. Grades should directly reflect student performance in demonstrating proficiency related to the curriculum. To this end, homework assigned should clearly align with the district curriculum. Assessment of student performance on homework should be handled consistently by all staff. Therefore, scores from homework in any course should not exceed 10 percent of the student's grade for any given grading period.

The Board believes that each stakeholder has a given set of responsibilities as they relate to homework. Defining those roles and responsibilities lessens the burdens on each party and provides direction for helping students achieve.

Responsibilities of Staff

• Assign meaningful and appropriate homework that is challenging and aligns with the learning objectives.
• Provide ongoing and clear guidance to ensure students understand the directions and reasons for the homework.
• Provide timely and specific feedback for all homework assignments.
• Recognize student effort.
• Inform parents of the homework policy and their roles related to homework.
• Promote quality work.
• Assist students in being successful and in believing they are capable of doing the work.

FIGURE 7.2
Sample District Homework Policy *(continued)*

Responsibilities of Parents

- Establish routines related to study times and study habits.
- Provide a suitable environment and study area.
- Reduce distractions.
- Provide encouragement.
- Communicate with the school/teacher if difficulties arise.

Responsibilities of Students

- Keep track of all homework assignments (with a planner or computer).
- Follow routines related to study times and study habits.
- Establish an environment for learning. (Keep distractions to a minimum.)
- Believe you can do the work.
- Ask for assistance if necessary.
- Produce high-quality work at all times.
- Complete all assignments on time.

School-based Homework Policies
The Board believes that there should be consistent homework practices throughout the district. To this end, building principals are asked to align their school-based homework policies with the district policy and to work with parents and site councils to annually review all practices related to homework. The school-based homework policy should be communicated to students and their parents/guardians during the fall of each year, and reminders should be sent on at least two other occasions.

Recommendation Two:
Design homework assignments that support academic learning and communicate their purpose.

Your students should know the purpose of homework assignments. Are they focusing on increasing their speed at long division? Are they accessing prior knowledge for an introduction to the general theory of relativity? Are they extending what they have learned about food webs? Many times, students do not understand the purpose of homework assignments. When students don't know why they are doing an assignment, homework can seem like busywork—they simply want to get through it. Therefore, connecting homework assignments to a meaningful purpose is a powerful instructional practice. Here, we discuss three possible purposes for assigning homework: (1) to give students opportunities to practice skills, (2) to prepare students for a new topic, or (3) to elaborate on introduced material.

Homework assigned to provide practice is usually associated with learning a skill, as opposed to learning information. When practice is the purpose of homework, it is imperative that students first reach a level of self-sufficiency in performing the skill. It makes little sense to assign practice homework when students are not capable of engaging in unsupervised practice. Homework assigned as practice commonly increases students' speed and accuracy relative to the skill they are learning. Practicing a skill requires a different kind of assignment and a different focus from the student than he or she would use to learn new information. To increase speed and accuracy with a particular skill, a student might break an assignment into chunks and time herself as she completes each section. Knowing that she is practicing to reach a goal gives the assignment meaning. Homework is no longer just busywork. Rather, the student is working toward improving speed and internalizing a skill.

When you assign homework to introduce a topic, the goal is to help students access prior knowledge about that topic. This type of homework assignment requires a different focus from students than is required with homework to practice a skill or to improve speed and accuracy. These homework assignments might ask students to reflect on what they have learned from other classes, from reading, and from their personal experiences. When using homework to introduce a topic, you might also ask students to think about what they want to learn or to observe a phenomenon, such as the phases of the moon, in order to prepare for upcoming learning.

A homework assignment that asks students to elaborate on a topic might require them to engage in activities that extend their knowledge, such as conducting research, comparing items, constructing support for an argument, or representing knowledge in a graphic organizer. As an example, if students are studying a famous explorer or inventor, their teacher might assign homework that requires students to identify specific ways that the explorer or inventor demonstrated qualities that were discussed in class. These might include persistence, attention to detail, lasting impact on society, and willingness to risk.

All three of these purposes for homework are legitimate. The key is to identify a purpose for each homework assignment you give and communicate that purpose to students.

Recommendation Three:
Provide feedback on assigned homework.

As we discussed in Chapter 1, feedback is an essential part of learning. Providing feedback on homework assignments benefits students, particularly when that feedback is in the form of written comments or grades (Walberg,

1999). If you assign homework, comment on it. Timely and specific feedback on homework can improve student achievement. Obviously, teachers do not have enough time to provide extensive feedback on every homework assignment, so make this task more realistic by using different methods to comment on homework. For example, you might set up opportunities for students to share their work with one another and offer feedback. This approach works well when students are preparing for new information because they can share ideas and broaden their knowledge base before they dig in to the new information. When students are practicing a skill for homework, you might ask them to keep track of their accuracy or speed. As students record and watch their progress over time, they can identify areas where they need more work. Students might also keep a homework portfolio that you collect and comment on once a week.

Providing feedback does not necessarily mean grading homework. Giving feedback in the form of comments, conversations with peers and/or teachers, and self-feedback using a rubric can encourage students to take risks and provide teachers with information regarding students' conceptual understanding of the topic (Brookhart, 2008; Hattie & Timperley, 2007; Shute, 2008).

Rubrics and Checklists

The teacher rubric provided in Figure 7.3 is intended to be a tool used for reflection on the way in which you currently assign homework in your classroom. It is designed so that a 3 represents best practice as indicated by the research. A 4 indicates both teacher best practice as described in a 3 and how that practice transfers into student behaviors. You can also use this rubric as a growth tool, seeing where you are now and what the next level might look like. This will provide you with valuable information as you build your professional growth plan.

Using the teacher rubric will give you the chance to reflect on your practice. You can also ask your students how they perceive the way you assign homework. Figure 7.4 provides a student checklist you might want to use. Periodically give this checklist to your students, and ask them to react honestly to the statements. This checklist can help your students better understand how homework helps them learn, and it can provide valuable feedback to you about how your students view the process of assigning homework.

Tools, Templates, and Protocols

If you are using this handbook as part of a school PLC or book study, Figure 7.5 provides statements that can serve as discussion prompts. Likewise, if you are using this book for individual growth, think about these prompts as they relate to your classroom practice. For example, if your answer to the first statement is a 0 or 1, then what steps should you take to move toward the other end of the spectrum, "to a great extent"? Use your individual or team results from Figure 7.5 to form the basis of a professional growth plan (see Figure 7.6).

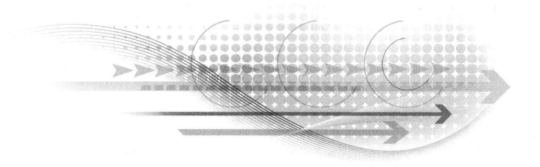

FIGURE 7.3
Teacher Rubric: Assigning Homework

Develop and communicate a district or school homework policy. *Establishing a clear set of guidelines that is based on the age of the learner, the expectations for completion, and the relationship between homework and grades provides a manageable framework for collaboration between home and school.*

4	3	2	1
I have a classroom homework policy that is aligned with the school/district homework policy. My students have read, discussed, and understand my classroom homework policy.	I have a classroom homework policy that is aligned with the school/district homework policy.	I have a classroom homework policy that is not aligned with the school/district homework policy.	I do not have a classroom homework policy.
I consistently follow the guidelines of the district/school homework policy. My students understand their role as articulated in that policy.	I consistently follow the guidelines of the district/school homework policy.	I occasionally follow the guidelines of the district/school homework policy.	I seldom follow the guidelines of the district/school homework policy.

Design homework assignments that support academic learning and communicate their purpose. *Homework should be assigned to help students prepare for instruction, to review or practice, or to extend learning opportunities.*

4	3	2	1
I consistently communicate the purpose of homework to both students and parents. My students and their parents consistently communicate with me when problems related to homework arise.	I consistently communicate the purpose of homework to both students and parents.	I occasionally communicate the purpose of homework to both students and parents.	I seldom communicate the purpose of homework to both students and parents.

FIGURE 7.3
Teacher Rubric: Assigning Homework (continued)

Design homework assignments that support academic learning and communicate their purpose. *Homework should be assigned to help students prepare for instruction, to review or practice, or to extend learning opportunities.*

4	3	2	1
I consistently assign homework that aligns with the learning objectives. My students see the clear alignment between the classroom learning and their homework.	I consistently assign homework that aligns with the learning objectives.	I occasionally assign homework that aligns with the learning objectives.	I seldom assign homework that aligns with the learning objectives.

Provide feedback on assigned homework. *If homework is assigned, it should be commented on.*

4	3	2	1
I consistently provide corrective feedback on all homework assignments. My students can provide both self- and peer feedback on homework.	I consistently provide corrective feedback on all homework assignments.	I occasionally provide corrective feedback on all homework assignments.	I seldom provide corrective feedback on all homework assignments.

FIGURE 7.4
Student Checklist: Assigning Homework

		Always	Sometimes	Rarely	Never
HOMEWORK POLICY	I understand my responsibilities as described in the school homework policy.				
	My parents or guardians understand their responsibilities as described in the school homework policy.				
	I understand my responsibilities as described in the classroom homework policy.				
	My parents or guardians understand their responsibilities as described in the classroom homework policy.				
COMMUNICATION	When homework is assigned, I see the connection to what we are learning in class.				
	I understand the purpose of homework assignments.				
	My parents or guardians understand the purpose of homework assignments.				
	When issues arise related to homework, my parents or guardians communicate with my teacher.				
FEEDBACK	I receive corrective feedback on all homework assignments.				
	I can provide feedback to myself and my peers related to homework assignments.				

FIGURE 7.5
Assessing Myself: Assigning Homework

I have a classroom homework policy aligned to the district/school policy.

Not at all   To a great extent

0   1   2   3   4

I communicate the purpose of homework assignments to both students and parents.

Not at all   To a great extent

0   1   2   3   4

I ensure the homework I assign clearly aligns with the learning objectives I am teaching.

Not at all   To a great extent

0   1   2   3   4

I maintain open communications with parents related to homework.

Not at all   To a great extent

0   1   2   3   4

I provide corrective feedback on all homework assignments.

Not at all   To a great extent

0   1   2   3   4

I help my students provide self- and peer feedback on homework assignments.

Not at all   To a great extent

0   1   2   3   4

FIGURE 7.6
Professional Growth Plan: Assigning Homework

1. How will I make sure my classroom homework policy is aligned to the district/school policy?

2. How do I communicate the purpose of homework assignments to both students and parents?

3. How do I ensure the homework I assign clearly aligns with the learning objectives I am teaching?

4. How do I maintain open communications with parents related to homework?

5. How will I provide corrective feedback on all homework assignments?

6. In what ways will I help my students provide self- and peer feedback on homework assignments?

Providing Practice

Why This Strategy?

Practice is the act of repeating a specific skill or reviewing small amounts of information to increase recall, speed, and accuracy. This strategy refers to the need for students to devote time to reviewing what they have learned so it becomes immediately accessible for cognitive use. This information can be stored in a student's working memory or long-term memory, depending on how often the information is used.

The popular adage "practice makes perfect" seems very logical. The truth, however, is that practice makes permanent. The adage really should be "Practice makes permanent. Perfect practice makes perfect." There are three phases to practice: the introductory phase, the shaping or guided practice phase, and independent practice. After students are introduced to a skill or process, they are given guided practice time to shape that skill, reinforced by constant and corrective feedback. Once they have an understanding of the process, they are ready for independent practice. When students move too quickly from guided practice to independent practice, they often develop misconceptions or errors that then become ingrained as they practice independently. Teachers must spend additional class time correcting those errors and misconceptions. It would be both clearer for the student and more efficient for the teacher to spend some more time in the guided practice phase before moving to independent practice.

Have you ever taught a child how to ride a bicycle? You start out with a shiny new bicycle and training wheels that touch the ground. The child learns how to work the pedals and brakes and how to steer. While the child is learning this, you are walking beside the bicycle and holding it for additional support, coaching on every step. After the child shows some ability to pedal, brake, and steer, you raise the training wheels a couple of inches. Now, while still learning to pedal, brake, and steer, the child is also beginning to learn how to balance the bicycle. As this is happening, you are still walking or running beside the bicycle and providing additional support. As the child begins to get the hang of balancing, you don't simply remove the training wheels; rather, you raise them up a few more inches. Now the child is almost riding independently, but you are still running alongside and providing support, feedback, and encouragement as needed. The training wheels are also still there to provide support. Finally, the child is ready for independent practice. The training wheels come off, and you stand to the side as the child strikes out on his or her own. Is the child now an accomplished bicycle rider? No.

He or she still falls on occasion, and there are sometimes problems with direction, but the child is able to ride the bicycle well enough to begin to hone his or her skills and move toward mastery. Now sitting comfortably and nervously on the front porch, you occasionally yell words of encouragement and feedback.

Think about this as a metaphor for teaching skills and processes in class that have multiple steps and that we want our students to be able to perform with automaticity. Following the writing process, understanding the scientific inquiry process, performing with good intonation in music, and knowing which formula to apply to solve problems all come to mind as skills or processes we want our students to know at a deep and enduring level. Students need to be taught in a similar manner as we taught the child to ride a bicycle. The steps need to be clearly articulated, practiced, and accompanied by feedback as students move from guided practice toward automaticity.

You might be surprised by the number of practice sessions students need before they can use new knowledge effectively. We can represent the relationship between practice sessions and learning as a curved line (Figure 7.7), where the vertical axis shows improvement in learning and the horizontal axis represents the number of practice sessions in which the student has engaged (Anderson, 1995; Newell & Rosenbloom, 1981).

The graph shows that when students first begin practicing a skill, their learning progresses rapidly. However, students probably need at least 20 practice sessions before you can be reasonably sure they grasp the new skill enough to use it effectively on their own. Only after a great deal of practice can students perform a skill with speed and accuracy.

Practice is important for mastering skills, but, like homework, practice must have certain characteristics to produce the desired results. The following recommendations for practice help teachers make the most of this strategy as they help students develop understanding in the classroom:

1. **Clearly identify and communicate the purpose of practice activities.** Practice must tightly align with learning objectives and provide students with opportunities to deepen their understanding or become faster and more proficient at a skill.

2. **Design practice sessions that are short, focused, and distributed over time.** Short practice sessions encourage students to make efficient use of their practice time. Focused practice is designed to target specific aspects of more complex skills and processes.

3. **Provide feedback on practice sessions.** It is critical that students receive specific feedback during formative practice sessions to help

them understand which aspect(s) of the skill or process they are not performing appropriately.

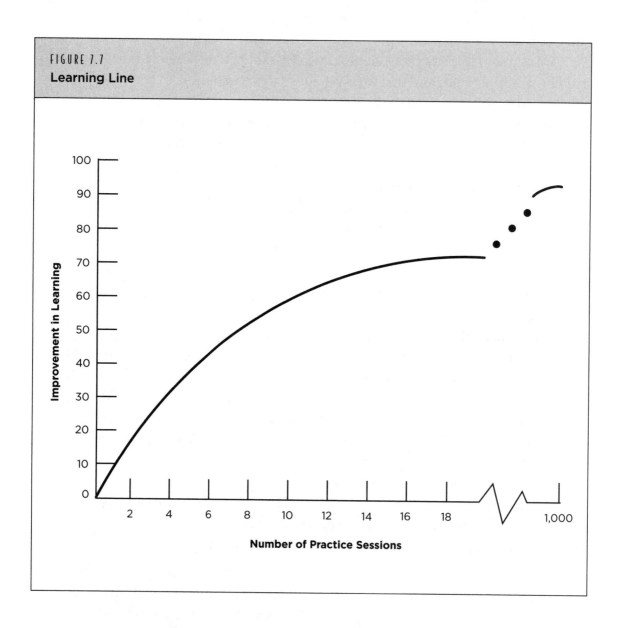

FIGURE 7.7
Learning Line

Reflecting on My Current Practice

The questions listed in Figure 7.8 are provided as a means to assist you as you provide practice in your classroom.

FIGURE 7.8

Reflecting on Current Practice: Providing Practice

1. Do I clearly identify the purpose of practice?

2. Do I provide specific time for guided and independent practice?

3. Do I provide practice sessions that are short, focused, and distributed over time?

4. Do I provide a way for students to track and monitor their progress?

5. Do I provide specific feedback on the individual steps in a process?

Bringing the Strategy to Life in the Classroom

Recommendation One:
Clearly identify and communicate the purpose of practice activities.

One of the most significant decisions a teacher makes is to identify which skills are important enough to practice. Since practice takes a great deal of time and effort, your students probably can't afford to practice every skill they encounter. This time constraint means that students will not master all the skills you teach. There is nothing wrong with that. However, if students do not have time to master everything, then you must distinguish between content they will practice in depth and content they will simply be introduced to and may look up on their own. If you do not make this distinction, students will spend too much time on some skills and too little time on others.

Just as it is crucial to clearly set the objective for your lesson, as we discussed in Chapter 1, it is equally important to provide a clear purpose for practice activities. In the following vignette, see how a kindergarten teacher redirects a practice session and how it makes a difference in student learning.

Ms. Verdi is introducing the letter G to her kindergarten students. In one center, the students are coloring a worksheet that includes a number of things, including a giant, a giraffe, a car, and a school. The students are supposed to color the pictures of objects that begin with the letter G.

The students are highly engaged in their worksheets. Ms. Verdi kneels down next to Nancy and asks her what she is learning. Nancy looks up from her coloring and says, "I am coloring."

"I see that," says Ms. Verdi, "but what are you learning while you color?"

Nancy replies, "I am coloring big things. Giraffes are big, and giants are big."

Ms. Verdi immediately stands and says to the children in the center, "Remember, today we are learning about the letter G. Some of the pictures on your worksheet begin with the letter G. Let's all look at the pictures, one at a time, and say their names. Which ones start with the letter G? Those are the ones we want to color. Remember, today is G day!"

A few minutes later, Ms. Verdi returns to talk with Nancy. "What are you learning as you color this worksheet?" she asks again.

"I am coloring the pictures that begin with the letter G. Some of these pictures don't start with a G, and I am not supposed to color those. Today we are learning about the letter G."

Recommendation Two:
Design practice sessions that are short, focused, and distributed over time.

At first, practice sessions should be close together—*massed practice*. Over time, you can space them apart—*distributed practice*. The relationship between massed and distributed practice can be represented graphically (Figure 7.9).

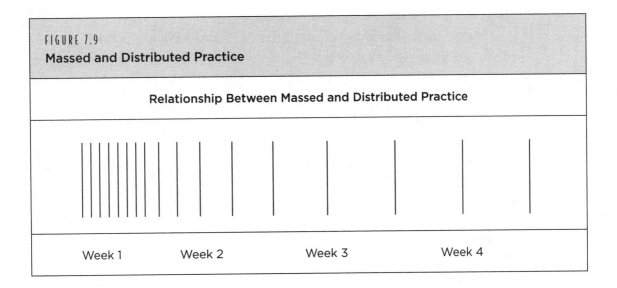

FIGURE 7.9
Massed and Distributed Practice

Relationship Between Massed and Distributed Practice

Week 1   Week 2   Week 3   Week 4

When students are first learning a new skill or process, they should practice it immediately and often. That is, they should engage in massed practice. For example, in a computer technology class, pairs of students might work at the computer and practice using a spreadsheet program as many times as possible before the end of a period. The teacher might also provide time for students to practice the next day—perhaps not as long as at first but for a substantial amount of time. The teacher should gradually increase the interval of time between practice sessions. Instead of practicing every day, students should practice every other day, then every third day, and so on. Lengthening the intervals of time between practice sessions involves students in distributed practice. Over time, students will internalize the new skill.

In the following vignette, see how Ms. Tann, a 4th grade math teacher, uses the idea of massed and distributed practice to help ensure her students truly know their multiplication facts rather than just memorize them for the weekly quiz.

"Okay students, we have been working on learning how to multiply by 5s. Everyone has been able to complete the mad minute on their 5s. Before we move to our 6s, we are going to review all the facts we've learned."

Students move to centers around the room and work on their facts in a variety of ways. Some are doing peer quizzes, some are engaged with manipulatives, and some are doing individual worksheets.

Angie and Sam are working on peer quizzes using flash cards. As Angie quizzes Sam, he says, "Last week when we learned the 4s, I aced the test. Now I am having a hard time with a few of these."

Angie says, "I'm glad you went first. I had to look at the back of a few of the cards myself." As they continue to work on their flash cards, they both begin to improve as they remember what they learned in the past.

When it is time to transition between centers, Ms. Tann asks, "How many of you missed a few of the facts you had learned last week and the week before?" Quite a few hands go up. Ms. Tann continues, "This is why we are going to review all the facts we have learned on a regular basis. Just memorizing facts for the test does not mean you actually own those facts. We need to keep coming back to them every week to make sure they become second nature to you."

Recommendation Three:
Provide feedback on practice sessions.

Every skill or process has variations, and students must understand them in order to use the skill or process successfully. Frequent and well-crafted feedback is essential as students are shaping their learning. For example, to perform three-column addition well, you must understand variations in that process: what to do when you have to carry from the first column to the second, what to do when you don't have to carry from the first column to the second, and so on. It is through targeted feedback that students are given guidance regarding what they are doing well and what they need to correct or modify in order to be successful.

The following vignette exemplifies the importance of consistent practice and high-quality feedback.

Ngoc, a level 3 ELL student, is working on improving her fluency and comprehension in her 9th grade language arts class. She times herself as she reads a passage and then takes a comprehension test on the passage. After she finishes, she sits down with her teacher, Mr. Hanover, to discuss the results.

Mr. Hanover says, "Congratulations Ngoc. Your reading speed improved again, and you were able to finish the passage within the target time. I see your practice is starting to pay off." Looking back on her previous four sessions, Ngoc is able to see the progress she has made in fluency and appreciates the recognition for her effort. "However," Mr. Hanover continues, "as your fluency speed increased, it seems your comprehension score went down a bit. What do you think that means?"

Ngoc replies, "I guess I was focusing so much on reading faster that I might have skipped over some words I didn't really understand."

"What do you think you should do next?" Mr. Hanover asks.

"Well, I think I have shown I can read faster, but I need to make sure I remember the reading strategies we learned about checking for clues as I read and looking at pictures for hints. That will probably help me keep up my speed and also do better on the comprehension test."

In this scenario, Mr. Hanover provides a way for Ngoc to monitor her progress as she practices her reading fluency and comprehension. She is given a number of practice sessions under his guidance to identify her strengths and address errors as they arise. Combining designated guided practice time with clear and direct feedback allows Ngoc to make decisions about where additional practice is needed. It also allows her to monitor the progress she is making toward mastery.

Rubrics and Checklists

The teacher rubric provided in Figure 7.10 is intended to be a tool used for reflection on the way in which you currently provide practice in your classroom. It is designed so that a 3 represents best practice as indicated by the research. A 4 indicates both teacher best practice as described in a 3 and how that practice transfers into student behaviors. You can also use this rubric as a growth tool, seeing where you are now and what the next level might look like. This will provide you with valuable information as you build your professional growth plan.

Using the teacher rubric will give you the chance to reflect on your practice. You can also ask your students how they perceive the way you provide practice. Figure 7.11 provides a student checklist you might want to use. Periodically give this checklist to your students, and ask them to react honestly to the statements. This checklist can help your students better understand how practice helps them learn, and it can provide valuable feedback to you about how your students view the process of providing practice.

Tools, Templates, and Protocols

If you are using this handbook as part of a school PLC or book study, Figure 7.12 provides statements that can serve as discussion prompts. Likewise, if you are using this book for individual growth, think about these prompts as they relate to your classroom practice. For example, if your answer to the first statement is a 0 or 1, then what steps should you take to move toward the other end of the spectrum, "to a great extent"? Use your individual or team results from Figure 7.12 to form the basis of a professional growth plan (see Figure 7.13).

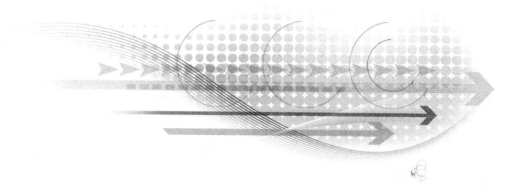

FIGURE 7.10

Teacher Rubric: Providing Practice

Clearly identify and communicate the purpose of practice activities. *Practice must tightly align with learning objectives and provide students with opportunities to deepen their understanding or become faster and more proficient with a skill.*

4	3	2	1
I consistently provide practice activities for my students that are aligned with the learning objectives they are to achieve. My students can articulate how what they are practicing is connected to the learning objective.	I consistently provide practice activities for my students that are aligned with the learning objectives they are to achieve.	I occasionally provide practice activities for my students that are aligned with the learning objectives they are to achieve.	I seldom provide practice activities for my students that are aligned with the learning objectives they are to achieve.
I consistently provide practice opportunities that are designed to deepen my students' understanding of a skill or process. My students understand how their practice over time helps them improve.	I consistently provide practice opportunities that are designed to deepen my students' understanding of a skill or process.	I occasionally provide practice opportunities that are designed to deepen my students' understanding of a skill or process.	I seldom provide practice opportunities that are designed to deepen my students' understanding of a skill or process.
I consistently provide students with a way to track their speed and accuracy of a skill or process. My students can monitor their own progress as they move toward mastery.	I consistently provide students with a way to track their speed and accuracy of a skill or process.	I occasionally provide students with a way to track their speed and accuracy of a skill or process.	I seldom provide students with a way to track their speed and accuracy of a skill or process.

FIGURE 7.10
Teacher Rubric: Providing Practice (continued)

Design practice sessions that are short, focused, and distributed over time. *Short practice sessions encourage students to make efficient use of their practice time. Focused practice is designed to target specific aspects of more complex skills and processes.*

4	3	2	1
I consistently design practice sessions that are focused on specific aspects of more complex skills and processes. My students understand how practicing the specific aspects leads to mastery of the skills or processes for the desired learning objective.	I consistently design practice sessions that are focused on specific aspects of more complex skills and processes.	I occasionally design practice sessions that are focused on specific aspects of more complex skills and processes.	I seldom design practice sessions that are focused on specific aspects of more complex skills and processes.
I consistently plan time for massed practice when I introduce a complex skill or process. My students understand the importance of frequent repetitions as they begin learning a skill or process.	I consistently plan time for massed practice when I introduce a complex skill or process.	I occasionally plan time for massed practice when I introduce a complex skill or process.	I seldom plan time for massed practice when I introduce a complex skill or process.
I consistently plan time for distributed practice as my students move toward mastery of a complex skill or process. My students understand the importance of distributed practice to move toward mastery of a skill or process.	I consistently plan time for distributed practice as my students move toward mastery of a complex skill or process.	I occasionally plan time for distributed practice as my students move toward mastery of a complex skill or process.	I seldom plan time for distributed practice as my students move toward mastery of a complex skill or process.

FIGURE 7.10

Teacher Rubric: Providing Practice (continued)

Provide feedback on practice sessions. *It is critical that students receive specific feedback during formative practice sessions to help them understand which aspect(s) of the skill or process they are not performing appropriately.*

4	3	2	1
I consistently provide specific feedback during formative practice sessions. My students understand how feedback helps them improve their work.	I consistently provide specific feedback during formative practice sessions.	I occasionally provide specific feedback during formative practice sessions.	I seldom provide specific feedback during formative practice sessions.
I consistently collect evidence about my students' proficiency at using the skill or process. My students are able to track the speed and accuracy of their work over time.	I consistently collect evidence about my students' proficiency at using the skill or process.	I occasionally collect evidence about my students' proficiency at using the skill or process.	I seldom collect evidence about my students' proficiency at using the skill or process.

FIGURE 7.11
Student Checklist: Providing Practice

		Always	Sometimes	Rarely	Never
PURPOSE	I understand how what we are practicing is connected to our learning objective.				
	I understand how practice helps me improve as I learn a skill or process.				
	I understand how to monitor how well I am learning a skill or process.				
MASSED AND DISTRIBUTED PRACTICE	I understand how a process is made up of individual skills.				
	I have enough time to learn part of the process multiple times before moving on to the next step.				
	I am given numerous opportunities over time to build mastery of a skill or process.				
FEEDBACK	I use corrective feedback my teacher provides to improve my skills.				
	I can provide feedback to myself and my peers related to the skill or process we are learning.				

FIGURE 7.12
Assessing Myself: Providing Practice

I clearly identify the purpose of practice.

Not at all   To a great extent

0   1   2   3   4

I provide specific time for guided and independent practice.

Not at all   To a great extent

0   1   2   3   4

I provide practice sessions that are short, focused, and distributed over time.

Not at all   To a great extent

0   1   2   3   4

I provide a way for students to track and monitor their progress.

Not at all   To a great extent

0   1   2   3   4

I provide specific feedback on the individual steps in a process.

Not at all   To a great extent

0   1   2   3   4

FIGURE 7.13
Professional Growth Plan: Providing Practice

1. How do I clearly identify the purpose of practice?

2. How do I provide specific time for guided and independent practice?

3. How do I provide practice sessions that are short, focused, and distributed over time?

4. How do I provide ways for students to track and monitor their progress?

5. How do I provide specific feedback on the individual steps in a process?

Part III

Helping Students Extend and Apply Knowledge

The strategies in this section emphasize the importance of helping students move beyond "right answer" learning to an expanded understanding and use of concepts and skills in real-world contexts. These strategies help students become more efficient and flexible in using what they have learned. The strategies in this section include

- Identifying Similarities and Differences
- Generating and Testing Hypotheses

When students are involved in identifying similarities and differences and/or generating and testing hypotheses, they are very often thinking and applying their knowledge at a higher level or with more rigor. Teachers should intentionally use the strategies in this section to help students take their learning to a higher and more meaningful level.

List of Figures

Chapter 8

8.1	Reflecting on Current Practice: Identifying Similarities and Differences	242
8.2	Venn Diagram	247
8.3	Comparison Matrix	248
8.4	Graphic Organizers for Classifying	252
8.5	Graphic Organizer for Creating Metaphors	257
8.6	Graphic Organizer for Creating Metaphors Example	258
8.7	Graphic Organizer for Creating Analogies	263
8.8	Teacher Rubric: Identifying Similarities and Differences	265
8.9	Student Checklist: Identifying Similarities and Differences	269
8.10	Assessing Myself: Identifying Similarities and Differences	270
8.11	Professional Growth Plan: Identifying Similarities and Differences	272

Chapter 9

9.1	Character Traits Advance Organizer	276
9.2	Reflecting on Current Practice: Generating and Testing Hypotheses	279
9.3	*Three Little Pigs* Advance Organizer	282
9.4	Disease Spread Chart	286
9.5	Teacher Rubric: Generating and Testing Hypotheses	292
9.6	Student Checklist: Generating and Testing Hypotheses	295
9.7	Assessing Myself: Generating and Testing Hypotheses	296
9.8	Professional Growth Plan: Generating and Testing Hypotheses	298

8

Identifying Similarities and Differences

Identifying Similarities and Differences

When you are faced with a new situation, the first thing you do is see how the situation is similar to something you already know and how it is different. Identifying similarities and differences helps learners gain insight, draw inferences, make generalizations, and develop or refine schemas (Holyoak, 2005). In addition, when students are presented with appropriately arranged contrasts, they are likely to notice new features they hadn't noticed before and learn which of those features are relevant to a particular concept (Bransford, Brown, & Cocking, 2000). There are four strategies in the Identifying Similarities and Differences category: comparing, classifying, creating metaphors, and creating analogies. Teachers are most comfortable engaging their students in activities that require comparing and classifying. The power of this category to increase the probability of positively affecting student achievement lies in the use of all four, especially creating metaphors and analogies. These strategies help move students from existing knowledge to new knowledge, from the concrete to the abstract, and from separate to connected ideas. Students use what they already know as an anchor for new learning. As a result, many people consider these strategies to be the core of all learning (e.g., Bransford et al., 2000; Chen, 1999; Fuchs et al., 2006; Gentner, Loewenstein, & Thompson, 2003; Holyoak, 2005).

Why This Strategy?

Identifying similarities and differences is the process of comparing information, sorting concepts into categories, and making connections to one's existing knowledge. Simply put, identifying similarities and differences helps us make sense of the world. We ask, "Is this like that?" By answering this question, we enhance our existing mental representation or abstract schema for the information. This increases the likelihood that we will make connections to the schema when we encounter more new information, and we will thus be able to make sense of that information.

What seems to be most effective is the practice of embedding this strategy as part of an instructional sequence that includes activating prior knowledge, introducing new knowledge, asking students to connect new and previous learning by identifying similarities and differences, and asking students to apply and demonstrate their understanding (Mbajiorgu, Ezechi, & Idoko, 2007; Rule & Furletti, 2004). Additional practices that facilitate student learning tie into research on other strategies, including providing supporting cues (e.g., posters of problem features, prompts for reflection, labeled diagrams), prompting students to reflect, and providing corrective feedback until students demonstrate understanding and proficiency (Valle & Callahan, 2006).

In this chapter, we provide opportunities for you to deepen your understanding of the four strategies that make up this category. Each of these strategies involves identifying how items, events, processes, or concepts are similar and different. When we compare and contrast, we examine how things are alike and different based on certain characteristics. For example, Heather's car is silver, has front-wheel drive, and has a bike rack on top; Bob's car is red, has four-wheel drive, and has ski racks on top. When we classify, we consider similarities and differences and then group items according to categories—hibiscus and Black-Eyed Susans are perennials; pansies and marigolds are annuals. Metaphors link two things that appear to be quite different on the surface but, after further scrutiny, are found to have some likeness, such as love and a rose. Analogies involve relationships and similarities between pairs of elements. For example, a ruler is to length as a cup is to volume. We then explicitly identify the relationship that unites the two pairs, as in this case, units of measurement.

Students need explicit instruction and structures when they first begin identifying similarities and differences. As they progress, however, students can use the process on their own to stimulate a wide-ranging exchange of ideas. Research also shows that graphic and symbolic representations help students understand and effectively use the four strategies for identifying similarities and differences. We encourage you to use these strategies in your lesson planning and delivery to enhance students' learning. We also encourage you to provide students with multiple opportunities to use each of the strategies. We run the risk of providing only surface-level use of this powerful category by only emphasizing comparing and classifying with our students. Though important, these strategies alone do not help students elaborate on their learning. It is only by helping students reach automaticity with the full complement of strategies that they are fully equipped to identify similarities and differences.

The following recommendations for identifying similarities and differences provide guidance for teachers as they create a learning evironment for student success. Teacher are encouraged to

1. **Teach students a variety of ways to identify similarities and differences.** Instruction should include providing students with clear modeling of each step in the process. Use familiar context or content when modeling so students focus on the process itself and don't have to think about understanding the content in addition to the process. Provide multiple opportunities to practice with corrective feedback.

2. **Guide students as they engage in the process of identifying similarities and differences.** Present students with a direct approach to identifying similarities and differences. Using a direct approach provides guidance, stimulates discussions about the similarities and differences, and encourages students to ask questions about the comparisons. Teachers can also provide structured tasks by identifying items to be compared and characteristics on which to base the comparison and having students draw conclusions.

3. **Provide supporting cues to help students identify similarities and differences.** Provide additional support to students by directing their attention to important features of the targeted knowledge. Do this by providing posters of important problem features, labeled diagrams, and prompts that help students reflect on what they are learning. Provide supportive cues to point out patterns in information, introduce a set of guiding questions to help students understand a metaphor, or use everyday objects as analogs.

Reflecting on My Current Practice

The questions listed in Figure 8.1 are provided as a means to assist you as you implement the instructional practices for identifying similarities and differences.

FIGURE 8.1

Reflecting on Current Practice: Identifying Similarities and Differences

1. Do I provide explicit instruction related to comparing, classifying, creating metaphors, and creating analogies?

2. Do I help students establish an understanding of identifying similarities and differences by teaching them to compare before providing instruction about classifying, creating metaphors, and creating analogies?

3. Do I teach comparing, classifying, creating metaphors, and creating analogies with familiar context and content?

4. Do I model comparing, classifying, creating metaphors, and creating analogies prior to having students practice each of the four strategies?

5. Do I provide multiple opportunities for students to practice each of the four strategies?

FIGURE 8.1

Reflecting on Current Practice: Identifying Similarities and Differences *(continued)*

6. Do I use a direct approach to provide guidance and stimulate discussions about similarities and differences?

7. Do I provide the steps for each of the processes involved in comparing, classifying, creating metaphors, and creating analogies?

8. Do I provide corrective feedback while students are learning and practicing the steps associated with comparing, classifying, creating metaphors, and creating analogies?

9. Do I use graphic organizers to help students represent their learning for each of the four strategies?

10. Do I help students see patterns and connections as they create metaphors and analogies?

Bringing the Strategy to Life in the Classroom: Comparing

Recommendation One:
Teach students a variety of ways to identify similarities and differences.

To compare is to identify similarities and differences between or among things or ideas. We engage in the process of comparing on a routine basis. We compare movies we have seen, restaurants where we have eaten, or ski runs on our favorite mountains.

In the classroom, we can use this process deliberately and rigorously to deepen students' understanding of the content they are learning. We can compare Heathcliff in *Wuthering Heights* to Mr. Rochester in *Jane Eyre*. We can compare the shape of the graph of $y = 2x + 3$ to the shape of $y = 2x - 3$. We can compare strategies used in the Battle of Gettysburg to those used at Antietam during the Civil War. We can compare the duties and responsibilities of state governments to those of the national government.

Students intuitively understand the process of comparing on some level because they compare things every day: "Friday's lunch in the cafeteria was better than today's"; "The new Batman movie is way better than the new Spider-Man movie"; "Ms. Bloomer's calculus class is a lot harder than Mr. Stacy's." To push students beyond the kind of comparing that they do automatically every day, we need to teach a systematic process and hold students accountable for rigorously using it. A model for comparing should include a set of steps for students to follow:

1. Select the items to be compared.
2. Select the characteristics of each item you will compare.
3. Explain how the items are similar and different with respect to those characteristics.

Comparing activities have broad applications. The key to an effective comparison is to identify important characteristics—those that will enhance students' understanding of the similarities and differences between items. If students are comparing Malcolm X and Martin Luther King Jr. during a history class, then describing similarities and differences between the two men in terms of where they were born might be interesting but does not add much to students' learning. A more useful characteristic to compare might be their religious views or roles in the civil rights movement.

We can make many comparisons at a surface level that do not contribute much to our learning. For example, we could compare Lewis and Clark's

Corps of Discovery expedition to Zebulon Pike's Arkansas River expedition on the basis of who went on the expeditions, how long each trip lasted, what kind of clothes the members of the expedition wore, and which expedition was written about the most. We might learn that Lewis and Clark became more famous than Pike, even though the latter's expedition was better dressed. Does this information add to an understanding of these expeditions' importance? Probably not. It is far more likely that students will have a much better understanding of the two expeditions if they base their comparison on more meaningful characteristics, such as each expedition's purpose, the areas they explored, and the outcomes that resulted.

Everyday comparisons can help students understand the steps in the comparing process. For example, if students are comparing Friday's cafeteria lunch to Tuesday's lunch, then they can compare them based on a set of characteristics, such as nutritional content, variety of foods, and type of cuisine. Explaining how the items are similar and different in terms of these specific characteristics uncovers the information that lies behind the claim that Friday's cafeteria lunch was "better" than Tuesday's. Understanding and following steps in a process for comparing something familiar helps students when they use the process with more rigorous or unfamiliar content knowledge. If students are taught a new process and new content simultaneously, then they will likely fail to learn either at a deep and enduring level. However, if the process is taught and practiced with familiar content first, then students have the opportunity to focus on and become proficient with the process, which enables them to transfer that skill to new learning situations.

Recommendation Two:
Guide students as they engage in the process of identifying similarities and differences.

When students first learn how to compare, a little guidance can go a long way. For example, you might identify the items to be compared and the characteristics to use in the comparison. In this case, students describe how the items are similar and different based on those predetermined characteristics. You also might ask students to summarize what they have learned and then create a class summary to ensure that students have captured the information you want them to have in place. Although these structured comparisons are somewhat limiting since students are working with a teacher-defined set of items and characteristics, this approach is useful because it is a tool to help students scaffold their understanding.

After students have had an opportunity to practice more structured comparison activities, you can provide less structure and guidance. For example, you might identify the items for students to compare and then ask them to choose the characteristics upon which they will base their comparison. Students have more responsibility and begin to think and work more independently. As they become more comfortable with the strategy of comparing, students must grapple with the issue of choosing meaningful characteristics to use in their comparisons.

A simple example of a structured activity would be to have students compare apples and oranges. Although they seem very different at first glance, there are several characteristics—such as color, function, shape, and size—that can be used as the basis of a comparison. If you were to compare function, then you could ask students to compare apples and oranges based on their use as a snack food. As students work in cooperative groups, they might state that apples and oranges are alike as snack foods because they are easy to carry, healthful, and inexpensive. Students might also suggest that apples and oranges are different as snack foods because orange skins aren't eaten, oranges are messier to eat, and oranges are easier to share.

Notice that, in this example, students are comparing a specific characteristic: apples and oranges as a snack food. A common mistake teachers make is merely asking students to compare two items without the specificity of criterion. Without the criterion, the rigor of the activity is lost. With the criterion, students have a focus for the work they are doing and therefore leave with a much deeper understanding of the content they are comparing. Another step in this process is to have students provide a summary of the comparison. By doing this in writing or orally, students have an additional opportunity to process the information and create deeper connections.

Recommendation Three:
Provide supporting cues to help students identify similarities and differences.

Students can use graphic organizers as a visual tool to help them make comparisons. The most common is the Venn diagram (Figure 8.2), which uses two or more intersecting circles to show how items are similar and different. Similarities are shown in the intersection of the circles, and differences are indicated in the nonoverlapping parts of each circle. The most basic type of Venn diagram is used to compare two things. If students want to compare various characteristics of rain forests and deserts—plant life, animal life, and climate—then they could use Venn diagrams to compare one characteristic at a time. This would mean that three different diagrams would be necessary—one for plant life, one for animal life, and one for climate.

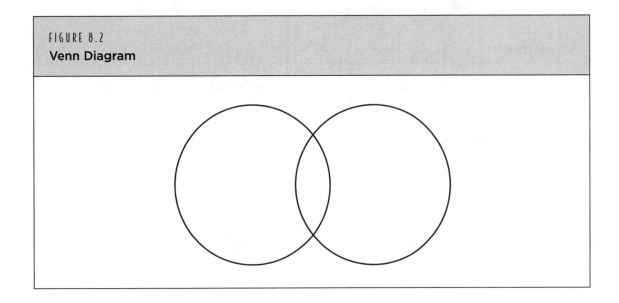

FIGURE 8.2
Venn Diagram

As the content students are learning becomes more complex, a Venn diagram may not be the best graphic organizer to help students represent what they are comparing. Instead of making multiple Venn diagrams to compare multiple characteristics, they can use a comparison matrix to graphically represent similarities and differences among items (Figure 8.3). A comparison matrix helps students systematically organize and compare information about multiple items or events.

You may need to provide more detailed instructions when students use a comparison matrix. For example, if students are asked to compare three sections of Colorado, they could place the terms *grassland prairie*, *foothills*, and *mountains* across the top of the comparison matrix. Next, they could place the characteristics to be compared down the left-hand side of the graphic organizer. Characteristics might include natural resources, human resources, and geographic features. Comparing the natural resources in the three areas, students might note that one natural resource found in each area is pastureland. However, a difference is the amount of grass that grows, due to the annual moisture received. Mountainous regions receive more moisture than foothills, and both mountains and foothills exceed grassland prairies in the amount of moisture received. As students complete the comparison matrix, they have a more complete set of information for reference and future use. In

FIGURE 8.3
Comparison Matrix

Characteristics	Items to Be Compared			Comparisons
	#1	#2	#3	
1.				*Similarities:*
				Differences:
2.				*Similarities:*
				Differences:
3.				*Similarities:*
				Differences:
4.				*Similarities:*
				Differences:

Source: From *Classroom Instruction That Works: Research-Based Strategies for Increasing Student Achievement* (p. 19), by R. J. Marzano, D. J. Pickering, & J. E. Pollock, 2001, Alexandria, VA: ASCD. Copyright 2001 by McREL. Adapted with permission.

addition, leaving space for students to write a summary helps them reflect on what they have learned.

Bringing the Strategy to Life in the Classroom: Classifying

Recommendation One:
Teach students a variety of ways to identify similarities and differences.

Classifying involves grouping things into definable categories based on similar characteristics. Like comparing, it is something we do in our day-to-day lives. We classify the clothes we put in our closet. We classify the food we put on our kitchen shelves. We classify the music in our digital playlists.

Certain rules govern these classifications: classical music goes together, Bob Dylan tunes have their own category, country goes with country. Even though we use rules to classify our music, clothes, and foods, most of us don't expend much intellectual effort to decide if the canned tomatoes should go with the canned fruit or the canned vegetables. In the classroom, students should use a systematic process to classify important pieces of content knowledge in order to deepen their understanding between and among the items being classified. They might classify organisms according to kingdom, phylum, class, order, family, genus, and species, or they might classify mathematical functions as linear, quadratic, trigonometric, exponential, or logarithmic. The more robust the activity, the greater depth of knowledge students acquire.

If we want students to move beyond classification schemes that are defined for them, such as food groups or the animal kingdom, then we need to give them opportunities to classify items using categories they create. By having students create their own categories, we cause them to think more deeply about the subject, which increases rigor in the classroom. Before students can be asked to complete these types of assignments, they need to be taught explicit steps for classifying.

1. Identify the items you wish to classify.
2. Select what seems to be an important item, describe its key attributes, and identify other items that have the same attributes.
3. Create a category by specifying the attribute(s) that the items must have for membership in that category.
4. Select another item, describe its key attributes, and identify other items that have the same attributes.

5. Create a second category by specifying the attribute(s) that the items must have for membership in that category.
6. Repeat the previous two steps until all items are classified and the specific attributes have been identified for membership in each category.
7. If necessary, combine categories or split them into smaller categories and specify attributes that determine membership in the category.

How things are classified influences our perceptions and behavior. When rules for category membership change, we change the way we think about items within those categories. Imagine we classified food items in a grocery store according to color. Purposefully grouping items into different categories can give us a different perspective on those items. When a green, square object is grouped with other square objects, we tend to notice it is square. When the green, square object is grouped with other green objects, we tend to notice it is green. In the classroom, the process of classifying can influence how students think about and see the information they are learning. When the perspectives for classifying are changed, the activity is inherently more robust.

Just as with comparing, it is important to begin the process of classifying by providing students with activities that involve familiar content. Use everyday examples to help students understand the process of grouping items and describing the rules for membership in a category. For example, students can classify local fast food restaurants into different categories based on specific characteristics. By considering some classification systems that we take for granted, students begin to understand that classifying the world around us can influence their thinking and behavior. How would our behavior change if library books were grouped by size? How does our thinking change if we group elephants with things in a circus before African wildlife? Thinking about what defines a particular group and why an item fits into that group helps students learn more about the content they are studying. The more students are able to move items among categories, the more critical thinking is required. In addition, the operations involved in classifying can provide students with opportunities to move from using concrete materials to more abstract ideas and concepts (Chen, 1999).

Recommendation Two:
Guide students as they engage in the process of identifying similarities and differences.

When students first learn to classify, teachers should structure the activity with predetermined items and categories. This helps focus students' attention on why items belong in certain categories. A structured classification activity can be appropriate for students in many situations. For example, if you want students to learn the specific characteristics of each of the major food groups, you might provide a list of foods and ask students to explain where each belongs and why. Students' performance on this type of activity is based on how accurately they place the items into the categories.

After students have had some practice completing structured classification activities, you can give them items to classify but ask them to form the categories themselves. This type of activity often extends students' understanding of the content they are studying. For example, asking students to group foods into the food groups can tell you how well they know the given rules for membership in each category. However, asking students to temporarily disregard these food groups and form their own helps them delve into what they understand about the characteristics of various foods. This latter activity requires students to think in a different way and forces them to answer the question "How would I group these items, and why?" More robust classification activities require students to provide their own groups for classification and describe why items are placed into those groups.

Recommendation Three:
Provide supporting cues to help students identify similarities and differences.

Graphic organizers are tools students can use as a visual guide to the classifying process. Two popular graphic organizers for classification are shown in Figure 8.4. The first example requires students to break material into discrete categories and then list examples that might be found in each category. The second example, however, provides opportunities for the division of categories into sets and subsets, a process that requires higher-level thinking and application. For example, younger students might use the first graphic organizer to place rocks in the three major categories of igneous, metamorphic, and sedimentary. This could be a simple matching exercise, or students might use the graphic organizer to place each rock type in the proper classification as the content is presented. Older students could use the second graphic organizer to go deeper in the classification process. They can again classify the three types of rocks under the large heading of "Rocks." Students might find, for example, that some igneous rocks formed due to fast cooling and others formed as a result of slow cooling. This means that students would need to indicate the split on the graphic organizer.

FIGURE 8.4

Graphic Organizers for Classifying

Categories				

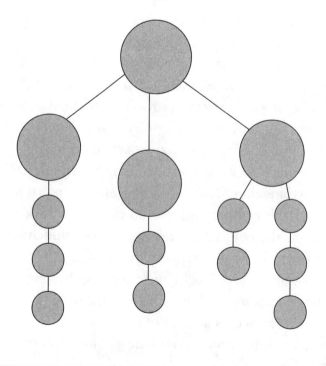

Bringing the Strategy to Life in the Classroom: Creating Metaphors

Recommendation One: Teach students a variety of ways to identify similarities and differences.

When we create metaphors, we identify a general or basic pattern in a specific topic and then find another topic that seems quite different at the literal level but has the same general pattern. Authors frequently use metaphors to give readers strong images. Shakespeare's *Macbeth* describes life with a metaphor:

> Life's but a walking shadow, a poor player
> That struts and frets his hour upon the stage
> And then is heard no more: it is a tale
> Told by an idiot, full of sound and fury,
> Signifying nothing. (V.v.24–28)

Macbeth likens life to a theatrical performance that exists for an "hour upon the stage" and then disappears, implying that life lacks substance and is merely a brief drama that does not leave a lasting mark. This passage further compares life to a tale full of noise and excitement and commotion but one that is meaningless in the end. The abstract relationship—a brief moment full of commotion that dissolves into nothingness—connects life to the images in Macbeth's description. Creating metaphors isn't just for Shakespeare. We can use metaphors and help students create metaphors to better understand academic content from history (the United States is freedom and promise) to mathematics (the graph of the sine function is a roller coaster). In metaphors, students need to identify specific information about each thing being compared. They then need to uncover and describe the general patterns or information that link the two things.

Students encounter metaphors in many different contexts. Authors use metaphors to give readers strong mental images, such as "he was walking on thin ice," "the fog was pea-soup thick," or "her eyes were pools of blue." Metaphors are also commonly used in specific content areas. In science, teachers might feel particularly descriptive and say "a cell is a city" or "a DNA molecule is a ladder." In health or biology class, students might connect the heart to a pump, the kidney to a water filter, or the eye to a camera. Teaching students to develop metaphors provides them with a powerful tool to explore ideas and information at deeper levels by aligning new information with something familiar. Students benefit from discrete steps to help them create metaphors.

1. Identify the important or basic elements of the information or situation with which you are working.
2. Write that basic information as a more general pattern by replacing words for specific things with words for more general things and by summarizing information whenever possible.
3. Find new information or a situation to which the general pattern applies.

Common metaphors can help students understand the steps to create their own metaphors. Students have probably heard sayings such as "You're walking on thin ice" or "It's raining cats and dogs." They themselves make metaphorical comparisons every day—"My brother is a tyrant," "Calculus is a monster," "Cafeteria lunches are dog food," "Love is a rose." Use these familiar examples to help students learn a deliberate process for making these connections. For example, if we want students to understand an abstract concept such as love, then giving them a concrete example as an anchor often provides a conceptual framework to aid in their understanding. As students identify the important information for both, they begin to recognize similarities between the two. Students can make a list that might look like the following:

Concrete Example	Abstract Example
ROSE	*LOVE*
• is sweet	• is special
• can brighten your day	• makes you feel good
• grows and blossoms	• grows and blossoms
• withers and dies	• needs to be tended
• has thorns	• can hurt you

Stating the relationship between "love" and "a rose" in more general terms—*love is a special emotion that can make you happy or can hurt you*—helps students understand the reasoning behind the connection they are making in the metaphor.

Recommendation Two:
Guide students as they engage in the process of identifying
similarities and differences.

The original learning associated with creating metaphors occurs within the language arts classroom. However, the application of this process as an instructional strategy can only be taken to its fullest potential when it is applied in all content areas as a means to help students create a mental model that serves as a frame for conceptual understanding.

Modeling the process of creating metaphors within the various content areas helps students understand how to identify the literal parts of a metaphor and describe the abstract relationship. Once students are familiar with the process, the teacher should identify one element of the metaphor and the abstract pattern, giving students a kind of scaffold to build on as they complete the metaphor. You can vary how structured the metaphor tasks are, according to students' level of understanding and skill.

When Mrs. Cleaver first learned about using metaphors, she thought that the process was not appropriate for her 1st graders. However, one day she realized that she had been using metaphors in class without intending to. She was trying to help students understand that, just as letters stand for sounds, numbers stand for things. She had been extending and refining students' understanding of symbol systems by showing them how things that may seem different are in fact similar at a general level—and her students were getting it.

The next week, Mrs. Cleaver teaches her students the process of using metaphors by using fairy tales with plots that follow the same general pattern. From then on, she periodically challenges her students to look for general patterns as they learn. She is amazed at what her students observe. One student notices that digits can be put together to make a new number in the same way that letters can be put together to make a new word. With further prompting from Mrs. Cleaver, students notice that if they change the order of the letters of some words, the meaning changes. For example, *tap* can become *pat*. Similarly, if they turn around the order of digits in a number, it, too, has a new meaning. For example, 453 can become 354.

Mrs. Cleaver starts a bulletin board on which she lists the general statements discovered by the class, along with specific examples from students. Periodically, she adds a general statement to see if students can apply it to specifics. For example, "If you put things together 'any old way,' you don't get much meaning, but if you put things together in an organized way, then you make patterns that have meaning." She hopes that students will see that words in random order say nothing, but in an organized sequence, they make a sentence. Likewise, numbers in a random order do not have any meaning, but if you follow a pattern such as counting by twos, then you get meaning. Mrs. Cleaver admits that students are beginning to see connections everywhere, even connections she has not noticed.

After students have had some practice completing metaphors, gradually remove the scaffolding by presenting one element of the metaphor and asking students to provide the second element and a description of the abstract relationship.

Disease is . . .
The brain is . . .
The Great Wall of China is . . .
Sedimentary rock is . . .

To complete metaphors such as these, students must use what they know about the given element and make connections to similar things, events, or processes. Explaining the relationships will help students analyze their reasoning and refine their metaphors. It is important to give students guidance until they are comfortable with the rigor of more complex metaphor activities. For example, you might allow students to work in pairs or monitor their individual progress and offer assistance as necessary.

Recommendation Three:
Provide supporting cues to help students identify similarities and differences.

Students can use a graphic organizer to help them understand and use metaphors. The one shown in Figure 8.5 is a good example that will assist students as they work with two dissimilar situations that each fit the general pattern.

The following vignette demonstrates how students can apply this strategy and create a metaphor of their own to deepen their understanding. Notice how, after giving students a model for creating metaphors, Mr. Cogburn provides an opportunity for students to work in groups and gain confidence in the process of creating metaphors.

Mr. Cogburn's biology students are working in cooperative groups, analyzing a problem and developing a viable solution. The problem focuses on a patient who developed a malignant tumor in his brain. The tumor could not be removed through surgery, but if it remained, it would kill the patient. Students hypothesized that by using high-intensity radiation, the tumor could be reduced or even eradicated. After reviewing information from journals and other research studies, the students determined that radiation with a high enough intensity to destroy the tumor would also destroy the surrounding tissue. The students are not making progress, and frustration is becoming obvious.

FIGURE 8.5
Graphic Organizer for Creating Metaphors

Initial Situation	General Pattern	New Situation

Mr. Cogburn reassembles his class and says, "Remember when we were working with metaphors last week? Let's look at the information that we have and put it in specific and general terms." He provides his students with the graphic organizer found in Figure 8.6.

The students begin to discuss various ideas that match the general pattern. As students offer their ideas, Rojelio says, "This is like the story we were reading in Ms. Savolt's English class! Remember the short story we read about the dictator and the men who overthrew him?" The room erupts in simultaneous conversations. Mr. Cogburn allows students a few minutes to recall the story and make connections before he asks Rojelio to retell the story.

"Well," begins Rojelio, "there was this evil ruler, and the men in the kingdom wanted to overthrow him. They plotted to overtake the castle that was in the center of the village by moving down the main road. Then they found out from one of the scouts that there were mines along the road and if too many men and their equipment marched down the road at the same time, then the mines would be detonated, destroying the land in the areas and killing the people. So they worked together to come up with a plan to move toward the castle from several different directions. They would arrive at the castle at the same time, not be harmed by the land mines, and be able to overthrow the evil ruler. Their plan worked."

As Rojelio finishes retelling the story, Ali says, "These two situations are alike. We can use the information from the story to help us figure out how to save this patient's life." By building this metaphor, it suddenly became obvious to the class that the man's life could be saved if low-level radiation was sent to the tumor all at once from several directions.

FIGURE 8.6

Graphic Organizer for Creating Metaphors Example

Initial Situation: Man with a Tumor	General Pattern	New Situation: Attacking the Fortress
The man has a tumor that must be removed or he will die.	Something bad must be destroyed.	
High-intensity radiation will destroy the tumor, but it will also destroy surrounding tissue.	If a full-strength approach is used, good and bad things will be destroyed.	
Low-intensity radiation will protect the surrounding tissue but will not destroy the tumor.	If a weak approach is used, nothing will be destroyed.	
A way needs to be found to use radiation to kill the tumor but allow for the remaining tissue to be unharmed.	We need to look at all possibilities for destroying the bad thing.	

Bringing the Strategy to Life in the Classroom: Creating Analogies

Recommendation One: Teach students a variety of ways to identify similarities and differences.

Creating analogies is the process of identifying relationships between pairs of concepts (e.g., identifying relationships between relationships). Like metaphors, analogies help us make connections between things that might seem very different. Typically, an analogy follows the pattern A:B::C:D (read "*A* is to *B* as *C* is to *D*"). The "as" portion of the pattern is where students explicitly state the relationship. For example: Happy is to sad as big is to small. *Happy* and *big* are opposites of *sad* and *small*, respectively. The relationship between the two is one of opposites.

Analogies can help explain an unfamiliar concept by making a comparison to something that we understand. For example, concentrations of particulates in water are commonly stated in measures that are difficult to comprehend: one part per million, one part per billion, and so on. What does one part per trillion mean? An analogy to familiar items and relationships that we can imagine helps us make sense of this unfamiliar concept: One is to a trillion as one drop of milk is to the amount of milk in a row of milk tanker trucks ten miles long.

In this analogy, the relationship is a simple mathematical proportion that relates a quantity of one to a large number. "One part of lead per trillion parts of water" is an abstract statement, but "one drop of milk in a ten-mile line of milk tanker trucks" is more concrete and easy to visualize. The relationships are easier to imagine because we have concrete representations for things such as one drop of milk. We can use analogies for similar purposes in the classroom.

An analogy pushes us to think about how items and concepts are related, how those items and concepts interact, and how the relationship between one pair of items is similar to the relationship between a second pair of items. At first, content-area analogies might seem very complicated to students because they involve several elements and relationships between and among the elements, such as in the examples that follow.

Heart is to human as compressor is to heat pump. The heart is an organ within the human body that contracts to force blood to circulate throughout the body. A heat pump vaporizes a refrigerant and circulates air throughout the pump. The relationship is that both objects force a substance to circulate throughout the container in which it is housed.

One is to multiplication as zero is to addition. When a number is multiplied by one, the result is that number; when a number is added to zero, the result is that number. The relationship is that within addition and multiplication, there are operations that do not change the original number.

If we provide students with the steps for creating analogies, then we can help them work with academic content more efficiently.

1. Identify how the two elements in the first pair are related.
2. State the relationship in a general way.
3. Identify another pair of elements that share a similar relationship.

Analogy problems are common in testing situations. Students will encounter analogy problems on many state standards tests, the PSAT, and the SAT. The types of relationships that are common to most analogies include the following (Lewis & Greene, 1982):

Similar Concepts Adjacent concepts are synonyms or similar in meaning. *Hungry is to ravenous as tired is to exhausted.*	**Dissimilar Concepts** Adjacent concepts are opposites or dissimilar in meaning. *Grim is to cheerful as hilly is to flat.*
Class Membership Adjacent concepts belong to the same class or category. *Carrot is to potato as brown is to purple.*	**Class Name/Member** One element in a pair is a class name, and the other is a member of the class. *The number 3 is to natural numbers as pi is to irrational numbers.*
Part to Whole One element in a pair is a part of the other element in the pair. *Spark plug is to engine as variable is to function.*	**Change** One element in a pair turns into the other element in the pair. *Caterpillar is to butterfly as tadpole is to frog.*
Function One element in a pair performs a function on or for the other element in the pair. *Pilot is to airplane as forester is to chainsaw.*	**Quantity/Size** The two elements in the pair are comparable in terms of quantity or size. *One minute is to two years as one penny is to ten thousand dollars.*

Providing students with examples of these relationships can help them recognize patterns in the analogies they come across and learn the steps for creating their own analogies. Use some of these common analogous relationships to introduce the structure of an analogy to students. To illustrate, introduce the "Class Name/Member" relationship with a few examples, such as

> Whale is to mammal as snake is to reptile.
> Newt is to amphibian as salmon is to fish.
> *The Adventures of Huckleberry Finn* is to classic American literature as *Great Expectations* is to classic British literature.

Once students understand the structure of analogies, they can begin to discover the complexities of the relationships implied by the form A:B::C:D. They can then create new analogies that explain different relationships that align with information being learned.

Recommendation Two: Guide students as they engage in the process of identifying similarities and differences.

Analogies emphasize similarities, but they also reveal differences. The more students examine the details of the relationships between the elements in each pair of an analogy (and of the connection between the pairs), the better they will be at recognizing differences. For example, consider the following analogy: Brain is to human as central processing unit is to computer.

In a human, the brain controls activities that are vital for survival, such as movement, sleep, and thirst. Other parts of the body and the external environment send signals to the brain, which then interprets these signals. The brain makes things happen and communicates with other parts of the body by sending electrical signals. Similarly, the CPU in a computer processes information. It interprets signals or instructions, executes programs, makes decisions, stores information, and communicates with other parts of the computer.

Once students understand the process of creating analogies, they are better equipped to understand analogous situations. When students understand the relationship between *a* and *b*, it gives them the mental framework to understand the relationship between *c* and *d*. Here is a complex analogous situation that serves as a great example of "Similar Concepts": bunnies are to prairie as contributors are to Wikipedia. By exploring this example, students should gain a deeper understanding of both supply and demand and survival of the fittest.

Think of Wikipedia's community of volunteer editors as a family of bunnies left to roam freely over an abundant green prairie. In early, fat times, their numbers grow exponentially. However, more bunnies consume more resources, and at some point, the prairie becomes depleted, and the population crashes.

Instead of prairie grasses, Wikipedia's natural resource is an emotion. The first time people make an edit to Wikipedia, they realize that 330 million people are seeing it live. During the early days of Wikipedia, every new addition to the site had a roughly equal chance of surviving editorial scrutiny. Over time, though, a class system emerged; revisions made by infrequent contributors are now much likelier to be undone by elite Wikipedians. There has also been a rise of so-called wiki-lawyering: for your edits to stick, you've got to learn to cite the complex laws of Wikipedia in arguments with other editors. Together, these changes have created a community that is a bit inhospitable to newcomers. People begin to wonder if they should continue to contribute—suddenly, like rabbits out of food, Wikipedia's population stops growing.

Recommendation Three:
Provide supporting cues to help students identify similarities and differences.

Students can use a graphic organizer as an aid for creating analogies. The graphic organizer describing the crash of the housing market (Figure 8.7) shows the relationship *Housing crash of 2008 is to U.S. economy as exposure to germs is to human body.* This relationship is an example of Similar Concepts.

Teachers who help support students' learning by providing tools such as posters and guiding questions in concert with graphic organizers create an environment that supports students as they learn the strategies for identifying similarities and differences. In the vignette that follows, notice how the teacher uses posters, guiding questions, and graphic organizers to support student learning.

In Mr. Burron's art history class, students are studying the Renaissance. They had just completed an exploration of the work and styles of Sandro Botticelli and Leonardo da Vinci. Mr. Burron wants his students to develop a deeper understanding of both artists. He begins by telling his students they will be comparing the two artists. He asks them to refer to the comparison chart and rules for comparing what they wrote in their art history journals. After reviewing the rules for comparison, Mr. Burron instructs the class to work in their table groups to determine the characteristics that will be best to use. As students begin their table discussions, Mr. Burron walks around the room, monitoring the discussions. At one table, he overhears a discussion about whether it is important to know if the artist was married or not. At another table, he overhears a similar discussion about the level of education each man attained.

Mr. Burron stops the class discussion for a redirect and says, "Be sure, as you are thinking about the characteristics for comparison, that you are looking at the major attributes that would have contributed to their work and importance as artists. Though their level of formal education might be interesting to know, is it really one of the major characteristics of their work?"

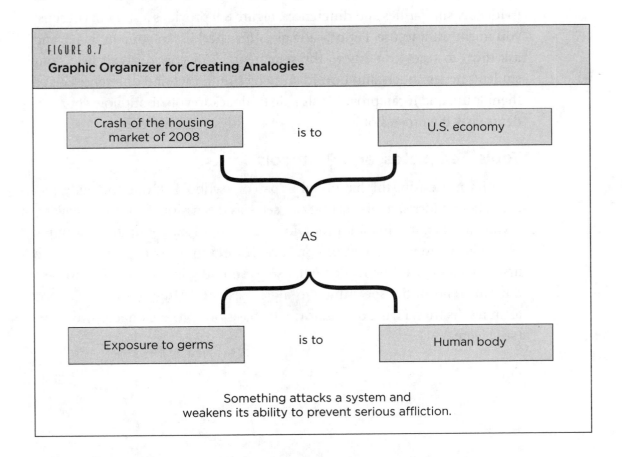

FIGURE 8.7
Graphic Organizer for Creating Analogies

Crash of the housing market of 2008   is to   U.S. economy

AS

Exposure to germs   is to   Human body

Something attacks a system and weakens its ability to prevent serious affliction.

As the students report out from their table discussions, Mr. Burron records their ideas on the board. He then displays a blank comparison matrix and has the students vote on which three characteristics they feel are the most appropriate for their comparisons. He enters those characteristics into the matrix, has the students copy it into their journals, and tells them to get to work.

Rubrics and Checklists

The teacher rubric provided in Figure 8.8 is intended to be a tool used for reflection on the way in which you currently identify similarities and differences in your classroom. It is designed so that a 3 represents best practice as indicated by the research. A 4 indicates both teacher best practice as described in a 3 and how that practice transfers into student behaviors. You can also use this rubric as a growth tool, seeing where you are now and what the next level might look like. This will provide you with valuable information as you build your professional growth plan.

Using the teacher rubric will give you the chance to reflect on your practice. You can also ask your students how they perceive the way you teach them to identify similarities and differences. Figure 8.9 provides a student checklist you might want to use. Periodically give this checklist to your students, and ask them to react honestly to the statements. This checklist can help your students better understand how identifying similarities and differences helps them learn, and it can provide valuable feedback to you about how your students view the process of identifying similarities and differences.

Tools, Templates, and Protocols

If you are using this handbook as part of a school PLC or book study, Figure 8.10 provides statements that can serve as discussion prompts. Likewise, if you are using this book for individual growth, think about these prompts as they relate to your classroom practice. For example, if your answer to the first statement is a 0 or 1, then what steps should you take to move toward the other end of the spectrum, "to a great extent"? Use your individual or team results from Figure 8.10 to form the basis of a professional growth plan (see Figure 8.11).

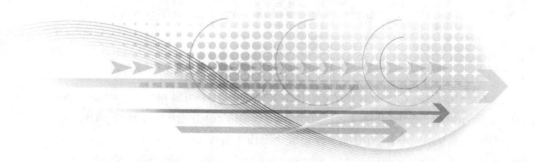

FIGURE 8.8
Teacher Rubric: Identifying Similarities and Differences

Teach students a variety of ways to identify similarities and differences. *Instruction should include providing students with steps in the process and modeling the process. Use familiar context/content when modeling so students focus on the process and don't have to think about understanding new content in addition to the process. Provide multiple opportunities to practice with corrective feedback.*

4	3	2	1
I consistently provide students with steps for the strategies of comparing, classifying, creating metaphors, and creating analogies. My students know the steps to comparing, classifying, creating metaphors, and creating analogies.	I consistently provide students with steps for the strategies of comparing, classifying, creating metaphors, and creating analogies.	I occasionally provide students with steps for the strategies of comparing, classifying, creating metaphors, and creating analogies.	I seldom provide students with steps for the strategies of comparing, classifying, creating metaphors, and creating analogies.
I consistently model and scaffold the strategies for the strategies of comparing, classifying, creating metaphors, and creating analogies. My students demonstrate and add to their skills over time.	I consistently model and scaffold the strategies for the strategies of comparing, classifying, creating metaphors, and creating analogies.	I occasionally model and scaffold the strategies for the strategies of comparing, classifying, creating metaphors, and creating analogies.	I seldom model and scaffold the strategies for the strategies of comparing, classifying, creating metaphors, and creating analogies.
I consistently use familiar context/content to teach and model the strategies for the strategies of comparing, classifying, creating metaphors, and creating analogies. My students demonstrate a more complete understanding of the process.	I consistently use familiar context/content to teach and model the strategies for the strategies of comparing, classifying, creating metaphors, and creating analogies.	I occasionally use familiar context/content to teach and model the strategies for the strategies of comparing, classifying, creating metaphors, and creating analogies.	I seldom use familiar context/content to teach and model the strategies for the strategies of comparing, classifying, creating metaphors, and creating analogies.

FIGURE 8.8
Teacher Rubric: Identifying Similarities and Differences *(continued)*

4	3	2	1
I consistently provide multiple practice sessions accompanied by corrective feedback so students internalize the strategies for the strategies of comparing, classifying, creating metaphors, and creating analogies. My students use the corrective feedback they receive to improve their use of the strategies.	I consistently provide multiple practice sessions accompanied by corrective feedback so students internalize the strategies for the strategies of comparing, classifying, creating metaphors, and creating analogies.	I occasionally provide multiple practice sessions accompanied by corrective feedback so students internalize the strategies for the strategies of comparing, classifying, creating metaphors, and creating analogies.	I seldom provide multiple practice sessions accompanied by corrective feedback so students internalize the strategies for the strategies of comparing, classifying, creating metaphors, and creating analogies.

Guide students as they engage in the process of identifying similarities and differences. *Present students with a direct approach to identifying similarities and differences. Using a direct approach provides guidance and stimulates discussions about similarities and differences and encourages students to ask questions about the comparisons. Teachers can also provide structured tasks by identifying items and characteristics to be compared and have students draw conclusions.*

4	3	2	1
I consistently provide students with explicit guidance in identifying similarities and differences to deepen their understanding and enhance their use. My students understand the importance of teacher guidance as they learn and use the strategies for identifying similarities and differences.	I consistently provide students with explicit guidance in identifying similarities and differences to deepen their understanding and enhance their use.	I occasionally provide students with explicit guidance in identifying similarities and differences to deepen their understanding and enhance their use.	I seldom provide students with explicit guidance in identifying similarities and differences to deepen their understanding and enhance their use.

FIGURE 8.8
Teacher Rubric: Identifying Similarities and Differences *(continued)*

4	3	2	1
I consistently use a direct approach to guide students and stimulate discussions about identifying similarities and differences. My students can identify similarities and differences and ask questions about each of the strategies.	I consistently use a direct approach to guide students and stimulate discussions about identifying similarities and differences.	I occasionally use a direct approach to guide students and stimulate discussions about identifying similarities and differences.	I seldom use a direct approach to guide students and stimulate discussions about identifying similarities and differences.
I consistently provide structured tasks and identify items and characteristics to compare so students can draw conclusions. My students can use the structured tasks to identify similarities and differences and draw conclusions.	I consistently provide structured tasks and identify items and characteristics to compare so students can draw conclusions.	I occasionally provide structured tasks and identify items and characteristics to compare so students can draw conclusions.	I seldom provide structured tasks and identify items and characteristics to compare so students can draw conclusions.

FIGURE 8.8

Teacher Rubric: Identifying Similarities and Differences (continued)

Provide supporting cues to help students identify similarities and differences. *Provide additional support to students by directing their attention to important features of the targeted knowledge by providing tools that help students reflect on what they are learning. Provide supportive cues to point out patterns in information, introduce a set of guiding questions to help students understand a metaphor, or use everyday objects as analogs.*

4	3	2	1
I consistently provide additional support through posters of important problem features, labeled diagrams, and prompts to help students identify similarities and differences. My students use the posters, labeled diagrams, and prompts as they identify similarities and differences.	I consistently provide additional support through posters of important problem features, labeled diagrams, and prompts to help students identify similarities and differences.	I occasionally provide additional support through posters of important problem features, labeled diagrams, and prompts to help students identify similarities and differences.	I seldom provide additional support through posters of important problem features, labeled diagrams, and prompts to help students identify similarities and differences.
I consistently provide supportive cues to point out patterns in information, introduce a set of guiding questions to help students understand a metaphor, or use everyday objects as analogs. My students use the patterns, guiding questions, and everyday objects to help them create metaphors and analogies.	I consistently provide supportive cues to point out patterns in information, introduce a set of guiding questions to help students understand a metaphor, or use everyday objects as analogies.	I occasionally provide supportive cues to point out patterns in information, introduce a set of guiding questions to help students understand a metaphor, or use everyday objects as analogs.	I seldom provide supportive cues to point out patterns in information, introduce a set of guiding questions to help students understand a metaphor, or use everyday objects as analogs.

FIGURE 8.9
Student Checklist: Identifying Similarities and Differences

		Always	Sometimes	Rarely	Never
VARIETY	I know the steps to compare, classify, create metaphors, and create analogies.				
	I can learn a new process better when I learn it with a familiar context/content.				
	Corrective feedback from my teacher helps me use the strategies associated with identifying similarities and differences.				
GUIDED ENGAGEMENT	I use guidance from my teacher as I learn and use the strategies for identifying similarities and differences.				
	I can identify similarities and differences and ask questions about each of the strategies.				
	I can use structured tasks to identify similarities and differences and draw conclusions.				
SUPPORTING CUES	I use graphic organizers and other tools to help me identify similarities and differences.				
	I can use patterns, guiding questions, and everyday objects to help me create metaphors and analogies.				

FIGURE 8.10

Assessing Myself: Identifying Similarities and Differences

I provide explicit instruction related to comparing, classifying, creating metaphors, and creating analogies.

Not at all   To a great extent

| 0 | 1 | 2 | 3 | 4 |

I help students establish an understanding of identifying similarities and differences by teaching them to compare before providing instruction about classifying, creating metaphors, and creating analogies.

Not at all   To a great extent

| 0 | 1 | 2 | 3 | 4 |

I teach comparing, classifying, creating metaphors, and creating analogies with familiar context and content.

Not at all   To a great extent

| 0 | 1 | 2 | 3 | 4 |

I model comparing, classifying, creating metaphors, and creating analogies prior to having students practice each of the four strategies.

Not at all   To a great extent

| 0 | 1 | 2 | 3 | 4 |

I provide multiple opportunities for students to practice each of the four strategies.

Not at all   To a great extent

| 0 | 1 | 2 | 3 | 4 |

FIGURE 8.10
Assessing Myself: Identifying Similarities and Differences *(continued)*

I use a direct approach to provide guidance and stimulate discussions about similarities and differences.

Not at all   To a great extent

0	1	2	3	4

I provide the steps for each of the processes involved in comparing, classifying, creating metaphors, and creating analogies.

Not at all   To a great extent

0	1	2	3	4

I provide corrective feedback while students are learning and practicing the steps associated with comparing, classifying, creating metaphors, and creating analogies.

Not at all   To a great extent

0	1	2	3	4

I use graphic organizers to help students represent their learning for each of the four strategies: comparing, classifying, creating metaphors, and creating analogies.

Not at all   To a great extent

0	1	2	3	4

I help students see patterns and connections as they create metaphors and analogies.

Not at all   To a great extent

0	1	2	3	4

FIGURE 8.11

Professional Growth Plan: Identifying Similarities and Differences

1. How can I provide explicit instruction related to comparing, classifying, creating metaphors, and creating analogies?

2. How can I help students establish an understanding of identifying similarities and differences by teaching them to compare before providing instruction about classifying, creating metaphors, and creating analogies?

3. How can I teach comparing, classifying, creating metaphors, and creating analogies using familiar context and content?

4. How can I model comparing, classifying, creating metaphors, and creating analogies prior to having students practice each of the four strategies?

5. How can I provide multiple opportunities for students to practice each of the four strategies: comparing, classifying, creating metaphors, and creating analogies?

FIGURE 8.11

Professional Growth Plan: Identifying Similarities and Differences *(continued)*

6. How can I use a direct approach to provide guidance and stimulate discussions about similarities and differences?

7. How can I provide the steps for each of the processes involved in comparing, classifying, creating metaphors, and creating analogies?

8. How can I provide corrective feedback while students are learning and practicing the steps associated with comparing, classifying, creating metaphors, and creating analogies?

9. How can I use graphic organizers to help students represent their learning for each of the four strategies?

10. How can I help students see patterns and connections as they create metaphors and analogies?

9

Generating and Testing Hypotheses

Generating and Testing Hypotheses

People generate and test hypotheses all the time. "If I do this, then what might happen?" "What would have happened if the Germans had won World War II?" "How might the world be different if JFK was never assassinated?" "How might Dickens's *Oliver Twist* be different if it were set in Boston rather than in London?"

Teachers ask students to generate and test hypotheses inductively or deductively. An inductive approach requires students to discover the principles, theories, or assumptions that are the primary focus of the lesson and then generate hypotheses or make inferences or predictions based on their discoveries. Inductive reasoning is used in the classroom to help students figure out things that are not explicit or overt. For example, we might observe how salt is used to cover icy roadways and hypothesize that salt somehow melts ice. The limitation of inductive reasoning is that, no matter how carefully we use the process, our conclusions may or may not be true. Misconceptions can easily form as students, investigating on their own, create an incomplete or incorrect understanding. Teachers who do not realize that misconceptions can be a byproduct of induction often fail to monitor and correct the inaccuracies in their students' understanding.

We don't mean to imply that the inductive approach is a bad teaching strategy. Rather, it is important to remember that when using the inductive approach, teachers must have a solid understanding of the content, communicate with students as they create an understanding from their observations, and continually provide formative assessment opportunities to ensure that students have not developed or reinforced misconceptions as they construct their own meaning from the instruction. The mental process for inductive reasoning is as follows:

1. What specific information do I have?
2. What connections or patterns can I find?
3. What general conclusions or predictions can I make?
4. When I get more information, do I need to change my conclusions or predictions?

Often, when students are engaged in inductive reasoning, they are using the process of inferring. An inference is a conclusion that is logical and defensible and is based on the information provided. It might be possible to test the validity of your inference, but this isn't a requirement. One could, for example, infer what Shakespeare might say if he saw *West Side Story*, but we would never actually be able to test that inference. Nonetheless, the inference must be logical, defensible, and based in fact.

In the following vignette, see how Ms. Stein has her language arts students use inductive reasoning to generate a hypothesis.

Ms. Stein's 3rd grade class loves reading Barbara Park's Junie B. Jones series of books. Even though she has multiple copies of each book, she can't keep up with the demand. One day, after reading *Junie B. Jones is a Graduation Girl*, Ms. Stein asks her students to go to their table groups and discuss the patterns and connections they have observed about Junie's personality throughout the series, incorporating specifics from the books to support their conclusions. Ms. Stein provides her students with a character traits advance organizer as a starting point (Figure 9.1). She then asks them to infer what it would be like if Junie were a new student in their classroom.

Francis and Ed infer that if Junie were in their class, then they would probably avoid being her friend. Ms. Stein asks them why they would make this statement.

Ed says, "Junie is always getting in trouble with Mrs., and if I were her friend, I probably would be in trouble with her too."

Ms. Stein asks, "Why do you think that's true, Ed?"

Ed replies, "It seems that on every other page of the books, Junie is doing something that attracts her teacher's attention, and not in a good way."

Ms. Stein says, "That's a good inference Ed and Francis. You were able to find an example in the book that makes your statement possible."

Barb and Kenneth say, "We think that if Junie were in our class, then you would probably quit before Thanksgiving."

Ms. Stein asks, "Why would you make that inference?"

Barb answers, "Because she causes her teacher so much grief."

Ms. Stein asks, "Have any of your teachers ever quit in the middle of the year because students were bad? You are right that Junie misbehaves a lot, but it isn't very likely that a teacher would quit in the middle of the year over one student's behavior."

After each group reports an inference, Ms. Stein ends the lesson by saying, "You did a good job overall today with inferring. It is really important to remember that you need to find places in the book that give you some evidence, but your inference also needs to make sense. Since we can't create a real Junie B. Jones and put her in our class, we can never really know how our inferences would turn out, but most of you were able to make really good inferences and support them with examples from the books."

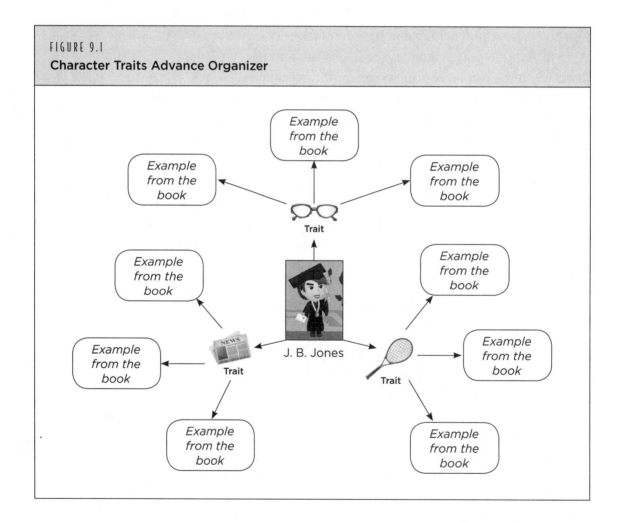

FIGURE 9.1
Character Traits Advance Organizer

Deductive reasoning, on the other hand, is the process of using generalizations and principles to infer unstated conclusions about specific information or situations. In other words, it is the process of using general statements to come to conclusions about specific information or situations. Deductive reasoning is used to help students develop the ability to transfer knowledge from one situation to another and apply general principles to specific situations. The mental process for deductive reasoning is as follows:

1. What specific topic am I studying?
2. What general information do I already know that might help me understand my specific topic?
3. Am I sure the general information applies to the specific topic I am studying?
4. If it does, how does the general information help me understand the specific topic?

In the following example, note how two teachers both are teaching the same principle—one with an inductive approach and the other with a deductive approach.

Both Ms. Winslow and Ms. Pine are teaching their students about the principle of buoyancy in their physics classes. Ms. Winslow decides to use an inductive approach and has her students add oil, milk, and ice to three separate beakers of water. She asks her students to observe what happens as they add their items to the three beakers and to generate hypotheses based on these discovered principles. Ms. Pine decides to use a deductive approach. She teaches her students about Archimedes' principle—"Any floating object displaces its own weight of fluid. Any object, wholly or partially immersed in a fluid, is buoyed up by a force equal to the weight of the fluid displaced by the object." With this knowledge as a basis, she has her students generate a hypothesis using the three beakers and the oil, milk, and ice. After they write their hypotheses in their science journals, they test their hypotheses by putting each item in a beaker and observing what occurs.

Why This Strategy?

Many teachers hear the phrase "generating and testing hypotheses" and immediately think of this category of strategies as something specific to the science classroom. The truth is that students engage in this process in many content areas (Bottge, Rueda, & Skivington, 2006; Simons & Klein, 2007; Ward & Lee, 2004). We might refer to hypothesizing by different names in other content areas—predicting, inferring, deducing, or theorizing—but the mental processes used are the same. When students create thesis statements, make predictions based on evidence, or consider the consequences of a certain action, they are using the process of generating and testing hypotheses.

The following recommendations provide guidance for teachers as they help students develop an understanding of this category of strategies. Teachers are encouraged to help students by providing structures that guide them through the process of generating hypotheses and making predictions:

1. **Engage students in a variety of structured tasks for generating and testing hypotheses.** A variety of tasks helps provide a context for students to generate and test hypotheses. These tasks may include processes such as systems analysis, problem solving, experimental inquiry, and investigation.

2. **Ask students to explain their hypotheses and their conclusions.** Asking students to explain the principles from which they work, the hypotheses they generate from these principles, and why their hypotheses make sense helps students deepen their understanding of the principles they are applying.

Reflecting on My Current Practice

The questions listed in Figure 9.2 are provided as a means to assist you as you implement the instructional practices for generating and testing hypotheses.

FIGURE 9.2

Reflecting on Current Practice: Generating and Testing Hypotheses

1. Do I intentionally have students use inductive or deductive reasoning when they generate hypotheses?

2. When students are engaged in inductive reasoning, do I monitor for and correct misconceptions?

3. Do I intentionally have students explain their thinking and justify their conclusions?

4. Do I explicitly teach the steps of systems analysis, problem solving, experimental inquiry, and investigation to my students?

5. Do I model the processes of systems analysis, problem solving, experimental inquiry, and investigation for my students?

6. Do I provide minilessons to help students better understand the individual steps of each strategy, how to develop a good hypothesis or prediction, and how to write a good explanation of their conclusions?

7. Do I use familiar content to teach the strategies of generating and testing hypotheses?

8. Do I provide students with useful and relevant graphic organizers to help them frame their thinking?

9. Do I provide guidance as my students generate and test their hypotheses?

Bringing the Strategy to Life in the Classroom

Recommendation One:
Engage students in a variety of structured tasks for generating and testing hypotheses.

Engaging students in a variety of tasks helps provide a context for them to generate and test hypotheses. These tasks include the processes of systems analysis, problem solving, experimental inquiry, and investigation. Two other processes, decision making and invention, are inherently part of problem solving. For example, as students complete the steps of problem solving, they must determine which solution is best. Invention requires the determination of a solution to meet a specific need or make improvements, a process similar to overcoming the constraints in a problem.

To ensure students' success with systems analysis, problem solving, experimental inquiry, and investigation, teachers should

- Model the processes for students.
- Use familiar content to teach the steps of the processes.
- Provide students with useful and relevant graphic organizers.
- Give students guidance as needed.

As we discussed in Chapter 1, it is important for students to focus not only on the "what" but also on the "why" of an activity. Be sure your students aren't so involved in an activity that they lose sight of the learning that is happening. As teachers intentionally incorporate the four processes of generating and testing hypotheses into lesson design and delivery, they provide opportunities for students to employ critical-thinking skills, to work collaboratively with peers, and to engage in oral discourse as they describe their learning and thinking. Explicit use of each of these strategies equips students with a mechanism for extending and applying their knowledge. We will look at each of the four processes—systems analysis, problem solving, experimental inquiry, and investigation—for generating and testing hypotheses and provide a classroom context for each.

Systems analysis. Systems analysis is the process of analyzing the parts of a system and the manner in which they interact. The steps in the process of systems analysis are as follows:

- Explain the purpose of the system, the parts of the system, and the function of each part.
- Describe how the parts affect one another.

- Identify a part of the system, describe a change in that part, and then hypothesize what would happen as a result of this change.
- When possible, test your hypothesis by actually changing the part or by using a simulation to change the part.

In the following vignette, see how Ms. Nunn uses familiar content as she teaches her students about systems analysis.

Ms. Nunn wants her 5th graders to look at literature from a systems analysis perspective. Because she had learned that, in order to teach students a process, she should begin with familiar content, she decides to use *The Three Little Pigs* to introduce the process. Ms. Nunn gives her students an advance organizer (Figure 9.3) to help them learn the relationships among the characters. She has her students work in groups of four and reread the story, taking notes about the main attributes of each character.

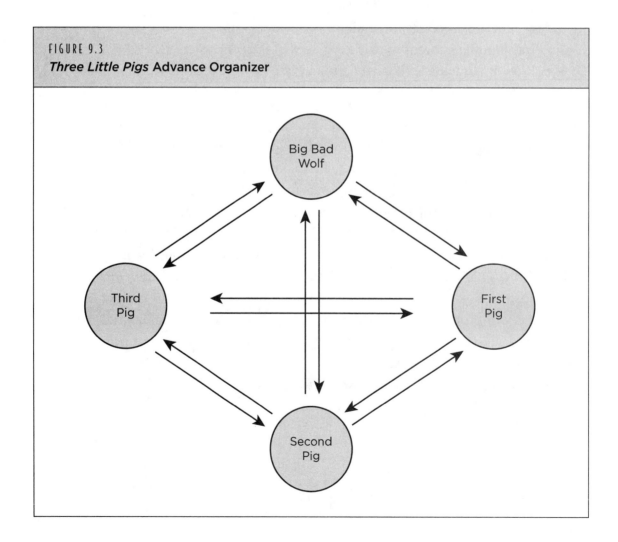

FIGURE 9.3
***Three Little Pigs* Advance Organizer**

After her students have a chance to gain a clear understanding of how the characters interact and how they are related, she tells the class that the story is a system and each character in the story is part of that system. She asks each small group to decide on one part (character) of the system (story) they are going to change and then rewrite the story, showing how that one change could affect the entire story. "As an example," Ms. Nunn says, "what if the wolf isn't alone? Maybe it is a pack of wolves. How might that change the story?"

The students get to work and think about what one thing they can change in the story. One group moves the setting of the story into a forest where the trees offer protection from wind. Another group decides that the second pig is a math whiz and knows how to use triangles to give his cottage more strength. A third group decides that the wolf has asthma. Each of the groups rewrites the fairy tale with the one change and shares it with the class. The teacher then shares Jon Scieszka and Lane Smith's *The True Story of the Three Little Pigs* so students can experience another version in which the wolf is not an antagonist.

"Now, as we move from our language arts block to our social studies block, let's use this same systems analysis process to look at the U.S. government," Ms. Nunn says. "We have learned about the three branches of the U.S. government: the executive, legislative, and judicial. The government is the system, and each branch is a part of the system. Using what we have learned, how would a change in one part of the system change the overall system?"

Problem Solving. Problem solving involves overcoming constraints or limiting conditions that are in the way of achieving goals. The steps in problem solving include the following:

- Identify the goal you are trying to accomplish.
- Describe the barriers or constraints that are preventing you from achieving your goal or are creating the problem.
- Identify different solutions for overcoming the barriers or constraints and hypothesize which solution is likely to work.
- Try your solution, either in reality or through a simulation.
- Explain whether your hypothesis was correct. Determine if you want to test another hypothesis using a different solution. In some cases, this may involve building or designing an invention.

In the following vignette, see how Mr. Norman's advanced design students use the strategy of problem solving as they design and realize a mural for their school.

The Springfield school board requested that the art department at the high school create a mural on the front wall of the new auditorium to welcome visitors. The school board provided a budget of $6,000 for the project and instructed the art department to produce an outstanding mural that represents the school by the end of the school year. Mr. Norman, the art department chair, meets with his advanced design students and presents the project and its constraints to them. He reminds them that the mural will be welcoming visitors for years to come. It is very likely that their own children will one day see this work when they are high school students.

Mr. Norman begins with the project's parameters:

- The work has to be completed and on the wall by June 1.
- The school board has provided $6,000.
- The work needs to welcome visitors and "shout" school pride.
- Initial design sketches and budget estimates are due in two weeks, when the class will decide which design will be presented to the board for approval.

He divides the class into three cooperative learning groups based on their artistic skills and expertise. One group is charged with creating a design that uses acrylic paints. Another group focuses on a design that uses ceramic tiles. The third group works on a design that uses mixed media. Each group gets to work immediately. They work in cooperative teams, and each group has students working on budget estimates, performing site reviews, and researching similar projects.

At the end of the two-week planning and design phase, the class meets to review the three plans. Though all three are very well received by both Mr. Norman and the class, the proposed design done in ceramic tiles is the hands-down favorite. There is a problem though. The estimated budget for the ceramic mural is just over $12,000, double the allotted budget.

Using the problem-solving process they had been taught in other classes, the students begin to identify barriers to solving this problem. Clearly, the budget is the biggest barrier. There is also a question about the weight of the mural and the students' ability to complete the work on schedule. They begin by looking at the easier issues to address: the weight of the mural and the timeframe. They ask architects about the weight issue and are told that to properly hold the weight of a ceramic mural of that size, either the wall needs to be reinforced or the mural needs to have additional supports from the ceiling and floor.

One possible solution to the schedule barrier is to make the mural smaller, which would require fewer tiles and therefore save time and also reduce weight. Another possible solution is to use larger tiles. A third solution is to involve two other classes to work under their direction and help with tile installation.

Finally, they look at the budget problem. Four possible solutions are proposed. They can go back to the school board, show them how amazing the mural would be, and ask them to double the budget. They can launch a massive schoolwide fundraiser, even though the school has just finished raising $30,000 to fund the instrumental music program. They can go to various vendors and ask for a greatly reduced price on materials. They can approach businesses that are run by school alumni and ask for donations.

The students look at each of the possible solutions and decide that their best course of action is to keep the mural's original size and provide additional supports from both the ceiling and floor. They will bring in students from additional classes to provide the labor needed to complete the project on time, and they will generate the additional funding necessary by going to alumni. As a result, they are able to work within an increased budget and complete the mural on time.

In this example, students identify the barriers that might prevent them from accomplishing their goal. They look at possible ways to overcome each barrier, and they decide which of the possible solutions is best to help them meet their goal. Ultimately, they produce a high-quality product, both on time and within budget. They recognize that the strategy they learned in their other classes had other applications in the classroom and the "real world."

Experimental inquiry. Experimental inquiry is the process of generating and testing explanations of observed phenomena. The steps in experimental inquiry include the following:

- Observe something of interest to you and describe what you observe.
- Apply specific theories or rules to what you have observed.
- Based on your explanation, generate a hypothesis to predict what would happen if you applied the theories or rules to what you observed or to a situation related to what you observed.
- Set up an experiment or engage in an activity to test your hypothesis.
- Explain the results of your experiment or activity. Decide if your hypothesis was correct and if you need to conduct additional experiments or activities or if you need to generate and test an alternative hypothesis to answer your question(s).

In the following vignette, note how Ms. Rose engages her students in experimental inquiry as they learn how diseases spread.

Ms. Rose's 7th grade life science class is learning how diseases spread within a population. She has taught them that bacteria, viruses, parasitic worms, and other pathogens can all invade the body and cause disease. In order to be successful, though, pathogens must be able to move from one host to another. "Every year at this time, we hear news reports about a new strain of influenza and how the virus spreads in the population," she explains. "Today, we will explore how population density affects the spread of influenza."

Ms. Rose has pairs of students hypothesize how an increase or decrease in population density would impact the rate of disease spread. "How long will it take for five people to become infected if we vary the total number of people in the room?" she asks. First, the students create a simple graphic organizer that will help them track their predictions for three situations and then enter their hypotheses on a chart (Figure 9.4). Next, each pair conducts the experiment using an online simulation. Finally, they record the actual time it takes for five people to become infected in each scenario as it plays out through a simulation.

After they complete the data collection, Ms. Rose asks, "What trend do you see in the data, and how would you explain it?"

Jackie and Zach are working together. They hypothesize that the greater the population density, the faster the disease will spread. After they run the simulation, they look at their data against their hypothesis. They see a big difference in the amount of time it takes to infect 15 as opposed to 25 people but a much smaller change between 25 and 35 people. Their observation

FIGURE 9.4
Disease Spread Chart

Number of People	Predicted Time Required to Infect Five People (hr)	Time Required to Infect Five People (hr)
15	19	16.2
25	13	7.6
35	9	6.4

is that their hypothesis is pretty solid. There seems to be a tipping point at which the disease begins to spread quickly. The conclusion they reach is that avoiding large crowds is one way to at least cut down on the likelihood of a disease spreading.

Investigation. Investigation is the process of identifying and resolving issues regarding past or current events about which there are confusions or contradictions. The steps in investigation include the following:

- Clearly identify the situation (i.e., concept to be defined, historical event to be explained, hypothetical future event to be defined or explained).
- Identify what is already known or agreed upon.
- Offer a hypothetical scenario, based on what you understand and know about the situation.
- Seek out and analyze evidence to determine if your hypothetical scenario is plausible.

In the following vignette, see how Mr. Adams uses investigation to deepen his students' understanding of a complex economic event.

Mr. Adams takes the opportunity to engage his 10th grade world history students in an investigation about the causes of the Great Depression. The class discusses events leading up to the Depression, and Mr. Adams presents some of the commonly held views about the cause. He explains that historical economists are split into three camps, and each camp maintains that they have identified the primary causal factor of the Great Depression. The primary causes Mr. Adams presents are the following:

- The decline in investment spending. Proponents of this theory believe people invested less and saved more, so investment fell short of savings, causing the level of public income to fall. As a result, consumers spent less, so businesses produced less and, in turn, cut workers' pay or laid off workers. As workers made less or lost their jobs, they spent even less, and so on, creating a downward spiral of income and spending.
- The high tariff passed during the Hoover administration. A summary of this argument is that the United States passed a tax on goods imported from other countries, but, at the same time, the United States was making loans to those same countries and trying to export our goods to them. As a result, other countries imposed high taxes on U.S. exports. Those countries could not make enough money to buy U.S. products or pay back their loans.

- Poor monetary policy. Some economists believe that the federal government interfered too much with the country's money supply (monetary policy) to keep the prices on goods from falling. Economists who support this argument think the government did not give the economy time to self-correct.

Although Mr. Adams doesn't expect his class to resolve a disagreement that economic historians have debated for years, he thinks the investigation will help his students gain a deeper understanding of the historical issues and economic concepts related to the Great Depression. Mr. Adams intentionally places students in cooperative groups of six students. Within each cooperative group, students divide into pairs, and each pair is assigned one of the possible causes. They are to use the textbook and a selection of Internet resources to provide evidence that supports their assigned cause as the primary reason for the Great Depression.

After pairs research their cause for the remainder of that class, he tells them that they will be working in three large expert groups during the next class. The purpose of that class is to compare information and build the most compelling case to support their argument. At the end of the second class, the cooperative groups reassemble, and each pair of students presents their argument within their cooperative group. Finally, students vote on which cause they think has the best supporting evidence.

Mr. Adams stresses that there really is no agreed-upon right or wrong answer to the primary cause of the Great Depression. The purpose of this activity is to learn about the topic much more deeply by exploring in depth each of the possible causes through the strategy of investigation.

Recommendation Two:
Ask students to explain their hypotheses and their conclusions.

Asking students to explain the principles from which they work, the hypotheses they generate from these principles, and why their hypotheses make sense helps students deepen their understanding of the principles they are applying (Darling-Hammond et al., 2008; Lavoie, 1999; Lavoie & Good, 1988; Lawson, 1988; Pitler, Hubbell, Kuhn, & Malenoski, 2007; Tweed, 2009). It is very important to have the students not only engage in the process of creating a hypotheses and conclusion but also explain why they think what they think.

Designing assignments so students have to describe how they generated their hypotheses and explain what they learned as a result of testing helps students focus on these important aspects of the process and increases their ability to use the process. It helps keep the focus on the learning and not just on the activity. To accomplish this, teachers should do the following:

- Provide students with templates for reporting their work, highlighting the areas in which they are expected to provide explanations.
- Provide sentence frames for students (especially young students) that help them articulate their explanations.
- Ask students to create audio recordings in which they explain their hypotheses and conclusions.
- Provide or collaboratively develop rubrics that identify the criteria on which students will be evaluated.
- Provide opportunities for students to create graphic organizers that help them make sense of the material.
- Establish events at which parents or community members can ask students to explain their thinking.

In the following vignette, Ms. Villalpando has students explain their hypotheses and why their conclusions are right or wrong. As you read this vignette, note how frequently the teacher corrects misconceptions and asks students to explain their rationale.

Ms. Villalpando is teaching her 4th grade students about density. She begins the lesson by asking her students to predict if a closed can of soda will sink or float when placed in an aquarium of water. The students discuss the problem in their table groups, and then Ms. Villalpando records their votes. About one-third of the students think the can will float, and the rest say it will sink.

"Someone who said the can will sink, explain your thinking," says the teacher.

Paul replies, "At our table, we said it would sink for two reasons. One is that the can is made of metal and should be heavy. The other reason is that the can is sealed and there is no air in it."

The teacher says, "I would like someone to tell me why they predicted the can would float."

"Well," Amanda replies, "We thought the can would float because of all of the air bubbles you see in soda when you pour it. I thought that air would make the can float." Other students nod in agreement.

Ms. Villalpando then performs the experiment, and the soda can quickly sinks to the bottom of the tank.

"We see that the can sank," observes the teacher. "Amanda's group thought the can would float because of all of the air bubbles in soda. That's a good thought, but those bubbles are only released after you open the can and release the pressure. Let's try one more experiment and see if that helps us with our understanding. This time, predict if a can of diet soda will sink or float. The can contains exactly the same amount of soda. At your tables, decide if it will sink or float and why."

This time, the vote is almost unanimous. All but two students predict the can will sink. "Why do you believe the can will sink?" she asks.

"Our table thinks that because both cans contain 12 ounces of soda, both are sealed, and since the first can sank, then the second one will too," says James.

"All right," says Ms. Villalpando. "Let's hear from someone who predicts the can will float. Why will this one float when the other one sank?"

Jacque replies, "I think this sounds silly, but Willow and I thought that the can will float because it is diet and not regular. Somehow diet is lighter than regular maybe?"

"Let's do the experiment and see," replies the teacher as she places the can of diet soda into the aquarium. Most of the class is surprised to see the can of diet soda float to the top of the tank.

"Most of you predicted that the can would sink. Why was your prediction incorrect?" asks the teacher.

"Is it possible that Jacque is right? Does diet soda just weigh less? I mean, 12 ounces is 12 ounces, right?" asks Andrew.

"Andrew, you are making a common error," explains Ms. Villalpando. "Soda is measured as a liquid, not as a solid. Twelve *fluid* ounces just refers to the volume of liquid in the can, not the weight. Both of the cans each hold the same volume, but they are not necessarily the same weight. And yes, Jacque was right. This 12-ounce can of soda contains 40 grams of sugar. I know that doesn't sound like a lot, since a gram is so small, but 40 grams of sugar is about the same as 17 of those sugar packets you see in restaurants. It was that extra weight that caused the soda to sink, while the diet soda, which contains zero grams of sugar, floated."

Rubrics and Checklists

The teacher rubric provided in Figure 9.5 is intended to be a tool used for reflection on the way in which you currently generate and test hypotheses in your classroom. The rubric is designed so that a 3 represents best practice as indicated by the research. A 4 indicates both teacher best practice as described in a 3 and how that practice transfers into student behaviors. You can also use this rubric as a growth tool, seeing where you are now and what the next level might look like. This will provide you with valuable information as you build your professional growth plan.

Using the teacher rubric will allow you to reflect on your practice. You can also ask your students how they perceive the way you teach them to generate and test hypotheses. Figure 9.6 provides a student checklist you might want to use. Periodically give this checklist to your students, and ask them to react honestly to the statements. This checklist can help your students better understand how generating and testing hypotheses helps them learn and deepen their understanding, and it can provide valuable feedback to you about how your students view the process of generating and testing hypotheses.

Tools, Templates, and Protocols

If you are using this handbook as part of a school PLC or book study, Figure 9.7 provides statements that can serve as discussion prompts. Likewise, if you are using this book for individual growth, think about these prompts as they relate to your classroom practice. For example, if your answer to the first statement is a 0 or 1, then what steps should you take to move toward the other end of the spectrum, "to a great extent"? Use your individual or team results from Figure 9.7 to form the basis of a professional growth plan (see Figure 9.8).

FIGURE 9.5

Teacher Rubric: Generating and Testing Hypotheses

Engage students in a variety of structured tasks for generating and testing hypotheses. *A variety of tasks helps provide a context for students to generate and test hypotheses. These tasks include processes such as systems analysis, problem solving, experimental inquiry, and investigation.*

4	3	2	1
I consistently engage students in a variety of structured tasks for systems analysis, problem solving, experimental inquiry, and investigation. My students can identify which process they are using for each structured task.	I consistently engage students in a variety of structured tasks for systems analysis, problem solving, experimental inquiry, and investigation.	I occasionally engage students in a variety of structured tasks for systems analysis, problem solving, experimental inquiry, and investigation.	I seldom engage students in a variety of structured tasks for systems analysis, problem solving, experimental inquiry, and investigation.
I consistently teach the steps in systems analysis, problem solving, experimental inquiry, and investigation to my students. My students can explain the steps for each process.	I consistently teach the steps in systems analysis, problem solving, experimental inquiry, and investigation to my students.	I occasionally teach the steps in systems analysis, problem solving, experimental inquiry, and investigation to my students.	I seldom teach the steps in systems analysis, problem solving, experimental inquiry, and investigation to my students.
I consistently model the processes of systems analysis, problem solving, experimental inquiry, and investigation for my students. My students can independently follow the steps for generating and testing hypotheses.	I consistently model the processes of systems analysis, problem solving, experimental inquiry, and investigation for my students.	I occasionally model the processes of systems analysis, problem solving, experimental inquiry, and investigation for my students.	I seldom model the processes of systems analysis, problem solving, experimental inquiry, and investigation for my students.

FIGURE 9.5

Teacher Rubric: Generating and Testing Hypotheses *(continued)*

4	3	2	1
I consistently provide opportunities for my students to use inductive and deductive reasoning while generating and testing hypotheses. My students understand the difference between inductive and deductive reasoning.	I consistently provide opportunities for my students to use inductive and deductive reasoning while generating and testing hypotheses.	I occasionally provide opportunities for my students to use inductive and deductive reasoning while generating and testing hypotheses.	I seldom provide opportunities for my students to use inductive and deductive reasoning while generating and testing hypotheses.
When using inductive reasoning, I consistently monitor for and correct misconceptions. My students use my feedback to clarify their thinking.	When using inductive reasoning, I consistently monitor for and correct misconceptions.	When using inductive reasoning, I occasionally monitor for and correct misconceptions.	When using inductive reasoning, I seldom monitor for and correct misconceptions.
I consistently provide appropriate graphic organizers to help my students organize and interpret their thinking. My students understand how to use the provided graphic organizers to guide their thinking.	I consistently provide appropriate graphic organizers to help my students organize and interpret their thinking.	I occasionally provide appropriate graphic organizers to help my students organize and interpret their thinking.	I seldom provide appropriate graphic organizers to help my students organize and interpret their thinking.

FIGURE 9.5

Teacher Rubric: Generating and Testing Hypotheses (continued)

Ask students to explain their hypotheses and their conclusions. *Asking students to explain the principles from which they work, the hypotheses they generate from these principles, and the reasons why their hypotheses make sense helps students deepen their understanding of the principles they are applying.*

4	3	2	1
I consistently have my students explain their hypotheses, either orally or in writing. My students are able to articulate, either orally or in writing, the principles from which they are working.	I consistently have my students explain their hypotheses, either orally or in writing.	I occasionally have my students explain their hypotheses, either orally or in writing.	I seldom have my students explain their hypotheses, either orally or in writing.
I consistently have my students explain their conclusions or findings. My students are able to explain their findings and explain why they were correct or incorrect.	I consistently have my students explain their conclusions or findings.	I occasionally have my students explain their conclusions or findings.	I seldom have my students explain their conclusions or findings.
I consistently make connections between the activity in which my students are engaged and the principles they are investigating. My students can explain not only what they are doing but also what they are learning.	I consistently make connections between the activity in which my students are engaged and the principles they are investigating.	I occasionally make connections between the activity in which my students are engaged and the principles they are investigating.	I seldom make connections between the activity in which my students are engaged and the principles they are investigating.

FIGURE 9.6

Student Checklist: Generating and Testing Hypotheses

		Always	Sometimes	Rarely	Never
VARIETY OF TASKS	I can identify which strategy I am using for each task or activity my teacher provides.				
	I know the steps for systems analysis, problem solving, experimental inquiry, and investigation.				
	When my teacher models generating and testing hypotheses, it helps me better understand the strategy.				
	I use the feedback my teacher provides to correct errors in my thinking.				
	I use graphic organizers provided by my teacher to help me organize my thinking.				
EXPLAIN HYPOTHESES AND CONCLUSIONS	Talking through my hypothesis helps me better understand what I am learning.				
	I am able to explain why my conclusion was right or wrong.				
	I can make the connection between what I am doing and what I am learning.				

FIGURE 9.7
Assessing Myself: Generating and Testing Hypotheses

I intentionally have students use inductive or deductive reasoning when they generate hypotheses.

Not at all   To a great extent

0	1	2	3	4

I monitor for and correct misconceptions when students are engaged in inductive reasoning.

Not at all   To a great extent

0	1	2	3	4

I intentionally have students explain their thinking and justify their conclusions.

Not at all   To a great extent

0	1	2	3	4

I explicitly teach the steps of systems analysis, problem solving, experimental inquiry, and investigation to my students.

Not at all   To a great extent

0	1	2	3	4

I model the processes of systems analysis, problem solving, experimental inquiry, and investigation for my students.

Not at all   To a great extent

0	1	2	3	4

FIGURE 9.7

Assessing Myself: Generating and Testing Hypotheses *(continued)*

I provide minilessons to help students better understand the individual steps of each strategy, how to develop a good hypothesis or prediction, and how to write a good explanation of their conclusions.

Not at all   To a great extent

0   1   2   3   4

I use familiar content to teach the strategies of generating and testing hypotheses.

Not at all   To a great extent

0   1   2   3   4

I provide students with useful and relevant graphic organizers to help them frame their thinking.

Not at all   To a great extent

0   1   2   3   4

I provide guidance as my students generate and test their hypotheses.

Not at all   To a great extent

0   1   2   3   4

FIGURE 9.8
Professional Growth Plan: Generating and Testing Hypotheses

1. How will I intentionally have students use inductive or deductive reasoning when they generate hypotheses?

2. How will I monitor for and correct misconceptions when students are engaged in inductive reasoning?

3. How will I intentionally have students explain their thinking and justify their conclusions?

4. How will I explicitly teach the steps of systems analysis, problem solving, experimental inquiry, and investigation to my students?

5. How will I model the processes of systems analysis, problem solving, experimental inquiry, and investigation for my students?

FIGURE 9.8
Professional Growth Plan: Generating and Testing Hypotheses *(continued)*

6. How will I provide minilessons to help students better understand the individual steps of each strategy, how to develop a good hypothesis or prediction, and how to write a good explanation of their conclusions?

7. How will I use familiar content to teach the strategies of generating and testing hypotheses?

8. How will I provide students with useful and relevant graphic organizers to help them frame their thinking?

9. How will I provide guidance as my students generate and test their hypotheses?

Part IV

Putting the Instructional Strategies to Use

In the foreword to *Classroom Instruction That Works* (2nd edition), John Hattie writes

> One of the key features of this book is that it is based on a conceptual model that integrates the various "bits" of teaching and learning. This allows the authors to focus on showing how and why various strategies work more effectively than others. The answer, of course, is not identifying one method and adopting that new technique; rather, it is more about developing a wider worldview, or model, of how different influences in the classroom must work together to help all students realize their learning gains. The message here is that the nine strategies of instruction presented in *Classroom Instruction That Works* are a powerful way of thinking about teaching and learning. This book highlights these instructional strategies rather than the different methods that may or may not use these strategies to various degrees. Having the flexibility to decide when and with whom to use the best strategy or mix of strategies is critical." (Dean et al., p. vii)

In the final section of this book, we will take you through an entire lesson, from the initial planning through its delivery. Follow along and see how our teacher intentionally makes decisions about instruction.

List of Figures

Chapter 10

10.1	The Framework for Instructional Planning.	304
10.2	Reflecting on Current Practice: Instructional Planning	306
10.3	District Guaranteed and Viable Curriculum	309
10.4	Lesson Plan	310
10.5	Demonstration Graph	312
10.6	Ms. Dempsey's Walk to the Office	313
10.7	Race Graphs	315
10.8	Assessing Myself: Instructional Planning	317
10.9	Professional Growth Plan: Instructional Planning	319

10

Instructional Planning Using the Nine Categories of Strategies

Instructional Planning

The instructional strategies presented in the previous chapters are like instruments in an orchestra. Each has its own characteristics, contributes to the orchestra in particular ways, and must be masterfully played both alone and in combination with other instruments to obtain the desired effect. The orchestra's conductor must know when to emphasize each of the instruments and how to bring out their particular qualities in order to accomplish the purpose of the music. An orchestra sounds best when the composer selects the most appropriate instruments and the conductor blends those instruments in just the right way to create the desired sound. To be skilled conductors of instruction, teachers must intentionally select the best mix of instructional strategies to meet the diverse needs of students in their classrooms.

As we described in Chapter 8, using a metaphor to connect prior knowledge with new learning is a powerful instructional tool. To be skilled in creating a lesson, teachers must intentionally select the best mix of instructional strategies to meet the diverse learning needs of students, just as a good coach must use different members of his or her volleyball team in various capacities. The coach must know when and how to emphasize a particular skill from each player. He or she matches skills in just the right way to create the desired outcome. Classroom teachers who are strategic in the selection and placement of instructional strategies provide a learning environment ripe for student success. In this chapter, we provide guidance for intentionally selecting and using the strategies for effective lesson design and delivery.

Why This Chapter?

This chapter provides explicit guidance to teachers as they work to accomplish the goal of helping all students succeed. The information in this chapter addresses the components of the instructional planning framework (Figure 10.1) and the intentional use of the nine categories of strategies to increase the probability of student success. It provides a process for teachers to follow as they put the information from the first nine chapters into practice. The practical application of the instructional strategies from the nine categories lays a foundation for designing intentional instruction for students at every grade level and within all content areas.

The first steps to lesson design require you to apply the three categories of instructional strategies found in the first component—Creating the Environment for Learning. The categories of setting objectives and providing feedback, reinforcing effort and providing recognition, and cooperative learning form the basis of every lesson designed and delivered over the course of the academic year. No lesson should be crafted without careful consideration

---

FIGURE 10.1
The Framework for Instructional Planning

Creating the Environment for Learning

| Setting Objectives and Providing Feedback | Reinforcing Effort and Providing Recognition | Cooperative Learning |

Helping Students Develop Understanding

Cues, Questions, and Advance Organizers

Nonlinguistic Representations

Summarizing and Note Taking

Assigning Homework and Providing Practice

Helping Students Extend and Apply Knowledge

Identifying Similarities and Differences

Generating and Testing Hypotheses

of the aforementioned strategies. The intentional application of each allows you to create a positive environment for student learning that is built on the research base described in the earlier chapters. Creating this positive environment increases the chance for students to say "yes" when they ask themselves, "Can I do the work?" and "Will I be accepted?"

After you have ensured that these three categories are in place, decisions must be made regarding which of the remaining strategies from the second and third components will best facilitate the next steps in student learning. This is the artistry of lesson design—utilizing the appropriate strategies at the appropriate time.

The next section of this chapter provides questions that will guide your lesson design. The following section contains a model lesson that will help you recognize how decisions are made as strategies are applied. As in previous chapters, the final section allows you to check your understanding against a set of questions and use that information to establish a professional plan.

Reflecting on My Current Practice

The questions listed in Figure 10.2 are provided as a means to assist you as you apply the information from the first nine chapters of this book into your lesson design and delivery.

FIGURE 10.2
Reflecting on Current Practice: Instructional Planning

1. Do I use information from the Common Core or state standards as a guide for my lesson design?

2. Do I identify the declarative and procedural knowledge found within the standards?

3. Do I intentionally plan to move my students to higher levels of cognitive complexity?

4. Is there a logical scope and sequence to the lessons I design?

5. Do I take into consideration the prerequisite knowledge that students must have when I design lessons?

6. Do my lessons reflect a differentiated approach through the types of questions asked, the level of cognitive demand, and the application of nonlinguistic representations and/or reciprocal teaching?

7. Do I explicitly ask students to use their prior knowledge acquired in previous lessons/units of study?

8. Do I intentionally provide adequate time for my students to practice the skills they are learning?

9. Do I provide a gradual release of information and responsibility (scaffolding) over the course of the lesson?

Bringing Instruction to Life in the Classroom

In the previous chapters, we discussed the components of the framework and described each of the strategies independently. Here, we will take a look inside a teacher's head as she plans her instruction. Share in her thought processes and the decisions she makes. Notice how the teacher intentionally brings various strategies into play to provide good instruction and support student learning.

The lesson in this scenario, Integrating Time/Distance Graphs, is a 6th grade mathematics lesson that will serve as the vehicle to illustrate the thought processes and decisions that must be made as a lesson is designed.

As she sits down to plan her lesson, Ms. Dempsey reviews her scope and sequence from the district's guaranteed and viable curriculum guide (Figure 10.3). She sees that the upcoming unit in mathematics will focus on the Common Core State Standard of representing and analyzing quantitative relations between dependent and independent variables. Prior to applying the strategies from the first component, the teacher reviews the information contained in the Common Core State Standards and clusters for mathematics and determines what students must know, understand, and be able to do upon completion of the lesson.

After reviewing the Common Core State Standards, Ms. Dempsey pulls out the embedded prerequisite skills. She asks herself, 'Do my students understand what a variable is, what slope indicates, how to use graphs, and how to analyze real-world problems?' She determines that all but four of her students have shown mastery of the prerequisite skills for this unit and are ready to move on. Ms. Dempsey knows that she will need to create additional learning opportunities for the four students who have not yet reached mastery. In order to help them, she selects appropriate lessons from the Khan Academy website (www.khanacademy.org) to provide additional guided practice that will help them acquire the needed prerequisites.

As Ms. Dempsey begins to plan instruction, she analyzes the types of knowledge and cognitive complexity outlined in the Common Core State Standards for Mathematics. She knows that it is important to identify the declarative and procedural knowledge so she can best match learning objectives and instruction to types of knowledge.

In the lesson plan shown in Figure 10.4, the teacher creates objectives that reflect these two types of knowledge. The objectives listed under the "Know" heading indicate that students must have a working knowledge of independent and dependent variables—what they are and the similarities and differences between them. In addition, the objectives beneath the "Understand" heading designate those things about which students must develop deeper content knowledge. The "Be Able To" heading indicates the procedural knowledge that students must acquire and have adequate time to practice.

As Ms. Dempsey plans this lesson, she intentionally selects strategies for specific purposes. In this case, Ms. Dempsey applies what she learned about cues, questions, and advance organizers to ensure that she is designing instruction so her students are able to think at all levels of Bloom's Taxonomy. She also keeps in mind the information she learned about providing practice—students require ongoing and sustained opportunities to master a skill through the application of massed and distributed practice. Ms. Dempsey's lesson design and activities mirror best practice, giving her students the greatest chance for success.

FIGURE 10.3
District Guaranteed and Viable Curriculum

Grade Six – Mathematics

ESSENTIAL CONTENT:

COMMON CORE DOMAIN 6.EE Expressions and Equations

COMMON CORE STANDARD(S) AND CLUSTER(S):

Represent and analyze quantitative relationships between dependent and independent variables.

   CCSS.Math.Content.6.EE.C.9 Use variables to represent two quantities in a real-world problem that change in relationship to one another; write an equation to express one quantity, thought of as the dependent variable, in terms of the other quantity, thought of as the independent variable. Analyze the relationship between the dependent and independent variables using graphs and tables, and relate these to the equation. *For example, in a problem involving motion at constant speed, list and graph ordered pairs of distances and times, and write the equation d = 65t to represent the relationship between distance and time.*

MATHEMATICAL PRACTICE(S):
 • Make sense of problems and persevere in solving them.
 • Model with mathematics.

LESSON BIG IDEAS:
 • Mathematical situations and structures can be translated and represented abstractly using variables, expressions, and equations

FIGURE 10.4
Lesson Plan

Interpreting Time/Distance Graphs

LEARNING OBJECTIVES (STUDENT-FRIENDLY)

We will:

Know
  • independent variable (identify and provide basic description)
  • dependent variable (identify and provide basic description)

Understand
  • A change in one variable may (or may not) be related to a change in the second variable.
  • A graph shows the relationship of one quantity to another.
  • The shape of a graph helps us understand the nature of the change.

Be Able To
  • Interpret time and distance (position) graphs and communicate ideas verbally and in writing.

VOCABULARY:
  • independent variable – identify and provide basic description
    - answers the question "What do I change?"
  • dependent variable – identify and provide basic description
    - answers the question "What do I observe?"
  • rate of change

MATERIALS/RESOURCES:
  • motion detector
  • graph paper
  • practice handouts: graphs to stories and stories to graphs
  • poster board to use with motion detector
  • teacher-prepared notes

Ms. Dempsey knows that effort is an often overlooked strategy that is essential to the full development of an environment for learning. She works hard to intentionally place stories and examples of what it means and looks like to work hard within almost every lesson she creates. She also knows it is important for her students to have a clear understanding of what effort means to them personally. As a means of maintaining a consistent message about effort, Ms. Dempsey calls attention to the mathematical practices listed on her teacher-prepared notes and asks her students to share stories of how perseverance has played a role in their prior mathematics lessons. She engages students in conversations about what effort will look like in this lesson and how effort impacts their learning. Finally, she has students use the student checklist from page 54 in this book as an additional advance organizer for the discussion.

After appropriately using the strategies to create an environment for learning, Ms. Dempsey then plans instruction to help students develop understanding and extend and apply their knowledge. Let's now follow Ms. Dempsey as she delivers a 90-minute lesson.

As Ms. Dempsey's students walk into the classroom, they see the learning objectives for the period written on the board. Ms. Dempsey reviews with her students what they should know, understand, and be able to do by the end of the period. Knowing the importance of oral discourse, Ms. Dempsey asks her students to discuss the objectives with their table partners. Groups are instructed to write any questions that come up during the discussion so they can be answered when the large group reconvenes at the end of class.

Ms. Dempsey reminds her students of a previous lesson in which they worked with the concept of slope and how difficult it was for some. She reminds them that several teams had to keep working in order to complete the assignments, and because they stuck with the assignments, they were ultimately successful. Ms. Dempsey says, "Remember that math doesn't come easily to some of us, but if we put in the effort and keep trying, then everyone is capable of learning math. Remember the story that I told you about how I wanted to give up when I was learning fractions in 4th grade. Even though I struggled at first, I didn't quit, and now I love math. I want you to do the same."

As a means of immediately engaging her students in the learning and activating their prior knowledge, she provides the following cue: "Estimate how long it will take me to walk 20 feet across the classroom if I walk at a steady pace." After calling on several pairs of students, a class average time is established.

Ms. Dempsey then asks, "How long will it take me to walk 200 feet down the hallway to the cafeteria at the same steady pace?" Once again, students contribute their thinking, and a second class average is established.

She creates a graph using the data points from the two examples (Figure 10.5). Then she explains the steady pace (rate) is a constant, so the line on the graph is at a constant slope. Ms. Dempsey tells her students that the time it takes to travel across the room or down the hall is the independent variable.

The distance traveled is the dependent variable. This means that the dependent variable (distance) on the *y*-axis depends on the independent variable (time) on the *x*-axis. In this example, there is a steady pace so the slope of the line is constant.

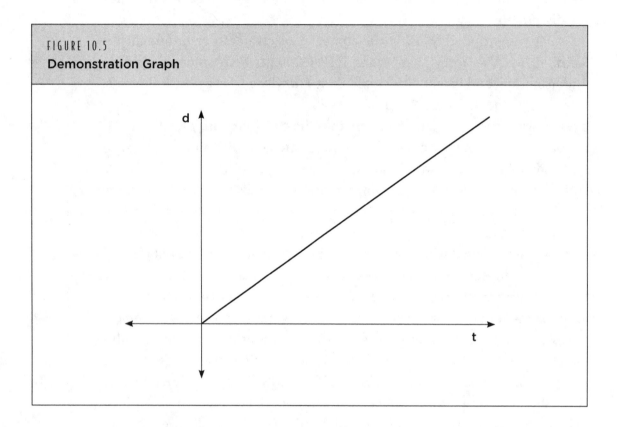

FIGURE 10.5
Demonstration Graph

Ms. Dempsey asks her students to come up with real-life examples of dependent and independent variables where a change in one causes a change in the other. After some discussion among table teams, one student reports, "We remember that when we attended Coach Moore's summer weight-lifting program, he had us chart the effort we applied as we lifted every day. The *x*-axis was the effort we applied day by day, and the *y*-axis was the amount of weight could lift. Over the three weeks, most of us were able to lift a lot more weight than we could at the beginning. We think the effort we applied is the independent variable and the amount of weight is the dependent variable." Ms. Dempsey provides recognition by saying, "That is a really good and specific example of independent and dependent variables."

Ms. Dempsey then says, "Remember, we use graphs as a nonlinguistic representation of the things we observe and explain. When you look at a graph, you can hypothesize what happened. What hypothesis or story can you create to explain this graph of my walk from our classroom to the office? After today's activity, you will be asked to check your hypothesis and explain why it was correct or incorrect." (See Figure 10.6.)

She continues, "Today we are going to explore how graphs can tell a story and how stories can be expressed as graphs using dependent and independent variables."

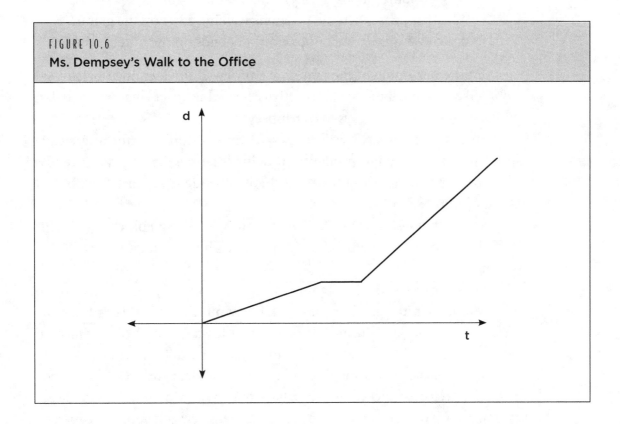

FIGURE 10.6
Ms. Dempsey's Walk to the Office

Ms. Dempsey has her students move into cooperative groups, and she reminds them that one of the important roles for everyone in the group is to ensure that each member knows the information by the end of the activity. She quickly reviews what they have learned about using a motion detector and asks them to use the detector to graph each of the following situations:

- One student walks at a constant rate toward the motion detector.
- The same student walks at a faster constant rate toward the detector.
- A student walks at a constant rate away from the detector.
- A student stands in one place in front of the detector.

Students work in their cooperative groups to create graphs for each of the four situations, making sure to identify the dependent and independent variables on the proper axis. Once the graphs are completed, Ms. Dempsey passes out clarifying questions for students to use as they deepen their understanding of the concepts:

- Why are some motion graphs steeper than others?
- What generalization can be made about the steepness of the graph and motion?
- Why do some graphs have a horizontal segment?
- What happens when the person is walking away on the graph?
- Which variable (time or position) depends on the other variable?

"At the beginning of the period, we reviewed the learning objectives. I would like you to tell me how this activity helped us meet what was stated in our learning objectives," says Ms. Dempsey.

Troy offers, "When I walked toward the motion detector at a steady speed and saw the graph produced, it helped me see that the distance was the dependent variable and time was the independent variable. That is part of our objectives."

LaQuisha says, "I got it that when I stopped, the graph changed. This helped me see that the shape of the graph shows how the dependent variable is changing."

Ms. Dempsey says, "I am going to share a short story, and I want you to think about what the graph would look like. I put my pet turtle Ertle on the table directly in front of the motion detector. Ertle walks away from the motion detector at a turtlely pace, gets tired, and stops for a bit. He then begins walking a little faster in the same direction. Based on what we learned from the motion detector, predict what you believe that graph would look like. Create that graph by yourself and then compare your answer with your table mates."

Students work individually to complete their graphs and then discuss what they believe to be the correct answer. After asking a few tables to report out, Ms. Dempsey displays the graph that she has created. She asks students to explain to their partners why their graphs were correct or incorrect.

Ms. Dempsey says, "You did a great job predicting what a graph would look like for the story about my turtle. Now I have a story that will challenge you, but I know you can come up with the correct answers. Four athletes ran the 100-meter dash. Graph 1 displays the results of the race. The challenge is for your group to explain the order each runner finished and how they each ran the race. If everyone in your team feels confident that he or she can explain this graph, and you feel your group is ready for a bigger challenge, work from Graph 2 instead." (See Figure 10.7.)

FIGURE 10.7
Race Graphs

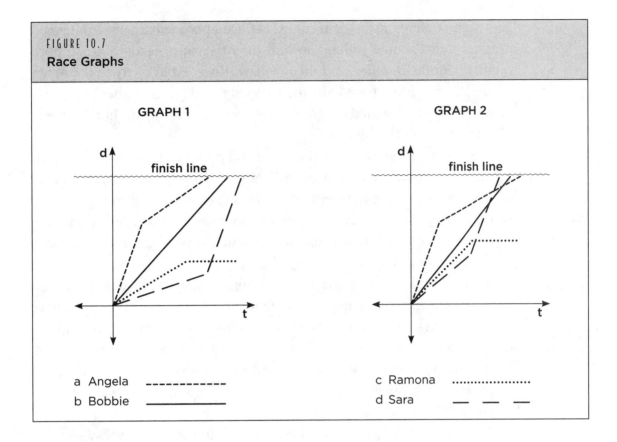

GRAPH 1

GRAPH 2

a Angela   - - - - - - - - - -
b Bobbie   _____

c Ramona   ·····················
d Sara   — — —

After the groups finish their assignment and explain their thinking, Ms. Dempsey remarks, "You have done a great job working in teams, and it appears everyone has a pretty good understanding of graphs to stories. For this next task, I would like you to work alone."

She begins, "This is a story about a mother who sent her child to the store to get milk and eggs. The child walks three blocks at a steady pace to the local convenience store. He stops at the convenience store only to discover the store is closed, so he decides to walk an additional two blocks to the market. He purchases both milk and eggs at the market and then walks directly home. Since he is carrying milk and eggs, he walks at a slower pace. Your task is to create a graph that represents this story. You are to work alone. Remember to determine the dependent and independent variables and place them on the correct axes of your graph."

"During the opening of the lesson," says Ms. Dempsey, "I asked you to create a hypothesis or story to explain the graph of my walk from our classroom to the office. We have learned a lot of good information during the past 70 minutes. Based on what we have learned, please review your story and make any corrections you believe are necessary."

After students make corrections, Ms. Dempsey tells them, "The graph indicates that I started walking toward the office at a steady pace, stopped to talk to another teacher, and then realized I needed to hurry to the office, so I walked at a faster pace." She then asks her students to let her know how accurately they interpreted the graph by giving a thumbs up or thumbs down. All students give a thumbs up.

Ms. Dempsey goes over to the board and points to the lesson objectives. "We said we would be able to identify and provide a basic description of independent and dependent variables and understand rate of change. Within your groups, go back to the questions you wrote when I asked you to talk about the objectives. Please take a few minutes in your group to make sure all your questions have been answered.

"In your math journals, explain three things you are absolutely sure you know, two things you are pretty confident you understand, and, if you have one, a lingering question that needs to be answered. When you finish writing, turn to your elbow partner and share the three things you have learned. If you think you understand one of the learning objectives better after you talked with your elbow partner, go back to your journals and make changes to your 3-2-1.

"Thank you for putting so much effort into your work today in class. Please place your math journals in the basket by the door as you leave."

Tools, Templates, and Protocols

If you are using this handbook as part of a school PLC or book study, Figure 10.8 provides statements that can serve as discussion prompts. Likewise, if you are using this book for individual growth, think about these prompts as they relate to your classroom practice. For example, if your answer to the first statement is a 0 or 1, then what steps should you take to move toward the other end of the spectrum, "to a great extent"? Use your individual or team results from Figure 10.8 to form the basis of a professional growth plan (see Figure 10.9).

FIGURE 10.8
Assessing Myself: Instructional Planning

I use information from the Common Core or state standards as a guide for my lesson design.

Not at all   To a great extent

0   1   2   3   4

I identify the declarative and procedural knowledge found within the standards.

Not at all   To a great extent

0   1   2   3   4

I intentionally plan to move my students to higher levels of cognitive complexity.

Not at all   To a great extent

0   1   2   3   4

I design a logical scope and sequence to my lessons.

Not at all   To a great extent

0   1   2   3   4

I take into consideration the prerequisite knowledge that students must have when I design lessons.

Not at all   To a great extent

0   1   2   3   4

FIGURE 10.8
Assessing Myself: Instructional Planning (continued)

My lessons reflect a differentiated approach through the types of questions asked, the level of cognitive demand, and the application of nonlinguistic representations and/or reciprocal teaching.

Not at all   To a great extent

0   1   2   3   4

I explicitly ask students to use their prior knowledge acquired in previous lessons/units of study.

Not at all   To a great extent

0   1   2   3   4

I intentionally provide adequate time for my students to practice the skills they are learning.

Not at all   To a great extent

0   1   2   3   4

I provide a gradual release of information and responsibility (scaffolding) over the course of the lesson.

Not at all   To a great extent

0   1   2   3   4

| FIGURE 10.9 |
| Professional Growth Plan: Instructional Planning |

1. How will I use information from the Common Core or state standards as a guide for my lesson design?

2. How will I identify the declarative and procedural knowledge found within the standards?

3. How will I intentionally plan to move my students to higher levels of cognitive complexity?

4. How will I ensure there is a logical scope and sequence to the lessons I design?

5. How will I take into consideration the prerequisite knowledge that students must have when I design lessons?

FIGURE 10.9
Professional Growth Plan: Instructional Planning *(continued)*

6. How will I ensure that my lessons reflect a differentiated approach through the types of questions asked, the level of cognitive demand, and the application of nonlinguistic representations and/or reciprocal teaching?

7. How will I explicitly ask students to use their prior knowledge acquired in previous lessons/units of study?

8. How will I intentionally provide adequate time for my students to practice the skills they are learning?

9. How will I provide a gradual release of information and responsibility (scaffolding) over the course of the lesson?

Conclusion

This handbook has presented suggestions for classroom practice in nine research-based categories of instructional strategies. We have provided tools and protocols so you can examine your intentional use of instructional strategies, see how they impact your students, and work with others in your school or district to implement these strategies. Ultimately, this process of testing the effectiveness of what we do and considering new ways of doing things is key to success in the classroom. Instructional strategies do not produce effective teaching. Rather, effective teaching is the byproduct of a thoughtful individual, skilled in the craft of good teaching, who makes intentional decisions about the best practice for his or her students at all times.

Handbooks such as this one are only tools. With this in mind, we encourage you to continue your exploration into the effectiveness of the instructional strategies and consider other strategies as well. If possible, involve others in your learning. Nothing is more powerful than a group of dedicated educators sharing their insights about classroom practice.

We have included examples to demonstrate how teachers might intentionally plan and use these strategies in concert and provide students with the best opportunity to be successful in the classroom. We began this book with the following: every day, when students enter the school building, they ask themselves two important questions: "Will I be accepted?" and "Can I do the work." It is our hope that, building on the information in this handbook and in *Classroom Instruction That Works* (2nd edition), you will increase the likelihood that each and every one of your students will be able to answer both of those questions every day with a resounding *yes*.

References

Alderman, M. K. (2008). *Motivation for achievement* (3rd ed.). New York: Routledge.

Anderson, J. R. (1995). *Learning and memory: An integrated approach.* New York: Wiley.

Anderson, V., & Hidi, S. (1988/1989). Teaching students to summarize. *Educational Leadership, 46,* 26–28.

Antil, L. R., Jenkins, J. R., Wayne, S. K., & Vadasy, P. F. (1998). CL: Prevalence, conceptualizations, and the relation between research and practice. *American Educational Research Journal, 35,* 419–454.

Aronson, E., Stephan, C., Stikes, J., Blaney, N., & Snapp, M. (1978). *The jigsaw classroom.* Beverly Hills, CA: Sage.

Atkinson, J. W. (1964). *An introduction to motivation.* New York: American Book-Van Nostrand-Reinhold.

Bailey, L. B., Silvern, S. B., Brabham, E., & Ross, M. (2004). The effects of interactive reading homework and parent involvement on children's inference responses. *Early Childhood Education Journal, 32*(3), 173–178.

Bandura, A. (1986). *Social foundations of thought and action: A social cognitive theory.* Englewood Cliffs, NJ: Prentice-Hall.

Bangert-Drowns, R. L., Kulik, C.-L. C., Kulik, J. A., & Morgan, M. (1991). The instructional effect of feedback in test-like events. *Review of Educational Research, 61,* 213–238.

Balli, S. J. (1998). When mom and dad help: Student reflections on parent involvement with homework. *Journal of Research and Development in Education, 31*(3), 142–148.

Balli, S. J., Demo, D. H., & Wedman, J. F. (1998). Family involvement with children's homework: An intervention in the middle grades. *Family Relations: Interdisciplinary Journal of Applied Family Studies, 47*(2), 149–157.

Beesley, A. D., & Apthorp, H. S. (Eds.). (2010). *Classroom instruction that works, second edition: Research report.* Denver, CO: Mid-continent Research for Education and Learning.

Boch, F., & Piolat, A. (2005). Note taking and learning: A summary of research. *The WAC Journal, 16,* 101–113.

Bottge, B., Rueda, E., & Skivington, M. (2006). Situating math instruction in rich problem-solving contexts: Effects on adolescents with challenging behaviors. *Behavioral Disorders, 31,* 394–407.

Bouffard, T., Boisvert, J., Vezeau, C., & Larouche, C. (1995). The impact of goal orientation on self-regulation and performance among college students. *British Journal of Educational Psychology, 65*(3), 317–330.

Bransford, J., Brown, A., & Cocking, R. (1999). *How people learn: Brain, mind, experience, and school.* Washington, DC: National Academies Press.

Bransford, J., Brown, A., & Cocking, R. (2000). *How people learn: Brain, mind, experience, and school* (Expanded ed.). Washington, DC: National Academies Press.

Broer, N., Aarnoutse, C., Kieviet, F., & van Leeuwe, J. (2002). The effects of instructing the structural aspects of text. *Educational Studies, 28*(3), 213–238.

Brookhart, S. M. (2008). *How to give effective feedback.* Alexandria, VA: ASCD.

Brophy, J. (1981). Teacher praise: A functional analysis. *Review of Educational Research, 51*(1), 26.

Brophy, J. (2004). *Motivating students to learn* (2nd ed.). Boston: McGraw-Hill.

Brown, A. L., Campione, J. C., & Day, J. D. (1981). Learning to learn: On training students to learn from text. *Educational Researcher, 10*, 14–21.

Chen, Z. (1999). Schema induction in children's analogical problem solving. *Journal of Educational Psychology, 91*(4), 703–715.

Clark, J., & Paivio, A. (1991). Dual coding theory and education. *Educational Psychology Review, 3*, 149–210.

Cohen, E. (1994). *Designing group work: Strategies for the heterogeneous classroom.* New York: Teachers College Press.

Cooper, H., Lindsay, J. J., Nye, B., & Greathouse, S. (1998). Relationships among attitudes about homework, amount of homework assigned and completed, and student achievement. *Journal of Educational Psychology, 90*(1), 70–83.

Covington, M. V. (1992). *Making the grade: A self-worth perspective on motivation and school reform.* New York: Cambridge University Press.

Darling-Hammond, L., Barron, B., Pearson, P. D., Schoenfeld, A. H., Stage, E. K., Zimmerman, T. D., et al. (2008). *Powerful learning: What we know about teaching for understanding.* San Francisco: John Wiley & Sons.

Dean, C. B., Hubbell, E. R., Pitler, H., & Stone, B. (2012). *Classroom instruction that works: Research-based strategies for increasing student achievement* (2nd ed.). Alexandria, VA: ASCD.

DeVries, D. L., & Edwards, K. J. (1973). Learning games and student teams: their effects on classroom process. *American Educational Research Journal, 10*(4), 307–318.

Diperna, J. C. (2006). Academic enablers and student achievement: Implications for assessment and intervention services in the schools. *Psychology in the Schools, 43*(1), 7–17.

Dweck, C. (2006). *Mindset: The new psychology of success.* New York: Random House.

Dweck, C. (2010). Mind-sets and equitable education. *Principal Leadership, 10*(5), 26–29.

Eccles, J. S., Wigfield, A., & Schiefele, U. (1998). Motivation to succeed. In N. Eisenberg (Ed.), *Handbook of child psychology: Volume 3—Social, emotional, and personality development* (5th ed.) (pp. 1017–1096). New York: Wiley.

Elliot, E. S., McGregor, H. A., & Gable, S. L. (1999). Achievement goals, study strategies, and exam performance: A mediational analysis. *Journal of Educational Psychology, 91*, 549–563.

Fillippone, M. (1998). Questioning at the elementary level. Master's thesis, Kean University. (ERIC Document Reproduction Service No. ED 417 421).

Flanders, N. (1970). *Analyzing teacher behavior.* Reading, MA: Addison-Wesley

Fraser, B. J., Walberg, H. J., Welch, W. W., & Hattie, J. A. (1987). Synthesis of educational productivity research [Special issue]. *International Journal of Educational Research, 11*(2), 145–252.

Fuchs, L. S., Fuchs, D., Finelli, R., Courey, S. J., Hamlett, C. L., Sones, E. M., & Hope, S. (2006). Teaching third graders about real-life mathematical problem solving: A randomized controlled study. *Elementary School Journal, 106*, 293–312.

Gentner, D., Loewenstein, J., & Thompson, L. (2003). Learning and transfer: A general role for analogical encoding. *Journal of Educational Psychology, 95*, 393–408.

Gerlic, I., & Jausovec, N. (1999). Multimedia: Differences in cognitive processes observed with EEG. *Educational Technology Research and Development, 47*(3), 5–14.

Greene, B. A., Miller, R. B., Crowson, H. M., Duke, B. L., & Akey, K. L. (2004). Predicting high school students' cognitive engagement and achievement: Contributions of classroom perceptions and motivation. *Contemporary Educational Psychology, 29*(4), 462–482.

Hattie, J. (1992). Measuring the effects of schooling. *Australian Journal of Education, 36*(1), 5–13.

Hattie, J., & Timperley, H. (2007). The power of feedback. *Review of Educational Research, 77*(1), 81–112.

Henderlong, J., & Lepper, M. R. (2002). The effects of praise on children's intrinsic motivation: A review and synthesis. *Psychological Bulletin, 128*, 774–795.

Hidi, S., & Anderson, V. (1987). Providing written summaries: Task demands, cognitive operations, and implications for instruction. *Review of Educational Research, 56*, 473–493.

Holyoak, K. J. (2005). Analogy. In K. J. Holyoak & R. G. Morrison (Eds.), *The Cambridge handbook of thinking and reasoning* (pp. 117–142). New York: Cambridge University Press.

Howard, B. C. (1996, February). *A meta-analysis of scripted cooperative learning.* Paper presented at the Annual Meeting of the Eastern Educational Research Association, Boston, MA.

Igel, C., (2010). *The effect of cooperative learning instruction on K–12 student learning: A meta-analysis of quantitative studies from 1998–2009.* Unpublished doctoral dissertation, University of Virginia, Charlottesville, VA.

Jewitt, C. (2008). Multimodality and literacy in school classrooms. In J. Green, G. J. Kelly, & A. Luke (Eds.), *Review of research in education: Vol. 32. What counts as knowledge in educational settings: Disciplinary knowledge, assessment, and curriculum* (pp. 241–267). Thousand Oaks, CA: Sage.

Johnson, D. W., & Johnson, R. T. (1999). *Learning together and alone* (5th ed.). Boston, MA: Allyn & Bacon.

Johnson, D. W., & Johnson, R. T. (2009). An educational psychology success story: Social interdependence theory and cooperative learning. *Educational Researcher, 38*(5), 365–379.

Kagan, S. (1985).*Cooperative learning resources for teachers.* Riverside, CA: University of California at Riverside.

Kagan, S. (1990). The structural approach to cooperative learning. *Educational Leadership, 47*(4), 12–15.

Kamins, M. L., & Dweck, C. S. (1999). Person versus process praise and criticism: Implications for contingent self-worth and coping. *Developmental Psychology, 35,* 835–847.

Karpicke, J. D., & Roediger H. R. III, (2008). The critical importance of retrieval for learning. *Science, 319,* 966–968.

Kohn, A. (2006). *The homework myth.* Cambridge, MA: Da Capo Press.

Koutselini, M. (2009). Teacher misconceptions and understanding of cooperative learning: An intervention study. *Journal of Classroom Interaction, 43*(2), 34–44.

Kress, G. (1997). *Before writing: Rethinking the paths to literacy.* London: Routledge.

Lavoie, D. R. (1999). Effects of emphasizing hypothetico-predictive reasoning within the science learning cycle on high school students' process skills and conceptual understanding in biology. *Journal of Research in Science Teaching, 36*(10), 1127–1147.

Lavoie, D. R., & Good, R. (1988). The nature and use of prediction skills in biological computer simulation. *Journal of Research in Science Teaching, 25,* 334–360.

Lawson, A. E. (1988). A better way to teach biology. *The American Biology Teacher, 50,* 266–278.

Lefrancois, G. R. (1997). *Psychology for teaching* (9th ed.). Belmont, CA: Wadsworth.

Lewis, D., & Greene, J. (1982). *Thinking better.* New York: Rawson, Wade Publishers, Inc.

Lou, Y., Abrami, P. C., Spence, J. C., Paulsen, C., Chambers, B., & d'Apollonio, S. (1996). Within class grouping: A meta-analysis. *Review of Educational Research, 66*(4), 423–458.

Manjoo, F. (2009, September 28). Where Wikipedia ends. *Time.*

Margolis, H., & McCabe, P. P. (2004). Self-efficacy: A key to improving the motivation of struggling learners. *Clearing House, 77*(6), 241–249.

Martorella, P. H. (1991). Knowledge and concept development in social studies. In J. P. Shaver (Ed.), *Handbook of research on social studies teaching and learning* (pp. 370–399). New York: Macmillan.

Marzano, R. J., Norford, J. S., Paynter, D. E., Pickering, D. J., & Gaddy, B. B. (2001). *A handbook for classroom instruction that works.* Alexandria, VA: ASCD.

Marzano, R. J., & Pickering, D. J. (1997). *Dimensions of learning teacher's manual* (2nd ed.). Alexandria, VA: ASCD.

Marzano, R. J., & Pickering, D. J. (2007, March). Special topic: The case for and against homework. *Educational Leadership, 64*(6), 74–79.

Marzano, R. J., Pickering, D. J., & Pollock, J. E. (2001). *Classroom instruction that works: Research-based strategies for increasing student achievement.* Alexandria, VA: ASCD.

Mbajiorgu, N. M., Ezechi, N. G., & Idoko, E. C. (2007). Addressing nonscientific presuppositions in genetics using a conceptual change strategy. *Science Education, 91*(3), 419–438.

Medina, J. (2008). *Brain rules: 12 principals for surviving and thriving at work, home, and school.* Seattle, WA: Pear Press.

Michalchik, V., Rosenquist, A., Kozma, R., Kreikemeier, P., & Schank, P. (2008). Representational competence and chemical understanding in the high school chemistry classroom. In J. K. Gilbert, M. Reiner, & M. Nakhleh (Eds.), *Theory and practice in science education* (pp. 233–282). New York: Springer.

Moore-Partin, T. C., Robertson, R. E., Maggin, D. M., Oliver, R. M., & Wehby, J. H. (2010). Using teacher praise and opportunities to respond to appropriate student behavior. *Preventing School Failure, 54*(3), 172–178.

National Association of Colleges and Employers. (2009). Job outlook 2009 survey. Retrieved from www.naceweb.org/Research/Job_Outlook/2009/Job_Outlook_2009.aspx

National Governors Association Center for Best Practices and Council of Chief State School Officers. (2010). Common Core State Standards.

Naylor, G. (1992). *Bailey's café*. New York: Harcourt Brace Jovanovich.

Newell, A., & Rosenbloom, P. S. (1981). Mechanisms of skill acquisition and the law of practice. In J. R. Anderson (Ed.), *Cognitive skills and their acquisition*. Hillsdale, NJ: Erlbaum.

Paivio, A. (2006). Dual coding theory and education. Draft chapter for the conference "Pathways to Literacy Achievement for High Poverty Children," The University of Michigan School of Education, September 29–October 1. Retrieved from http://readytolearnresearch.org/

Palincsar, A. S., & Brown, A. L. (1985). Reciprocal teaching: Activities to promote reading with your mind. In T. L. Harris & E. J. Cooper (Eds.), *Reading, thinking and concept development: Strategies for the classroom*. New York: The College Board.

Pashler, H., Rohrer, D., Cepeda, N. J., & Carpenter, S. K. (2007). Enhancing learning and retarding forgetting: Choices and consequences. *Psychonomic Bulletin and Review, 14*(2), 187–193.

Phan, H. P. (2009). Exploring students' reflective thinking practice, deep processing strategies, effort, and achievement goal orientations. *Educational Psychology, 29*(3), 297–313.

Pintrich, P. R., & Schrauben, B. (1992). Students' motivational beliefs and their cognitive engagement in classroom tasks. In D. Schunk & J. Meece (Eds.), *Students perceptions in the classroom: Causes and consequences* (pp. 149–183). Hillsdale, NJ: Lawrence Erlbaum.

Pintrich, P. R., & Schunk, D. H. (2002). *Motivation in education: Theory, research and applications* (2nd ed.). Upper Saddle River, NJ: Merrill Prentice-Hall.

Piolat, A., Olive, T., & Kellogg, R. T. (2005). Cognitive effort during note taking. *Applied Cognitive Psychology, 19*, 291–312.

Pitler, H., Hubbell, E. R., Kuhn, M., & Malenoski, K. (2007). *Using technology with classroom instruction that works*. Alexandria, VA: ASCD.

Richardson, A. (1983). Imagery: Definitions and types. In A. A. Sheikh (Ed.), *Imagery: Current theory, research, and application* (pp. 3–42). New York: John Wiley & Sons.

Rule, A. C., & Furletti, C. (2004). Using form and function analogy object boxes to teach human body systems. *School Science and Mathematics, 104*(4), 155–169.

Schunk, D. H. (1999). Social-self interaction and achievement behavior. *Educational Psychologist, 34*(4), 219–227.

Sharan, Y., & Sharan, S. (1992). *Expanding cooperative learning through group investigation*. New York: Teachers College Press.

Shute, V. J. (2008). Focus on formative feedback. *Review of Educational Research, 78*(1), 153–189.

Simons, K. D., & Klein, J. D. (2007). The impact of scaffolding and student achievement levels in a problem-based learning environment. *Instructional Science: An International Journal of the Learning Sciences, 35*(1), 41–72.

Simonson, B., Fairbanks, S., Briesch, A., Myers, D., & Sugai, G. (2008). Evidence-based practices in classroom management: Considerations for research to practice. *Education and Treatment of Children, 31*(3), 351–380.

Slavin, R. E. (1978). Student teams and achievement divisions. *Journal of Research and Development in Education, 12*, 39–49.

Slavin, R. E. (1983). *Cooperative learning*. New York: Longman.

Slavin, R. E. (1990). *Cooperative learning: Theory, research, and practice*. Boston: Allyn & Bacon.

Sternberg, R. J. (1977). *Intelligence, information processing and analogical reasoning: The componential analysis of human abilities*. Hillsdale, NJ: Erlbaum.

Tweed, A. (2009). *Designing effective science instruction: What works in science classrooms*. Arlington, VA: National Science Teachers Association.

Valenza, J. K. (2000). For the best answers, ask tough questions. *Philadelphia Inquirer*. Retrieved from http://faculty.philau.edu/kayk/KKay/articles/BestAnsers.pdf

Valle, A., & Callanan, M. A. (2006). Similarity comparisons and relational analogies in parent–child conversations about science topics. *Merrill-Palmer Quarterly, 52*(1), 96–124.

Walberg, H. J. (1999). Productive teaching. In H. C. Waxman & H. J. Walberg (Eds.), *New directions for teaching practice and research* (pp. 75–104). Berkeley, CA: McCutchen Publishing Corporation.

Walker, B. (2003). The cultivation of student self-efficacy in reading and writing. *Reading and Writing Quarterly: Overcoming Learning Difficulties, 19*(2), 173–187.

Ward, J. D., & Lee, C. L. (2004). Teaching strategies for FCS: Student achievement in problem-based learning versus lecture-based instruction. *Journal of Family and Consumer Sciences, 96*(1), 73–76.

White, R. T., & Tisher, R. P. (1986). Research on natural sciences. In M. C. Wittrock (Ed.), *Handbook of research on teaching* (pp. 874–905). New York: Macmillan.

Wigfield, A., & Eccles, J. (2000). Expectancy-value theory of achievement motivation. *Contemporary Educational Psychology, 25,* 68–81.

Woolfolk, A. (2004). *Educational psychology.* Boston: Pearson.

Wright, T. (2007). Star thrives despite doubts. *Greeley Tribune.* Retrieved from http://www.greeleytribune.com

Zimmerman, B. J. (2000). Self-efficacy: An essential motive to learn. *Contemporary Educational Psychology, 25,* 82–91.

Index

The letter *f* following a page number denotes a figure.

accountability in cooperative learning, 76–77, 79–80

achievement. *See* success

activities, objectives relation to, 4

advance organizers
  classroom practices, self-assessment, 127*f*
  descriptive pattern type, 135–136, 135*f*
  expository type, 113, 115
  function, 112
  graphic type, 113, 116, 118*f*, 119*f*
  narrative type, 113, 115
  professional growth plan, 128*f*
  recommendations for the classroom, 113
  reflection
    on current practice, questions for, 114*f*
    teacher rubric as a tool for, 120–121, 122–125*f*
  skimming strategy, 113, 116, 117*f*, 118*f*
  student checklist for understanding, 126*f*
  teacher-prepared notes as, 189
  text discussion elements, x
  Why This Strategy? 112–113

analytic questions, 100, 104

anticipation guide, 118*f*, 120*f*

argumentation frame, 167–168, 167*f*

benchmarks, examples of, 4

Bringing the Strategy to Life in the Classroom, introduction to, x–xi

classifying strategy
  guiding the process, 250–251
  methods for, teaching a variety of, 249–250
  supporting cues, providing, 251–252, 252*f*

combination note-taking, 193, 196*f*, 197*f*

comparing strategy
  guiding the process, 245–246
  methods for, teaching a variety of, 244–245
  supporting cues, providing, 246–248, 247*f*, 248*f*

concept graphic organizers, 134–135, 135*f*

control beliefs, 38

conversation frame, 171–173, 171*f*

cooperative learning
  classroom practices, self-assessment of, 89–90*f*
  consistent and systematic use of, 77, 80–81
  defined, 75
  function, 75–76
  group size in, 77, 80
  individual accountability in, 76–77, 79–80
  positive interdependence in, 77, 79–80
  professional growth plan, 91–92*f*
  recommendations for the classroom, 77
  reflection
    on current practice, questions for, 78*f*
    teacher rubric as a tool for, 81–82, 83–86*f*
  student checklist for understanding, 87–88*f*
  text discussion elements, x
  Why This Strategy? 76–77

creating analogies strategy
  guiding the process, 261–262
  methods for, teaching a variety of, 259–261, 260*f*
  supporting cues, providing, 262–263, 263*f*

creating metaphors strategy
  guiding the process, 255–256

creating metaphors strategy—(*continued*)
  methods for, teaching a variety of, 253–254
  supporting cues, providing, 256–258, 257*f*, 258*f*
criterion-referenced feedback, 24, 27–28, 28*f*
cues and questions
  analytic questions, 100, 104
  classroom practices, self-assessment of, 110*f*
  explicit cues, 100, 102–103
  focusing on important aspects of a topic, 100, 102
  function, 97–98
  inferential questions, 100, 103
  professional growth plan, 111*f*
  recommendations for the classroom, 100
  reflection
    on current practice, questions for, 101*f*
    teacher rubric as a tool for, 104–105, 106–108*f*
  student checklist for understanding, 109*f*
  text discussion elements, x
  Why This Strategy? 98–100

deduction, 276–277
definition frame, 165–167, 165*f*
descriptive graphic organizers, 134
descriptive pattern graphic organizer, 135–136, 135*f*
differences, identifying. *See* similarities and differences, identifying
distributed practice, 227, 227*f*

effort, reinforcing
  classroom practices, self-assessment of, 55*f*
  with explicit information on meaning of expending effort, 41, 45–47
  function, 37–38
  professional growth plan, 56*f*
  recommendations for the classroom, 41
  reflection
    on current practice, questions for, 42*f*
    teacher rubric as a tool for, 49, 51–53*f*
  student checklist for understanding, 54*f*
  by student tracking effort-achievement relationship, 41, 47–49, 48*f*
  by teaching the effort-achievement relationship, 41, 43–45
  text discussion elements, x
  Why This Strategy? 38–41
effort-achievement relationship, 38–41, 43–49, 48*f*
episode graphic organizer, 119*f*, 134
experimental inquiry in hypothesis testing, 285–287, 286*f*
explicit cues, 100, 102–103
expository form advance organizer, 113, 115

feedback, 211
feedback, providing
  classroom practices, self-assessment of, 34–35*f*
  connecting to future learning, 23, 26
  criterion-referenced, 24, 27–28, 28*f*
  engaging students in the process, 24, 28–29
  function, 23
  homework , 208, 214–215
  objectives relation to, 23
  with practice , 223, 228–229
  professional growth plan, 36*f*
  recommendations for the classroom, 23–24
  reflection
    on current practice, questions for, 25
    teacher rubric as a tool for, 29, 30–32*f*
  specificity in, 23, 26, 27*f*
  student checklist for understanding, 33*f*
  text discussion elements, x
  timeliness in, 24, 26–27
  Why This Strategy? 23–24
Frayer Model, 118, 121, 121*f*
function advance organizer, 112

generalization/principle graphic organizers, 134
graphic organizers, 113, 116, 118*f*, 119*f*, 131, 134–136

homework
  classroom practices, self-assessment, 220*f*
  feedback, providing, 208, 214–215
  function, 205
  professional growth plan, 221*f*
  purpose of, communicating the, 207, 213–214
  recommendations for the classroom, 207–208
  reflection
    on current practice, questions for, 210*f*
    teacher rubric as a tool for, 215, 217–218*f*
  school/district policies, establish and communicate, 207, 211–213, 212–213*f*
  student checklist for understanding, 219*f*
  supporting academic learning, 207, 213–214
  text discussion elements, x
  Why This Strategy? 205–207
hypotheses, generating and testing
  classroom practices, self-assessment, 296–297*f*
  experimental inquiry in, 285–287, 286*f*
  explanations to deepen understanding, 278, 288–290
  function, 274–277
  investigation in, 287–288
  problem solving in, 283–285
  professional growth plan, 298–299*f*

hypotheses, generating and testing—(*continued*)
    recommendations for the classroom, 281
    reflection
        on current practice, questions for,
            279–280*f*
        teacher rubric as a tool for, 290–291,
            292–294*f*
    student checklist for understanding, 295*f*
    systems analysis in, 281–283, 283*f*
    text discussion elements, x
    use tasks to provide context for, 278,
        281–288
    Why This Strategy? 277–278

illustrations, pictographs, and pictures, 131,
    139–140
imagery. *See* nonlinguistic representations
induction, 275–276
inferential questions, 100, 103
instructional planning
    classroom practices, self-assessment,
        317–318*f*
    intentional selection of strategies, 303–305
    lesson design example, 308–316
    professional growth plan, 319–320*f*
    reflection on current practice, questions for,
        306–307*f*
instructional planning framework components,
    vii, viii, 304*f*
interdependence in cooperative learning, 77,
    79–80
intrinsic motivation, 38
investigation in hypothesis testing, 287–288

kinesthetic activities, 131, 140–141

learning environment, creating, 1
learning objectives . *See* objectives, setting
luck, 38–39

manipulatives/physical models, 131, 136–137
massed practice, 227, 227*f*
mastery-goal orientation for recognition, 58,
    61–62
mental pictures, 131, 137–139
motivation, influencing, 37–38

narrative form advance organizer, 113, 115
narrative frame, 161–163, 162*f*
nonlinguistic representations, 134
nonlinguistic representations
    classroom practices, self-assessment,
        149–150*f*
    examples of using, 133–134
    function, 129
    graphic organizers, 131, 134–136

nonlinguistic representations—(*continued*)
    kinesthetic activities, 131, 140–141
    learning vocabulary with, 133
    mental pictures, 131, 137–139
    physical models/manipulatives, 131,
        136–137
    pictures, illustrations, pictographs, 131,
        139–140
    professional growth plan, 151*f*
    recommendations for the classroom, 131
    reflection
        on current practice, questions for, 132*f*
        teacher rubric as a tool for, 141, 143–146*f*
    student checklist for understanding, 147–148*f*
    text discussion elements, x
    Why This Strategy? 129–131
note taking
    classroom practices, self-assessment,
        202–203*f*
    function, 185
    professional growth plan, 204*f*
    recommendations for the classroom, 186
    reflection
        on current practice, questions for, 188*f*
        teacher rubric as a tool for, 196–197,
            198–200*f*
    revision and review opportunities, 186,
        193–196, 194*f*, 196*f*, 197*f*
    student checklist for understanding, 201*f*
    teach a variety of formats, 186, 189–193,
        190*f*, 192*f*
    text discussion elements, x
    using teacher-prepared notes, 186, 189
    Why This Strategy? 185–186

objectives, setting
    classroom practices, self-assessment of,
        18–19*f*
    communicating to students and parents, 5,
        8–9
    connecting to previous and future learning,
        5, 10–11
    engaging students to set personal objectives,
        5, 12
    feedback's relation to, 23
    function, 3
    professional growth plan, 20–21*f*
    recommendations for the classroom, 5
    reflection
        on current practice, questions for, 6–7
        teacher rubric as a tool for, 14–16
    specificity in, 5, 8
    student checklist for understanding, 17*f*
    text discussion elements, x
    Why This Strategy? 3–4
    worksheet, 22*f*

parents
   communicating learning objectives to, 5,
      8–10
   homework involvement for, 209, 211
peer feedback, 28–29. *See also* cooperative
   learning
physical models/manipulatives, 131, 136–137
pictographs, illustrations, and pictures, 131,
   139–140
pictures, illustrations, pictographs, 131, 139–140
practice
   classroom practices, self-assessment, 235*f*
   design for short, focused, and distributed,
      223, 227–228, 227*f*
   feedback, providing, 223, 228–229
   professional growth plan, 236*f*
   purpose of, identify and communicate, 223,
      226
   recommendations for the classroom, 223
   reflection
      on current practice, questions for, 225*f*
      teacher rubric as a tool for, 229, 231–233*f*
   student checklist for understanding, 234*f*
   text discussion elements, x
   Why This Strategy? 222–224, 224*f*
praise. *See also* recognition, providing
   aligning with expectations, 62–63, 65
   effective, 58
   guidelines for, 64*f*
   motivation and, 57
   specificity in, 62–63, 65
problem-solution frame, 168–171, 168*f*
problem solving in hypothesis testing, 283–285
process/cause-effect graphic organizers, 134

questions. *See* cues and questions

reciprocal teaching strategy for summarizing,
   154, 173–175
recognition, providing
   aligned with expectations, 58, 62–65
   classroom practices, self-assessment of,
      71–72*f*
   concrete symbols for, 58, 65–66
   function, 57
   mastery-goal orientation for, 58, 61–62
   praise guidelines, 64*f*
   professional growth plan, 73–74*f*
   recommendations for the classroom, 58
   reflection
      on current practice, questions for, 59–60*f*
      teacher rubric as a tool for, 66, 67–69*f*
   specificity in, 58, 62–65
   student checklist for understanding, 70*f*
   text discussion elements, x
   Why This Strategy? 57–58

recommendations for the classroom, 154
Reflecting on My Current Practice, introduction
   to, x
revision and review functions of note taking,
   186, 193–196, 194*f*, 196*f*, 197*f*
Rubrics and Checklists, introduction to, xi
rule-based summarizing strategy, 154, 158–160,
   158*f*, 159*f*

school/district policies, homework, 207,
   211–213, 212–213*f*
self-efficacy, 38
self-feedback, 28
similarities and differences, identifying
   classifying strategy, 249–252
   classroom practices, self-assessment,
      270–272*f*
   comparing strategy, 244–249, 247*f*, 248*f*
   creating analogies strategy, 259–264
   creating metaphors strategy, 253–258
   function, 239
   guiding the process
      classifying strategy, 250–251
      comparing strategy, 245–246
      creating analogies strategy, 261–262
      creating metaphors strategy, 255–256
      recommendations for the classroom, 241
   methods for, teaching a variety of
      classifying strategy, 249–250
      comparing strategy, 244–245
      creating analogies strategy, 259–261, 260*f*
      creating metaphors strategy, 253–254
      recommendations for the classroom, 241
   professional growth plan, 273–274*f*
   recommendations for the classroom, 241
   reflection
      on current practice, questions for,
         242–243*f*
      teacher rubric as a tool for, 264, 266–268*f*
   student checklist for understanding, 269*f*
   supporting cues, providing
      classifying strategy, 251–252, 252*f*
      comparing strategy, 246–248, 247*f*, 248*f*
      creating analogies strategy, 262–263, 263*f*
      creating metaphors strategy, 256–258,
         257*f*, 258*f*
      recommendations for the classroom, 241
   text discussion elements, x
   Why This Strategy? 239–241
skimming strategy, 113, 116, 117*f*, 118*f*
SQ3R Protocol, 117*f*
standards, examples of, 4
study groups, functions of, xi–xiii
success
   effort-achievement relationship, 38–41,
      43–49, 48*f*

success—(*continued*)
    motivation and, 37–38
summarizing
    classroom practices, self-assessment,
      181–182*f*
    function, 152–153
    professional growth plan, 183–184*f*
    reciprocal teaching, engage students in, 154,
      173–175
    recommendations for the classroom, 154
    reflection
      on current practice, questions for,
        156–157*f*
      teacher rubric as a tool for, 175–176,
        177–179*f*
    rule-based strategy, teach students the, 154,
      158–160, 158*f*, 159*f*
    student checklist for understanding, 180*f*
    summary frames
      argumentation frame, 167–168, 167*f*
      conversation frame, 171–173, 171*f*
      definition frame, 165–167, 165*f*
      elements of, 160–161
      narrative frame, 161–163, 162*f*
      problem-solution frame, 168–171, 168*f*
      recommendations for the classroom, 154
      topic-restriction-illustration frame, 163–
        165, 163*f*
    text discussion elements, x

summarizing—(*continued*)
    Why This Strategy? 153–154
summary frames
    argumentation frame, 167–168, 167*f*
    common, 160
    conversation frame, 171–173, 171*f*
    definition frame, 165–167, 165*f*
    elements of, 160–161
    narrative frame, 161–163, 162*f*
    problem-solution frame, 168–171, 168*f*
    recommendations for the classroom, 154
    topic-restriction-illustration frame, 163–165,
      163*f*
systems analysis in hypothesis testing, 281–283,
    283*f*

task value beliefs, 38
teacher-prepared notes, 186, 189
time-sequence graphic organizers, 134
Tools, Templates, and Protocols, introduction
    to, xi
topic-restriction-illustration frame, 163–165,
    163*f*

vocabulary, learning, 133

webbing, 191–192, 192*f*
Why This Strategy? introduction to, x

About the Authors

Howard Pitler is a Senior Director at McREL. He conducts workshops and training for K–12 teachers on research-based instructional strategies and technology integration, conducts technology audits for districts, and works with school and district leaders in using Power Walkthrough classroom observation software. Prior to coming to McREL, Howard served as an elementary and middle school principal. He holds an Ed.D. in Educational Administration from Wichita State University, an M.A. in Music Performance from Wichita State, and a B.A. in Music Education from Indiana State University. Howard is an Apple Distinguished Educator and a Smithsonian Laureate, and he was a 1997 National Distinguished Principal. He has been published in several journals, including *Principal*, *T.H.E. Journal*, *The Learning Principal*, and *Learning & Leading with Technology*, and he is coauthor of *Using Technology with Classroom Instruction that Works*. Howard has presented at a variety of national conferences, including ASCD, ISTE, and NSBA's T+L conference.

 **Bj Stone** is a principal consultant at McREL, and she works nationally and internationally with schools, districts, and educational agencies. She facilitates learning sessions with teachers, principals, district administrators, and leadership teams in the areas of research-based instructional strategies, vocabulary instruction, curriculum development, and assessment design. Bj has presented at local, state, and national conferences, including ASCD and the National Science Teachers Association. She was designated as a Teaching Fellow in a large National Science Foundation funded grant for preservice teachers and has been published in the *Journal of Teacher Education*. Preceding her work at McREL, Bj served as a middle and high school science teacher, a university instructor, and an assistant superintendent in charge of grants, curriculum and assessment development, and the design and delivery of professional development. Bj has a B.S. in Biology from the University of Northern Colorado. Her M.S. in Science Education and Ed.D. in Educational Leadership and Policy Study are also from the University of Northern Colorado.

About McREL

Mid-continent Research for Education and Learning (McREL) is a nationally recognized, nonprofit education research and development organization, headquartered in Denver, Colorado with offices in Honolulu, Hawai`i and Omaha, Nebraska. Since 1966, McREL has helped translate research and professional wisdom about what works in education into practical guidance for educators. Our 120-plus staff members and affiliates include respected researchers, experienced consultants, and published writers who provide educators with research-based guidance, consultation, and professional development for improving student outcomes.

Related ASCD Resources: Classroom Instruction That Works

At the time of publication, the following ASCD resources were available (ASCD stock numbers appear in parentheses). For up-to-date information about ASCD resources, go to www.ascd. org. You can search the complete archives of *Educational Leadership* at http://www.ascd.org/el.

ASCD EDge Group

Exchange ideas and connect with other educators on the social networking site ASCD EDge™ at http://ascdedge.ascd.org/

Online Courses

The Art and Science of Teaching (PD11OC102)
What Works in Schools: School Leadership in Action, 2nd Edition (PD11OC119)
What Works in Schools: Translating Research into Action, 2nd Edition (PD11OC103)

Print Products

The Art and Science of Teaching: A Comprehensive Framework for Effective Instruction by Robert J. Marzano (#107001)

Classroom Assessment and Grading That Work by Robert J. Marzano (#106006)

Classroom Instruction That Works (2nd edition) by Ceri B. Dean, Elizabeth Ross Hubbell, Howard Pitler, and Bj Stone (#111001)

Classroom Instruction That Works with English Language Learners by Jane Hill and Kathleen Flynn (#106009)

Classroom Management That Works: Research-Based Strategies for Every Teacher by Robert J. Marzano, Debra J. Pickering, and Jana Marzano (#103027)

Effective Supervision: Supporting The Art and Science of Teaching by Robert Marzano, David Livingston, and Tony Frontier (#110019)

A Handbook for the Art and Science of Teaching by John L. Brown and Robert J. Marzano (#108049)

A Handbook for Classroom Management That Works by Mark Foseid, Robert J. Marzano, Maria C. Foseid, Barbara Gaddy Carrio, and Jana Marzano (#105012)

School Leadership That Works: From Research to Results by Robert J. Marzano, Timothy Waters, and Brian McNulty (#105125)

Using Technology with Classroom Instruction That Works (2nd Edition) by Matt S. Kuhn, Elizabeth Hubbell, Howard Pitler, and Kim Malenoski (#107025)

What Works In Schools: Translating Research into Action by Robert J. Marzano (#102271)

Video

Classroom Instruction That Works DVD Series (Elementary, Middle, High School) (#612061)
Classroom Management That Works DVD and Facilitator's Guide (#604038)

THE WHOLE CHILD The Whole Child Initiative helps schools and communities create learning environments that allow students to be healthy, safe, engaged, supported, and challenged. To learn more about other books and resources that relate to the whole child, visit www.wholechildeducation.org.

For more information: send e-mail to member@ascd.org; call 1-800-933-2723 or 703-578-9600, press 2; send a fax to 703-575-5400; or write to Information Services, ASCD, 1703 N. Beauregard St., Alexandria, VA 22311-1714 USA.